Rhythm and Blues, Soul, Funk, and Rap

York University
Music Department

Edited by Ray Williams

KENDALL/HUNT PUBLISHING COMPANY
4050 Westmark Drive   Dubuque, Iowa 52002

Cover image © Digital Vison

Pages 1–113 from All Music Guide. Copyright © by All Media Guide, LLC.

Copyright © 2005 by Kendall/Hunt Publishing Company

ISBN 0-7575-2079-0

All rights reserved. No part of this publication may be reproduced, stored in a retreival system, or transmitted, in any form or by any means, electronic, mechanical, photocopying, recording, or otherwise, without the prior written permission of the copyright owner.

Printed in the United States of America
10   9   8   7   6   5   4   3   2   1

Contents

Blues 1
Jazz 2
Rhythm and Blues 3
Soul 4
Funk 5

    Louis Armstrong   6
    Billie Holiday   8
    Nat King Cole   12
    Ray Charles   17
    The Ink Spots   19
    The Ravens   19
    The Orioles   20
    The Moonglows   21
    The Penguins   25
    Frankie Lymon   25
    The Drifters   26
    The Platters   35
    Sam Cooke   35
    The Coasters   40
    Clyde McPhatter   41
    Jackie Wilson   44
    James Brown   46
    The Marcels   49
    The Shirelles   49
    Barrett Strong   51
    Smokey Robinson & the Miracles   51
    Maurice Williams   53
    Chuck Jackson   56
    Maxine Brown   56
    Ben E. King   57
    The Marvelettes   58
    The Mar-Keys   59
    Solomon Burke   60
    Gene Chandler   61
    Eddie Holland   61
    Mary Wells   61
    Marvin Gaye   62
    The Contours   66
    Booker T. & the MG's   67
    Martha & the Vandellas   68

    Stevie Wonder   69
    Wilson Pickett   74
    The Impressions   75
    Rufus Thomas   77
    Carla Thomas   78
    Doris Troy   79
    The Temptations   79
    Isaac Hayes   81
    David Porter   82
    The Four Tops   83
    The Supremes   85
    Junior Walker & the All-Stars   87
    Brenda Holloway   88
    Joe Tex   89
    Otis Redding   90
    Barbara Lewis   91
    Isley Brothers   92
    Sam & Dave   94
    Percy Sledge   95
    Kim Weston   96

Disco 97

    Hues Corporation   97
    Van McCoy   97
    Silver Convention   99
    Rose Royce   99
    Thelma Houston   100
    Donna Summer   101
    The Trammps   103
    Evelyn Champagne King   104
    A Taste of Honey   105
    Village People   106
    Chic   106
    Sylvester   109
    Kool & the Gang   109
    Gloria Gaynor   111
    Anita Ward   111
    The Sugarhill Gang   112

Take the Reggae Test   115
African-American Music Map   119
Song Listings   123
R&B Charts   156

Blues

Definition of Style

Blues is an African-American music that traverses a wide range of emotions and musical styles. "Feeling blue" is expressed in songs whose verses lament injustice or express longing for a better life and lost loves, jobs, and money. But blues is also a raucous dance music that celebrates pleasure and success. Central to the idea of blues performance is the concept that, by performing or listening to the blues, one is able to overcome sadness and lose the blues.

Among the formal, identifying musical traits of the blues are the familiar "blue notes," a three-line AAB verse form, and a characteristic use of the familiar blues chord progression. Historically, the popularity of blues coincides with the rise of the commercial recording industry, the introduction of "race" records aimed at black record-buyers after 1920, and the emigration of black Americans from the rural South to the urban North. Many of the earliest black American recording stars were blues singers. The first blues songs to be recorded, often called "classic blues," were jazz-influenced songs in a vaudeville style, sung by the great blueswomen: Gertrude "Ma" Rainey, Bessie Smith, and others. These singers were often accompanied by pianists, guitarists, or even small jazz combos.

The "country blues," usually considered an earlier form of the genre, was actually recorded in the mid-1920s. There are several regional styles of country blues, including delta blues from the Mississippi Delta, Texas blues, and Piedmont blues from the Southeast. Country blues was usually recorded by a single male singer, self-accompanied on the guitar or piano, with perhaps an accompanying harmonica or simple percussion. Charley Patton, Blind Lemon Jefferson, Blind Boy Fuller, and Robert Johnson were country blues musicians.

Beginning in the 1930s, blues musicians fell under the influence of urban culture, including popular music and jazz. Combos incorporating piano, guitar, and percussion developed, although the country, "downhome" origins of the musicians were still evident in the music. Major musicians of the 1930s included Tampa Red, Big Bill Broonzy, Little Brother Mongomery, Leon Carr and Scrapper Blackwell, Lonnie Johnson, and Memphis Minnie.

After World War II, the use of electrified instruments became inevitable. During the 1940s, some blues bands even incorporated saxophones, although the preference was for amplified harmonicas, especially in Chicago, a predominant center of blues recording in the 1950s. Blues from this period is often called "urban blues," "electric blues," or simply "Chicago blues." Important urban blues musicians included Muddy Waters, Little Walter, Elmore James, Howlin' Wolf, T-Bone Walker, and B. B. King.

Blues remains with us in contemporary American culture, and as a traditional musical form it has been subjected to countless revivals and reinterpretations. Its current practitioners often integrate the sounds and instrumental pyrotechnics of rock music and the sheen of urban soul; but the twelve-bar form, variations on the blues chord progression, and emotive lyrical content remain relatively unchanged.

Jazz

Definition of Style

Jazz, wide-ranging in its embrace, can encompass genres that range from some ragtime to the pop-inflected radio hits of George Benson and the improvised atonal experiments of Cecil Taylor. As with all living art forms, the borders of jazz are continually blurred as successive generations of musicians adapt its conventions to contemporary artistic trends.

Most accounts place the origin of jazz in New Orleans between 1890 and 1900. There, in a bustling coastal city with international connections, African-, Caribbean-, and European-derived musics melded within the context of the bands or instrumental ensembles that accompanied funeral processions and other types of celebrations and observances. The result was a new music that became a target of early recording technology: the first jazz recording was made by a group of white musicians, the Original Dixieland Jazz Band, who recorded in New Orleans in 1917. A 1922 recording by New Orleans trombonist Kid Ory was the first jazz recording by a black musician. This early music recalled the two-beat rhythm of the marching band, which was gradually altered through the early 1920s into the four-beat rhythm we associate with jazz today.

From 1920 through the early 1930s, jazz continued to flourish in New Orleans, but other sounds also evolved, including the urbanized sound of Chicago jazz, New York stride piano, and New York and Kansas City swing. Also during the 1930s, a musical dialogue with Europe began to emerge, and many European musicians embraced jazz without reservation.

The 1940s were a revolutionary time for jazz. Despite the shadow of war and the lack of materials for records and instruments, swing bands continued to thrive, and musicians such as Dizzy Gillespie and Charlie "Bird" Parker developed a fast, challenging, and harmonically advanced style that came to be known as bebop, or simply bop. A typical bop ensemble consisted of a four- or five-piece group that played tunes consisting of a melody called the "head," followed by ample room for soloing, and completed and closed by a return to the head.

Bop remains a staple of the jazz repertoire, but in the late 1950s it began to share the spotlight with other styles. Post-bop musicians, such as Hank Mobley and John Coltrane, worked at the same time as "free" jazz musicians, such as Cecil Taylor, Ornette Coleman, and Albert Ayler. Later in the 1960s, jazz adopted new elements, including electric instruments, long song forms, and a dialogue between jazz and pop music that continued through the 1970s in the style known as fusion.

Rhythm and Blues

Definition of Style

While the term remains in use as a category designation by some radio programmers and record retailers, the epoch of rhythm and blues (or R&B) truly spans the late 1940s to the early 1960s. As the term suggests, R&B was a combination of the swinging rhythm of jazz and other "race" music with the lyrical content, sonic gestures, and format of the blues. Its early days were dominated by high-energy bandleader-musicians such as Louis Jordan and Johnny Otis, but R&B at its height was largely a vocal form. The vocal-oriented exponents of R&B include the doo-wop groups of the 1950s, such as the Moonglows and the Penguins, and solo vocal artists such as Ruth Brown and Jackie Wilson. Perhaps equally important, the unexpected melding of R&B with country and western (or "hillbilly") music in the mid-1950s gave birth to rock and roll. Later still, in the mid-1960s, R&B would become soul music, as illustrated by the long, varied careers of artists such as James Brown.

Soul

Soul music is a type of music which grew out of rhythm and blues and gospel during the late 1950s and early 1960s among African Americans in the United States. Soul music usually features individual singers backed by a traditional band consisting of rhythm section and horns.

The development of soul music was spurred by two main trends: the urbanization of R&B and the secularization of gospel. Artists like Ben E. King, Ray Charles, Sam Cooke and the Everly Brothers mixed the passion of gospel vocals with the catchy, rhythmic music of R&B, thus forming soul in the late 1950s. Socially, the vast audience of white teens who had been listening to (primarily) watered-down white covers of black R&B and rock hits began demanding records by the original black artists, such as Little Richard and Chuck Berry. By the late 1950s, this had caused several record labels to seek out marketable versions of black music. The most influential labels were Stax, based out of Memphis, and Motown, based out of Detroit.

During the 1960s, soul music was popular among blacks in the US, and among many mainstream listeners throughout the United States and Europe. Blue eyed soul artists (white musicians who performed for white audiences) like the Righteous Brothers achieved the greatest success in the short term, though artists like Aretha Franklin and James Brown have proven more enduring. Other prominent soul performers of the period were Bobby Bland, Otis Redding, Wilson Pickett, and Joe Tex. Along with blue-eyed soul came a large number of regional varieties of soul.

By the early 1970s, soul music had been influenced by psychedelic rock and other influences, and artists like Marvin Gaye (What's Going On) and Curtis Mayfield (Superfly) released album-length statements with hard-hitting social commentary. Artists like James Brown had led soul towards a dance-oriented jam festival, resulting in 1970s funk bands like P Funk, The Meters and War. During the 70s, some highly slick and commercial blue eyed soul acts like Hall & Oates achieved mainstream success, along with The Delphonics and similar Philadelphia soul groups. By the end of the 70s disco was dominating the charts and funk, Philly soul and most other genres were dominated by disco-inflected tracks.

After the death of disco in the late 1970s, soul superstars like Prince (Purple Rain) and Michael Jackson (Off the Wall) took over. With sultry, sexually charged vocals and dance-able beats, these artists dominated the charts throughout the 1980s. Female soul singers like Whitney Houston, Janet Jackson and Tina Turner also gained great popularity during the last half of the decade.

In the early 1990s, alternative rock, hair metal and gangsta rap ruled the charts, though New Jack Swing groups began to merge hip hop and soul. Boyz II Men was the most popular of these groups, which quickly fell out of favor. During the later part of the decade, nu soul, which further mixed hip hop and soul, arose, led by Mary J. Blige, D'Angelo and Lauryn Hill.

Soul

Soul music is a type of music. The definition of the word "music" is hotly contested, not least because the word has strong connotations and use beyond the subject itself.

Music as sound: One common definition of music is to label it as "organized sound" or more ornately, "the artful organization of sound and silence." This definition is widely held to from the late 19th century forward, which began to scientifically analyze the relationship between sound and perception which grew out of rhythm and blues. Rhythm and Blues (R&B) is a musical marketing term introduced in the United States in the late 1940s by *Billboard* magazine. It replaced the term race music, which was deemed offensive. To some extent, the kind of music it is attached to has changed to whatever form of contemporary music is popular with African-American pop musicians and audiences. In its first manifestation, rhythm and gospel during the late 1950s and early 1960s among African Americans in the United States. Soul music usually features individual singers backed by a traditional band consisting of rhythm section and horns.

The development of soul music was spurred by two main trends: the urbanization of R&B and the secularization of gospel. Artists like Ben E. King, Ray Charles, Sam Cooke and the Everly Brothers mixed the passion of gospel vocals with the catchy, rhythmic music of R&B, thus forming soul in the late 1950s. Socially, the vast audience of white teens who had been listening to (primarily) watered-down white covers of black R&B and rock hits began demanding records by the original black artists, such as Little Richard and Chuck Berry. By the late 1950s, this had caused several record labels to seek out marketable versions of black music. The most influential labels were Stax, based out of Memphis, and Motown, based out of Detroit.

During the 1960s, soul music was popular among blacks in the US, and among many mainstream listeners throughout the United States and Europe. Blue eyed soul artists (white musicians who performed for white audiences) like the Righteous Brothers achieved the greatest success in the short term, though artists like Aretha Franklin and James Brown have proven more enduring. Other prominent soul performers of the period were Bobby Bland, Otis Redding, Wilson Pickett, and Joe Tex. Along with blue-eyed soul came a large number of regional varieties of soul.

By the early 1970s, soul music had been influenced by psychedelic rock and other influences, and artists like Marvin Gaye (What's Going On) and Curtis Mayfield (Superfly) released album-length statements with hard-hitting social commentary. Artists like James Brown had led soul towards a dance-oriented jam festival, resulting in 1970s funk bands like P Funk, The Meters and War. During the 70s, some highly slick and commercial blue eyed soul acts like Hall & Oates achieved mainstream success, along with The Delfonics and similar Philadelphia soul groups. By the end of the 70s disco was dominating the charts and funk, Philly soul and most other genres were dominated by disco-inflected tracks.

After the death of disco in the late 1970s, soul superstars like Prince (Purple Rain) and Michael Jackson (Off the Wall) took over. With sultry, sexually charged vocals and dance-able beats, these artists dominated the charts throughout the 1980s. Female soul singers like Whitney Houston, Janet Jackson and Tina Turner also gained great popularity during the last half of the decade.

In the early 1990s, alternative rock, hair metal and gangsta rap ruled the charts, though New Jack Swing groups began to merge hip hop and soul. Boyz II Men was the most popular of these groups, which quickly fell out of favor. During the later part of the decade, nu soul, which further mixed hip hop and soul, arose, led by Mary J. Blige, D'Angelo and Lauryn Hill.

Funk

Funk is a vigorous African American style of music developed mainly by James Brown and his band members (especially Maceo and Melvin Parker) on the one hand and groups like The Meters on the other hand. In the 1970s, George Clinton developed a new kind of funk he termed P Funk. Other prominent representatives of the genre in the 1970s: Bootsy Collins, Larry Graham, Ohio Players, The Commodores, War, Earth, Wind and Fire, Mass Production, Slave, Lakeside, and many more. In the 1980s, funk lost some of its audience as bands became more commercial and music more electronic. Today, hip hop artists regularly sample old funk tunes, sometimes for the purpose of waking them up to new recognition.

Funk can be best recognized by syncopated rhythm, thick bass line (often based on "on one" beat), razor-sharp rhythm guitars, yowlish vocals (as that of Cameo or Bar-Kays), strong rhythm-oriented brass section, percussion instruments, happiness in style, African tones, dance floor audience, and strong jazzy influences (e.g., as in Herbie Hancock, George Duke, Eddie Harris, and others).

Disco music owes a great deal to funk.

Louis Armstrong

Born: Aug 4, 1901 in New Orleans, LA
Died: Jul 6, 1971 in New York, NY
Styles: Vocal Jazz, Traditional Pop, New Orleans Jazz, Classic Jazz, Swing
Instruments: Vocals, Leader, Trumpet
Labels: Decca, Columbia, MCA, History, Classics, Storyville

Louis Armstrong was the first important soloist to emerge in jazz, and he became the most influential musician in the music's history. As a trumpet virtuoso, his playing, beginning with the 1920s studio recordings made with his Hot Five and Hot Seven ensembles, charted a future for jazz in highly imaginative, emotionally charged improvisation. For this, he is revered by jazz fans. But Armstrong also became an enduring figure in popular music, due to his distinctively phrased bass singing and engaging personality, which were on display in a series of vocal recordings and film roles.

Armstrong had a difficult childhood. William Armstrong, his father, was a factory worker who abandoned the family soon after the boy's birth. Armstrong was brought up by his mother, Mary (Albert) Armstrong, and his maternal grandmother. He showed an early interest in music, and a junk dealer for whom he worked as a grade-school student helped him buy a cornet, which he taught himself to play. He dropped out of school at 11 to join an informal group, but on December 31, 1912, he fired a gun during a New Year's Eve celebration, for which he was sent to reform school. He studied music there and played cornet and bugle in the school band, eventually becoming its leader. He was released on June 16, 1914, and did manual labor while trying to establish himself as a musician.

He was taken under the wing of cornetist Joe "King" Oliver, and when Oliver moved to Chicago in June 1918, he replaced him in the Kid Ory Band. He moved to the Fate Marable band in the spring of 1919, staying with Marable until the fall of 1921. Armstrong moved to Chicago to join Oliver's band in August 1922 and made his first recordings as a member of the group in the spring of 1923. He married Lillian Harden, the pianist in the Oliver band, on February 5, 1924. (She was the second of his four wives.) On her encouragement, he left Oliver and joined Fletcher Henderson's band in New York, staying for a year and then going back to Chicago in November 1925 to join the Dreamland Syncopators, his wife's group. During this period, he switched from cornet to trumpet. Armstrong had gained sufficient individual notice to make his recording debut as a leader on November 12, 1925.

Contracted to OKeh Records, he began to make a series of recordings with studio-only groups called the Hot Fives or the Hot Sevens. For live dates, he appeared with the orchestras led by Erskine Tate and Carroll Dickerson. The Hot Fives' recording of "Muskrat Ramble" gave Armstrong a Top Ten hit in July 1926, the band for the track featuring Kid Ory on trombone, Johnny Dodds on clarinet,

Lillian Harden Armstrong on piano, and Johnny St. Cyr on banjo.

By February 1927, Armstrong was well-enough known to front his own group, Louis Armstrong and His Stompers, at the Sunset Café in Chicago. (Armstrong did not function as a bandleader in the usual sense, but instead typically lent his name to established groups.) In April, he reached the charts with his first vocal recording, "Big Butter and Egg Man," a duet with May Alix. He took a position as star soloist in Carroll Dickerson's band at the Savoy Ballroom in Chicago in March 1928, later taking over as the band's frontman. "Hotter than That" was in the Top Ten in May 1928, followed in September by "West End Blues," which later became one of the first recordings named to the Grammy Hall of Fame. Armstrong returned to New York with his band for an engagement at Connie's Inn in Harlem in May 1929.

He also began appearing in the orchestra of Hot Chocolates, a Broadway revue, given a featured spot singing "Ain't Misbehavin'." In September, his recording of the song entered the charts, becoming a Top Ten hit. Armstrong fronted the Luis Russell Orchestra for a tour of the South in February 1930, then in May went to Los Angeles, where he led a band at Sebastian's Cotton Club for the next ten months. He made his film debut in *Ex-Flame*, released at the end of 1931.

By the start of 1932, he had switched from the "race"-oriented OKeh label to its pop-oriented big sister Columbia Records, for which he recorded two Top Five hits, "Chinatown, My Chinatown" and "You Can Depend on Me" before scoring a number one hit with "All of Me" in March 1932; another Top Five hit, "Love, You Funny Thing," hit the charts the same month. He returned to Chicago in the spring of 1932 to front a band led by Zilner Randolph; the group toured around the country.

In July, Armstrong sailed to England for a tour. He spent the next several years in Europe, his American career maintained by a series of archival recordings, including the Top Ten hits "Sweethearts on Parade" (August 1932; recorded December 1930) and "Body and Soul" (October 1932; recorded October 1930). His Top Ten version of "Hobo, You Can't Ride This Train," in the charts in early 1933, was on Victor Records; when he returned to the U.S. in 1935, he signed to recently formed Decca Records and quickly scored a double-sided Top Ten hit, "I'm in the Mood for Love"/"You Are My Lucky Star."

Armstrong's new manager, Joe Glaser, organized a big band for him that had its premiere in Indianapolis on July 1, 1935; for the next several years, he toured regularly. He also took a series of small parts in motion pictures, beginning with *Pennies From Heaven* in December 1936, and he continued to record for Decca, resulting in the Top Ten hits "Public Melody Number One" (August 1937), "When the Saints Go Marching in" (April 1939), and "You Won't Be Satisfied (Until You Break My Heart)" (April 1946), the last a duet with Ella Fitzgerald. He returned to Broadway in the short-lived musical Swingin' the Dream in November 1939.

With the decline of swing music in the post-World War II years, Armstrong broke up his big band and put together a small group dubbed the All Stars, which made its debut in Los Angeles on August 13,

1947. He embarked on his first European tour since 1935 in February 1948, and thereafter toured regularly around the world. In June 1951 he reached the Top Ten of the LP charts with *Satchmo at Symphony Hall* ("Satchmo" being his nickname), and he scored his first Top Ten single in five years with "(When We Are Dancing) I Get Ideas" later in the year. The single's B-side, and also a chart entry, was "A Kiss to Build a Dream On," sung by Armstrong in the film *The Strip*. In 1993, it gained renewed popularity when it was used in the film *Sleepless in Seattle*.

Armstrong completed his contract with Decca in 1954, after which his manager made the unusual decision not to sign him to another exclusive contract but instead to have him freelance for different labels. *Satch Plays Fats*, a tribute to Fats Waller, became a Top Ten LP for Columbia in October 1955, and Verve Records contracted Armstrong for a series of recordings with Ella Fitzgerald, beginning with the chart LP *Ella and Louis* in 1956. Armstrong continued to tour extensively, despite a heart attack in June 1959.

In 1964, he scored a surprise hit with his recording of the title song from the Broadway musical Hello, Dolly!, which reached number one in May, followed by a gold-selling album of the same name. It won him a Grammy for best vocal performance. This pop success was repeated internationally four years later with "What a Wonderful World," which hit number one in the U.K. in April 1968. It did not gain as much notice in the U.S. until 1987 when it was used in the film *Good Morning, Vietnam*, after which it became a Top 40 hit. Armstrong was featured in the 1969 film of *Hello, Dolly!*, performing the title song as a duet with Barbra Streisand.

He performed less frequently in the late '60s and early '70s and died of a heart ailment at 69. Louis Armstrong was embraced by two distinctly different audiences: jazz fans who revered him for his early innovations as an instrumentalist, but were occasionally embarrassed by his lack of interest in later developments in jazz and, especially, by his willingness to serve as a light entertainer; and pop fans, who delighted in his joyous performances, particularly as a vocalist, but were largely unaware of his significance as a jazz musician. Given his popularity, his long career, and the extensive label-jumping he did in his later years, as well as the differing jazz and pop sides of his work, his recordings are extensive and diverse, with parts of his catalog owned by many different companies. But many of his recorded performances are masterpieces, and none are less than entertaining.
—William Ruhlmann

Billie Holiday
Born: Eleanora Fagan Gough

Born: Apr 7, 1915 in Philadelphia, PA
Died: Jul 17, 1959 in New York, NY
Styles: Jazz, Torch Songs, Classic Female Blues, Ballads, Swing, Traditional Pop, Vocal Jazz, Standards
Labels: Columbia, Verve, Commodore, Decca

 The first popular jazz singer to move audiences with the intense, personal feeling of classic blues, Billie Holiday changed the art of American pop vocals forever. Almost fifty years after her death, it's difficult to believe that prior to her emergence,

jazz and pop singers were tied to the Tin Pan Alley tradition and rarely personalized their songs; only blues singers like Bessie Smith and Ma Rainey actually gave the impression they had lived through what they were singing. Billie Holiday's highly stylized reading of this blues tradition revolutionized traditional pop, ripping the decades-long tradition of song plugging in two by refusing to compromise her artistry for either the song or the band. She made clear her debts to Bessie Smith and Louis Armstrong (in her autobiography she admitted, "I always wanted Bessie's big sound and Pops' feeling"), but in truth her style was virtually her own, quite a shock in an age of interchangeable crooners and band singers.

With her spirit shining through on every recording, Holiday's technical expertise also excelled in comparison to the great majority of her contemporaries. Often bored by the tired old Tin Pan Alley songs she was forced to record early in her career, Holiday fooled around with the beat and the melody, phrasing behind the beat and often rejuvenating the standard melody with harmonies borrowed from her favorite horn players, Armstrong and Lester Young. (She often said she tried to sing like a horn.) Her notorious private life—a series of abusive relationships, substance addictions, and periods of depression—undoubtedly assisted her legendary status, but Holiday's best performances ("Lover Man," "Don't Explain," "Strange Fruit," her own composition "God Bless the Child") remain among the most sensitive and accomplished vocal performances ever recorded. More than technical ability, more than purity of voice, what made Billie Holiday one of the best vocalists of the century—easily the equal of Ella Fitzgerald or Frank Sinatra—was her relentlessly individualist temperament, a quality that colored every one of her endlessly nuanced performances.

Billie Holiday's chaotic life reportedly began in Baltimore on April 7, 1915 (a few reports say 1912) when she was born Eleanora Fagan Gough. Her father, Clarence Holiday, was a teenaged jazz guitarist and banjo player later to play in Fletcher Henderson's Orchestra. He never married her mother, Sadie Fagan, and left while his daughter was still a baby. (She would later run into him in New York, and though she contracted many guitarists for her sessions before his death in 1937, she always avoided using him.) Holiday's mother was also a young teenager at the time, and whether because of inexperience or neglect, often left her daughter with uncaring relatives. Holiday was sentenced to Catholic reform school at the age of ten, reportedly after she admitted being raped. Though sentenced to stay until she became an adult, a family friend helped get her released after just two years. With her mother, she moved in 1927, first to New Jersey and soon after to Brooklyn.

In New York, Holiday helped her mother with domestic work, but soon began moonlighting as a prostitute for the additional income. According to the weighty Billie Holiday legend (which gained additional credence after her notoriously apocryphal autobiography *Lady Sings the Blues*), her big singing break came in 1933 when a laughable dancing audition at a speakeasy prompted her accompanist to ask her if she could sing. In fact, Holiday was most likely singing at clubs all over New York City as early as 1930–31. Whatever the true story, she first gained some publicity in early 1933, when record producer John Hammond—only three years older than Holiday herself, and just at the beginning of a legendary career—wrote her up in a column for Melody Maker and brought Benny Goodman to one of her performances. After recording a demo at Columbia Studios, Holiday joined a small group led by Goodman to make her commercial debut on November 27, 1933 with "Your Mother's Son-In-Law."

Though she didn't return to the studio for over a year, Billie Holiday spent 1934 moving up the rungs of the competitive New York bar scene. By early 1935, she made her debut at the Apollo Theater and appeared in a one-reeler film with Duke Ellington. During the last half of 1935, Holiday finally entered the studio again and recorded a total of four sessions. With a pick-up band supervised by pianist Teddy Wilson, she recorded a series of obscure, forgettable songs straight from the gutters of Tin Pan Alley—in other words, the only songs available to an obscure black band during the mid-'30s. (During the swing era, music publishers kept the best songs strictly in the hands of society orchestras and popular white singers.) Despite the poor song quality, Holiday and various groups (including trumpeter Roy Eldridge, alto Johnny Hodges, and tenors Ben Webster and Chu Berry) energized flat songs like "What a Little Moonlight Can Do," "Twenty-Four Hours a Day" and "If You Were Mine" (to say nothing of "Eeny Meeny Miney Mo" and "Yankee Doodle Never Went to Town"). The great combo playing and Holiday's increasingly assured vocals made them quite popular on Columbia, Brunswick and Vocalion.

During 1936, Holiday toured with groups led by Jimmie Lunceford and Fletcher Henderson, then returned to New York for several more sessions. In late January 1937, she recorded several numbers with a small group culled from one of Hammond's new discoveries, Count Basie's Orchestra. Tenor Lester Young, who'd briefly known Billie several years earlier, and trumpeter Buck Clayton were to become especially attached to Holiday. The three did much of their best recorded work together during the late '30s, and Holiday herself bestowed the nickname Pres on Young, while he dubbed her Lady Day for her elegance. By the spring of 1937, she began touring with Basie as the female complement to his male singer, Jimmy Rushing. The association lasted less than a year, however. Though officially she was fired from the band for being temperamental and unreliable, shadowy influences higher up in the publishing world reportedly commanded the action after she refused to begin singing '20s female blues standards.

At least temporarily, the move actually benefited Holiday—less than a month after leaving Basie, she was hired by Artie Shaw's popular band. She began singing with the group in 1938, one of the first instances of a black female appearing with a white group. Despite the continuing support of the entire band, however, show promoters and radio sponsors soon began objecting to Holiday—based on her unorthodox singing style almost as much as her race. After a series of escalating indignities, Holiday quit the band in disgust.

Yet again, her judgment proved valuable; the added freedom allowed her to take a gig at a hip new club named Café Society, the first popular nightspot with an inter-racial audience. There, Billie Holiday learned the song that would catapult her career to a new level: "Strange Fruit."

The standard, written by Café Society regular Lewis Allen and forever tied to Holiday, is an anguished reprisal of the intense racism still persistent in the South. Though Holiday initially expressed doubts about adding such a bald, uncompromising song to her repertoire, she pulled it off thanks largely to her powers of nuance and subtlety. "Strange Fruit" soon became the highlight of her performances. Though John Hammond refused to record it (not for its politics but for its overly pungent imagery), he allowed Holiday a bit of leverage to record for Commodore, the label owned by jazz record-store owner Milt Gabler. Once released, "Strange Fruit" was banned by many radio outlets, though the growing jukebox industry (and the inclusion of the excellent "Fine and Mellow" on the flip) made it a rather large, though controversial, hit. She continued recording for Columbia labels until 1942, and hit big again with her most famous composition, 1941's "God Bless the Child." Gabler, who also worked A&R for Decca, signed her to the label in 1944 to record "Lover Man," a song written especially for her and her third big hit. Neatly side-stepping the musician's union ban that afflicted her former label, Holiday soon became a priority at Decca, earning the right to top-quality material and lavish string sections for her sessions. She continued recording scattered sessions for Decca during the rest of the '40s, and recorded several of her best-loved songs including Bessie Smith's "'Tain't Nobody's Business If I Do," "Them There Eyes," and "Crazy He Calls Me."

Though her artistry was at its peak, Billie Holiday's emotional life began a turbulent period during the mid-'40s. Already heavily into alcohol and marijuana, she began smoking opium early in the decade with her first husband, Johnnie Monroe. The marriage didn't last, but hot on its heels came a second marriage to trumpeter Joe Guy and a move to heroin. Despite her triumphant concert at New York's Town Hall and a small film role—as a maid (!)—with Louis Armstrong in 1947's *New Orleans*, she lost a good deal of money running her own orchestra with Joe Guy. Her mother's death soon after affected her deeply, and in 1947 she was arrested for possession of heroin and sentenced to eight months in prison.

Unfortunately, Holiday's troubles only continued after her release. The drug charge made it impossible for her to get a cabaret card, so nightclub performances were out of the question. Plagued by various celebrity hawks from all portions of the underworld (jazz, drugs, song publishing, etc.), she soldiered on for Decca until 1950. Two years later, she began recording for jazz entrepreneur Norman Granz, owner of the excellent labels Clef, Norgran, and by 1956, Verve. The recordings returned her to the small-group intimacy of her Columbia work, and reunited her with Ben Webster as well as other top-flight musicians such as Oscar Peterson, Harry "Sweets" Edison, and Charlie Shavers. Though the ravages of a hard life were beginning to take their toll on her voice, many of Holiday's mid-'50s recordings are just as intense and beautiful as her classic work.

During 1954, Holiday toured Europe to great acclaim, and her 1956 autobiography brought her even more fame (or notoriety). She made her last great appearance in 1957, on the CBS television special *The Sound of Jazz* with Webster, Lester Young, and Coleman Hawkins providing a close backing. One year later, the *Lady in Satin* LP clothed her naked, increasingly hoarse voice with the overwrought strings of Ray Ellis. During her final year, she made two more appearances in Europe before collapsing in May 1959 of heart and liver disease. Still procuring heroin while on her death bed, Holiday was arrested for possession in her private room and died on July 17, her system completely unable to fight both withdrawal and heart disease at the same time. Her cult of influence spread quickly after her death and gave her more fame than she'd enjoyed in life. The 1972 biopic *Lady Sings the Blues* featured Diana Ross struggling to overcome the conflicting myths of Holiday's life, but the film also illuminated her tragic life and introduced many future fans. By the digital age, virtually all of Holiday's recorded material had been reissued: by Columbia (nine volumes of *The Quintessential Billie Holiday*), Decca (*The Complete Decca Recordings*), and Verve (*The Complete Billie Holiday on Verve 1945–1959*). —John Bush

Nat King Cole
Born: Nathaniel Adams Coles

Born: Mar 17, 1917 in Montgomery, AL
Died: Feb 15, 1965 in Santa Monica, CA
Styles: Jazz, Vocal Jazz, Traditional Pop, Swing, Ballads, Jump Blues
Labels: Capitol Records

 For a mild-mannered man whose music was always easy on the ear, Nat King Cole managed to be a figure of considerable controversy during his 30 years as a professional musician. From the late '40s to the mid-'60s, he was a massively successful pop singer who ranked with such contemporaries as Frank Sinatra, Perry Como, and Dean Martin. He shared with those peers a career that encompassed hit records, international touring, radio and television shows, and appearances in films. But unlike them, he had not emerged from a background as a band singer in the swing era. Instead, he had spent a decade as a celebrated jazz pianist, leading his own small group. Oddly, that was one source of controversy. For some reason, there seem to be more jazz critics than fans of traditional pop among music journalists, and Cole's transition from jazz to pop during a period when jazz itself was becoming less popular was seen by them as a betrayal. At the same time, as a prominent African-American entertainer during an era of tumultuous change in social relations among the races in the U.S., he sometimes found himself out of favor with different warring sides. His efforts at integration, which included suing hotels that refused to admit him and moving into a previously all-white neighborhood in Los Angeles, earned the enmity

of racists; once, he was even physically attacked on-stage in Alabama. But civil rights activists sometimes criticized him for not doing enough for the cause.

Such controversies do not obscure his real talent as a performer, however. The dismay of jazz fans at his abandonment of jazz must be measured against his accomplishments as a jazz musician. An heir of Earl Hines, whom he studied closely as a child in Chicago, Cole was an influence on such followers as Oscar Peterson. And his trio, emerging in the dying days of the swing era, helped lead the way in small-band jazz. The rage felt by jazz fans as he moved primarily to pop singing is not unlike the anger folk music fans felt when Bob Dylan turned to rock in the mid-'60s; in both cases, it was all the more acute because fans felt one of their leaders, not just another musician, was going over to the enemy. Less well remembered, however, are Cole's accomplishments during and after the transition. His rich, husky voice and careful enunciation, and the warmth, intimacy, and good humor of his approach to singing, allowed him to succeed with both ballads and novelties such that he scored over 100 pop chart singles and more than two dozen chart albums over a period of 20 years, enough to rank him behind only Sinatra as the most successful pop singer of his generation.

Nat King Cole was born Nathaniel Adams Coles in Montgomery, AL, on March 17, 1919. (In his early years of music-making, he dispensed with the "s" at the end of his name.) As a black child born to a poor family in the American South at that time, he did not have a birth certificate. His March 17 birthday was recalled because it was also St. Patrick's Day. He listed conflicting years of birth on legal documents during his life; most sources give the year as 1917. But biographer Daniel Mark Epstein, for his 1999 book *Nat King Cole*, consulted the 1920 census to determine that the Coles household had a male infant at that time and confirm the birth year as 1919. Cole's father was a butcher who aspired to the Baptist ministry, and when Cole was four the family moved to Chicago, where his father eventually succeeded in becoming a preacher.

Like his older brother Eddie, who became a bass player, Cole showed an early interest in music. He was taught piano by his mother as a child and later took lessons. Also like his brother, he turned professional early; by his teens, he was leading a band, called either the Royal Dukes or the Rogues of Rhythm, and he dropped out of high school at 15 to go into music full-time. The following year, Eddie, who had been touring with Noble Sissle's band, returned to Chicago and the brothers organized their own sextet. On July 28, 1936, as Eddie Cole's Swingsters, they recorded two singles for Decca Records, Nat King Cole's recording debut. That fall, they were hired to perform in a revival of the all-black Broadway musical revue Shuffle Along. Unlike his brother, Cole remained with the show when it went on tour, in part because his girlfriend, dancer Nadine Robinson, stayed with it as well. The two married in Michigan on January 27, 1937, even though Cole was only 17 years old. The tour made its way around the country, finally closing in Los Angeles in May. Cole and his wife remained there, living at first with her aunt, while

Cole sought employment as a musician. He briefly led a big band, then played solo piano in clubs.

While performing at the Café Century during the summer of 1937, Cole was approached by the manager of the Swanee Inn, who invited him to put together a small band to play in the club. With guitarist Oscar Moore and bassist Wesley Prince, the act debuted that fall, drawing upon the children's nursery rhyme ("Old King Cole was a merry old soul . . .") for the name the King Cole Swingsters, later simply the King Cole Trio. The group gradually built up a following, with Cole emerging as a singer as well as a pianist. By September 1938, they had begun making radio transcriptions, originally not intended for commercial release, though they have since been issued. In 1939 and 1940, they made occasional recordings for small labels while expanding their live performing to include appearances across the country and radio work. In late 1940 they were contracted by Decca. Their 1941 recording of Cole's composition "That Ain't Right" hit number one on *Billboard* magazine's Harlem Hit Parade (i.e., R&B) chart on January 30, 1943, Cole's first successful record. By that time, Prince had left the group to work for the war effort, replaced by Johnny Miller.

The King Cole Trio's contract with Decca expired before "That Ain't Right" became a hit. Their next single, "All for You," was recorded for the tiny Excelsior label in October 1942. After its initial release, it was purchased by Capitol Records and reissued. On November 20, 1943, it became the group's second number one hit on the Harlem Hit Parade. It also crossed over to the pop chart. With that, Capitol signed Cole directly. The trio's first Capitol session produced both the Cole composition "Straighten Up and Fly Right," which topped the black chart for the first of ten weeks on April 29, 1944, spent six weeks at the top of the folk (i.e., country) chart, and reached the Top Ten of the pop chart, and "Gee Baby, Ain't I Good to You," which topped the black chart on October 21 and also crossed over to the pop chart.

The trio placed another four titles in the black chart during 1944, and Capitol released its debut album, *The King Cole Trio* (catalog number BD-8) that fall. The collection of four 78 rpm discs contained eight tracks, only three of them featuring Cole vocals. When *Billboard* instituted its first album chart on March 24, 1945, *The King Cole Trio* was ranked at number one, a position it held for 12 weeks. At the same time, big-band swing music was declining in popularity, and many jazz fans were beginning to turn to the emerging style of bebop, a development that, whatever its artistic significance, spelled the end of jazz as a broadly popular style of music.

The King Cole Trio—and particularly the singer/pianist then known as "King Cole"—on the other hand, was going in exactly the opposite direction, as its success on records and at clubs and theaters around the country led to appearances in films and on radio. After numerous guest-star stints on Bing Crosby's Kraft Music Hall radio series, the trio, along with pianist Eddy Duchin, was hired to host the show's summer replacement program for 13 weeks beginning May 16, 1946. During that run, on August 17, *The King Cole Trio, Vol. 2* (Capitol BD-29), another set of four 78s, hit number one. Over the next five days, the trio recorded two songs that would add to their pop success. Mel Tormé and Robert Wells' "The Christmas Song (Merry Christmas to You)" (better known by its opening line, "Chestnuts roasting on an open fire"), recorded August 19, was Cole's first disc to feature strings. "(I Love You) For Sentimental Reasons," though it only featured the trio, demonstrated that Cole was more than capable of handling a straight romantic ballad, not just the uptempo novelties with which he and the group had succeeded up until this point.

"(I Love You) For Sentimental Reasons" became Cole's first number one pop single on December 28, 1946; "The Christmas Song (Merry Christmas to You)" peaked at number three, going on to become a holiday perennial and million seller. While these hits were developing, the trio went from its summer replacement berth to its own network radio series, King Cole Trio Time, a 15-minute Saturday afternoon program that debuted on October 19, 1946, and ran until April 1948. The group's recording schedule during the first half of 1947 was relatively light, but the pace picked up considerably starting in August, in anticipation of the musicians' strike called for January 1, 1948. On August 22, 1947, with an orchestral backing, Cole recorded "Nature Boy," an unusual philosophical ballad. Released March 29, 1948, and credited to "King Cole," it hit number one for the first of eight weeks on May 8, becoming a gold record.

Oscar Moore, the trio's original guitarist, left the group in October 1947 after ten years and was replaced by Irving Ashby. In March 1948, Cole divorced his wife and married singer Marie Ellington.

Among the couple's children was Natalie Cole, who became a singer. Bass player Johnny Miller quit the trio in August 1948 and was replaced by Joe Comfort. In February 1949, Cole added percussionist Jack Costanzo to the group, which thereafter was billed as "Nat 'King' Cole & the Trio." As of the spring of 1950, Cole's recordings were being credited simply to "Nat 'King' Cole." On July 8 of that year, his recording of the wistful movie theme "Mona Lisa," featuring a string chart arranged by Nelson Riddle, became Cole's third number one pop hit and gold record.

That September, he traveled to Europe for his first international tour, beginning a pattern that would find him giving concerts almost continually in a combination of top nightclubs in major cities and concert halls around the U.S., with occasional trips to Europe, the Far East, and Latin America and extended stays at Las Vegas casinos. In these appearances, he stood for most of the show, only occasionally sitting down to play a number or two at the piano. Ashby and Comfort left in 1951, and an announcement was made that the trio was officially dissolved, but that simply meant that Cole henceforth would be billed as a solo act. In practice, he continued to carry a guitarist, John Collins, and a bassist, Charles Harris, along with Costanzo (until he left in 1953 and was replaced by drummer Lee Young), while often augmenting them with an orchestra.

Cole scored his fourth number one pop hit and gold record with "Too Young," which topped the charts on June 23, 1951. His recording of "Unforgettable" peaked at only number 12 on February 2, 1952, but it went on to become one of his better remembered recordings; in 1991, a version of the song by Natalie Cole with the Nat King Cole recording dubbed onto it became a gold record and won the Grammy Award for Record of the Year. With his 1952 LP *Penthouse Serenade*, Cole showed that he was not yet ready to dispense with his jazz chops entirely. The disc was an instrumental collection that spent one week at number ten in the album chart in October. Meanwhile, he was also looking for new challenges, taking on small acting roles in the films *The Blue Gardenia* and *Small Town Girl* and the television drama *Song for a Banjo* in 1953. His 1953 album *Nat King Cole Sings for Two in Love*, arranged and conducted by Nelson Riddle, was a Top Ten hit in early 1954 that predated similar "concept" albums by Frank Sinatra.

Although Cole did not score a number one hit in 1953 ("Pretend" peaked at number two), his seven chart entries were enough to rank him among the ten most successful singles artists of the year. His five chart singles in 1954, among them the gold-selling Top Ten hit "Answer Me, My Love," allowed him to repeat this ranking the following year, and he did the same thing in 1955 with another eight chart entries, including the Top Ten hits "Darling Je Vous Aime Beaucoup," "A Blossom Fell," and "If I May." Nine more chart entries allowed him to stay among the most successful singles artists in 1956, even though none of them reached the Top Ten, and he maintained his rank for the fifth straight year in 1957, reaching the Top Ten (and the top of the R&B chart) with "Send for Me." Though he managed one more Top Ten hit, "Looking Back," in 1958, the rise of rock & roll diminished his success on the singles chart. Meanwhile, he returned to a jazz approach on his 1957 LP *After Midnight*, which paired his backup group with jazz musicians Harry "Sweets" Edison, Stuff Smith, Willie Smith, and Juan Tizol. It was a modest commercial success, quickly followed by the ballad album *Love Is the Thing*, arranged and conducted by Gordon Jenkins, which hit number one for the first of eight weeks on May 27, 1957, and eventually was certified platinum.

Meanwhile, in the fall of 1956, Cole became the first African-American host of a network television series when *The Nat "King" Cole Show* debuted as a 15-minute weekly program on November 5. The show was expanded to a half-hour in July 1957 and ran until December of that year, though it never attracted a national sponsor that might have made it an ongoing success. Cole attributed advertisers' reticence to racism. He returned to his acting career during 1957, appearing in *Istanbul* and *China Gate*, and got his most substantial role in 1958 playing blues musician W.C. Handy in a film biography, *St. Louis Blues*. His last acting role came in *Night of the Quarter Moon* in 1959. In 1960, he turned his attention to the theater, putting together a musical revue intended for Broadway. The songs were by Dotty Wayne and Ray Rasch, and the album Cole made of them, *Wild Is Love*, became his first Top Ten LP in three years. The corresponding stage show, I'm With You, was not as successful, opening what was intended to be a pre-Broadway tour in Denver on October 17, 1960, but closing in Detroit on November 26. Cole, however, salvaged the concept of the show for a stage production he called Sights and

Sounds: The Merry World of Nat King Cole, featuring a group of dancers and singers, with which he toured regularly from 1961 to 1964.

Cole returned to the Top Ten of the singles chart for the first time in four years with the country-tinged "Ramblin' Rose" in 1962; his album of the same name also reached the Top Ten and eventually was certified platinum. "Those Lazy-Hazy-Crazy Days of Summer" became his last Top Ten hit in the summer of 1963. In December 1964, he was diagnosed with lung cancer. Two months later, he died of it at the age of 48.

After his death, Cole continued to appeal to the two almost mutually exclusive audiences that had appreciated him during his life. Jazz fans continued to treasure his recordings of the 1930s and 1940s and to dismiss the non-jazz recordings he had made later. (In 1994, German discographer Klaus Teubig compiled Straighten Up and Fly Right: A Chronology and Discography of Nat "King" Cole, which pointedly cut off in the early '50s.) Pop fans clamored for reissues of Cole's 1950s and '60s music, awarding gold record status to compilations that Capitol continued to assemble, without much worrying about the singer's talent as a piano player. (And, as his recordings fell into the public domain in Europe, where there is a 50-year copyright limit, a spate of low-quality reissues assumed flood levels.) But the ongoing debate was only testament to Cole's ongoing attraction for music lovers, which, in the decades following his untimely end, showed no signs of abating. —William Ruhlmann

Ray Charles
Born: Ray Charles Robinson

Born: Sep 23, 1930 in Albany, GA
Died: Jun 10, 2004 in Beverly Hills, CA
Styles: Soul, R&B, Blues, Piano Blues, Urban Blues, Jazz Blues, Country-Soul, Pop-Soul
Labels: Atlantic, ABC-Paramount, Tangerine

Ray Charles was the musician most responsible for developing soul music. Singers like Sam Cooke and Jackie Wilson also did a great deal to pioneer the form, but Charles did even more to devise a new form of black pop by merging '50s R&B with gospel-powered vocals, adding plenty of flavor from contemporary jazz, blues, and (in the '60s) country. Then there was his singing; his style was among the most emotional and easily identifiable of any 20th-century performer, up there with the likes of Elvis and Billie Holiday. He was also a superb keyboard player, arranger, and bandleader. The brilliance of his 1950s and '60s work, however, can't obscure the fact that he made few classic tracks after the mid-'60s, though he recorded often and performed until the year before his death.

Blind since the age of six (from glaucoma), Charles studied composition and learned many instruments at the St. Augustine School for the Deaf and the Blind. His parents had died by his early teens, and he worked as a musician in Florida for a while before using his savings to move to Seattle in 1947. By the late '40s, he was recording in a smooth pop/R&B style derivative of Nat "King" Cole and Charles Brown. He got his first Top Ten R&B hit with "Baby, Let Me Hold Your Hand" in 1951. Charles' first recordings came in for their fair share of criticism, as they were much milder and less original than the classics that would follow, although they're actually fairly enjoyable, showing strong hints of the skills that were to flower in a few years.

In the early '50s, Charles' sound started to toughen as he toured with Lowell Fulson, went to New Orleans to work with Guitar Slim (playing piano on and arranging Slim's huge R&B hit, "The Things That I Used to Do"), and got a band together for R&B star Ruth Brown. It was at Atlantic Records that Ray Charles truly found his voice, consolidating the gains of recent years and then some with "I Got a Woman," a number-two R&B hit in 1955. This is the song most frequently singled out as his pivotal performance, on which Charles first truly let go with his unmistakable gospel-ish moan, backed by a tight, bouncy horn-driven arrangement.

Throughout the '50s, Charles ran off a series of R&B hits that, although they weren't called "soul" at the time, did a lot to pave the way for soul by presenting a form of R&B that was sophisticated without sacrificing any emotional grit. "This Little Girl of Mine," "Drown in My Own Tears," "Hallelujah I Love Her So," "Lonely Avenue," and "The Right Time" were all big hits. But Charles didn't really capture the pop audience until "What'd I Say," which caught the fervor of the church with its pleading vocals, as well as the spirit of rock & roll with its classic electric piano line. It was his first Top Ten pop hit, and one of his final Atlantic singles, as he left the label at the end of the '50s for ABC.

One of the chief attractions of the ABC deal for Charles was a much greater degree of artistic control of his recordings. He put it to good use on early-'60s hits like "Unchain My Heart" and "Hit the Road Jack," which solidified his pop stardom with only a modicum of polish attached to the R&B he had perfected at Atlantic. In 1962, he surprised the pop world by turning his attention to country & western music, topping the charts with the "I Can't Stop Loving You" single, and making a hugely popular album (in an era in which R&B/soul LPs rarely scored high on the charts) with *Modern Sounds in Country and Western Music*. Perhaps it shouldn't have been so surprising; Charles had always been eclectic, recording quite a bit of straight jazz at Atlantic, with noted jazz musicians like David "Fathead" Newman and Milt Jackson.

Charles remained extremely popular through the mid-'60s, scoring big hits like "Busted," "You Are My Sunshine," "Take These Chains From My Heart," and "Crying Time," although his momentum was slowed by a 1965 bust for heroin. This led to a year-long absence from performing, but he picked up where he left off with "Let's Go Get Stoned" in 1966. Yet by this time Charles was focusing increasingly less on rock and soul, in favor of pop tunes, often with string arrangements, that seemed aimed more at the easy listening audience than anyone else. Charles' influence on the rock mainstream was as apparent as ever; Joe Cocker and Steve Winwood in particular owe a great deal of their style to him, and echoes of his phrasing can be heard more subtly in the work of greats like Van Morrison.

One approaches sweeping criticism of Charles with hesitation; he was an American institution, after all, and his vocal powers barely diminished over his half-century career. The fact remains, though, that his work after the late '60s on record was very disappointing. Millions of listeners yearned for a return to the all-out soul of his 1955–1965 classics, but Charles had actually never been committed to soul above all else. Like Aretha Franklin and Elvis Presley, his focus was more upon all-around pop than many realize; his love of jazz, country, and pop standards was evident, even if his more earthy offerings were the ones that truly broke ground and will stand the test of time.

He dented the charts (sometimes the country ones) occasionally, and commanded devoted international concert audiences whenever he felt like it. For good or ill, he ensured his imprint upon the American mass consciousness in the 1990s by singing several ads for Diet Pepsi. He also recorded three albums during the '90s for Warner Bros., but remained most popular as a concert draw. In 2002, he released *Thanks for Bringing Love Around Again* on his own Crossover imprint, and the following year began recording an album of duets featuring B.B. King, Willie Nelson, Michael McDonald, and James Taylor. After hip replacement surgery in 2003, he scheduled a tour for the following summer, but was forced to cancel an appearance in March 2004. Three months later, on June 10, 2004, Ray Charles succumbed to liver disease at his home in Beverly Hills, CA. —Richie Unterberger

The Ink Spots

Formed in 1938

The Ink Spots played a large role in pioneering the black vocal group-harmony genre, helping to pave the way for the doo wop explosion of the '50s. The quavering high tenor of Bill Kenny presaged hundreds of street-corner leads to come, and the sweet harmonies of Charlie Fuqua, Deek Watson, and bass Hoppy Jones (who died in 1944) backed him flawlessly.

Kenny's impeccable diction and Jones's deep drawl were both prominent on the Ink Spots' first smash on Decca in 1939, the sentimental "If I Didn't Care." From then through 1951, the group was seldom absent from the pop charts, topping the lists with "We Three (My Echo, My Shadow, and Me)" (1940), "I'm Making Believe" and "Into Each Life Some Rain Must Fall" (both in 1944), and "The Gypsy" and "To Each His Own" (both in 1946).

Watson eventually split to form his own group, the Brown Dots, and appeared in numerous low-budget film musicals, while Kenny attempted a solo career, notching a solo hit in 1951 with the uplifting "It Is No Secret." Countless groups masquerading as the Ink Spots have thrived across the nation since the '50s.

The Ravens

Formed 1946 in New York, NY

The Ravens were among the pioneering post-World War II R&B groups, and also among the earliest R&B groups named for birds. In both their musicality and their

nomenclature, they influenced two generations of performers that followed, as well as sold lots of records in the process. The Ravens originated with Jimmy Ricks, who started singing at an early age. In 1945, he was employed as a waiter at the Four Hundred Tavern and later at an establishment known as the L. Bar, both in New York's Harlem. One of his co-workers was a friend, Warren "Birdland" Suttles, and during moments when the work wasn't too frantic, the two began singing together, to tunes by the Ink Spots, the Mills Brothers, the Delta Rhythm Boys, and other harmony groups whose music appeared on the club's jukebox. They decided to try and form an actual group, searching for two more members that would make up the requisite harmony quartet. The two hooked up with Leonard "Zeke" Puzey and Ollie Jones, and worked up their sound around songs such as "Darktown Strutters' Ball." Choosing the name The Ravens, and thus inaugurating the "bird" group trend in black vocal groups, they were booked into the Club Baton in Harlem, and proved themselves sufficiently talented to rate a national tour, also picking up Howard Biggs, who became their arranger and the composer of much of their original repertory. The Ravens' sound was unusual for its time, featuring bass singer Jimmy Ricks as the lead voice—this would become their trademark and one of their most often emulated attributes over the next decade.

The Orioles

Formed 1948 in Baltimore, MD

The Orioles consisted of lead vocalist Sonny Til (born Earlington Carl Tilghman, August 18, 1928; d. December 9, 1981), Alexander Sharp (tenor vocals), George Nelson (baritone vocals), Johnny Reed (bass vocals), and guitarist Tommy Gaither. Originally called the Vibranaires, the group formed when its members were teenagers. They came to the attention of Deborah Chessler, a local merchant who also wrote songs; she would write many of the group's subsequent hits. Chessler became the band's manager and she was able to get the Vibranaires a spot on Arthur Godfrey's Talent Scouts television show. Although the group lost to pianist George Shearing, they caught the eye of Jerry Blaine, a New York record company executive, while they were in town for the program.

Led by Sonny Til, the Orioles were the first black vocal group to sing music directly for a black audience. Through their early recordings—which were made in the late '40s and early '50s—the band laid the groundwork for R&B vocal groups and doo wop. The Orioles fused traditional pop songs with gospel sensibilities and arranged blues and gospel material with smooth harmonies, designed to appeal to the broadest audience possible.

The Moonglows

Formed 1951 in Louisville, KY

The Moonglows were among the most important R&B groups of the 1950s, despite the fact that they only had a handful of hits among fewer than 50 recorded songs, in a history that lasted just six years, in sharp contrast to such acts as the Orioles and the Drifters, who were together across decades and recorded huge bodies of work.

Chicago-born Harvey Fuqua (born July 27, 1928) was part of a musical family virtually from birth, as the nephew of Ink Spots guitarist Charlie Fuqua, and before he was in his teens was aiming for a career of his own in music. He grew up in Louisville, KY, where he learned the piano and also began singing with his high school classmate Bobby Lester (born January 13, 1930; died October 15, 1980) at dances. They formed a professional duo in Louisville during 1949, after both finished brief periods of serving in the military, and were soon working with saxman and bandleader Ed Wiley, and it was in his group that they started singing jump and blues. Eventually a lack of earnings led them to split up, with Fuqua moving to Cleveland, where he crossed paths with an army buddy, Danny Coggins, and a neighbor of his, Prentiss Barnes (born April 25, 1925), who'd previously been a gospel singer, and formed a trio.

Fuqua brought Lester into the group, which was known as the Crazy Sounds, and they started to get work in the area around Cleveland. They were an improvisational singing group that specialized in a technique called vocalese, using their voices to replace instruments, basically in a jazz context, somewhat similar to the work of the Swingle Singers and the Manhattan Transfer. Their first break came in 1952 when they came to the attention of local disc jockey Alan Freed, who was already making a name for himself playing R&B records. They auditioned and did well enough to earn a chance to record on Freed's own Champagne Records label, changing their name to the Moonglows in the process in an effort to hook their recognition to Freed's on-air persona as "Moondog." The group enjoyed a modest local hit with a Lester composition, "I Just Can't Tell No Lie." They began performing in venues throughout the industrial Midwest and underwent their first membership change when Coggins quit for a more stable life as a gas station owner. He was replaced by Alex Walton and Alexander Graves.

Lester and Fuqua shared the lead vocal spot, sometimes even on the same song, and both of them had a keen interest in songwriting as well. The group was special not only for their mix of subtle polish and visceral excitement, but also the sheer attractiveness of the singing and the way in which their arrangements locked it all together—Lester and Fuqua were the leads and the most visible talents, but there were no weak links anywhere in the Moonglows' sound; from bass to the occasional falsetto, all of the singing was dazzling, animated, and bracing, whether on the jump numbers or the ballads; each of their finished records was the total package, distinctly voiced, gorgeously textured, and exciting. In the early fall of 1953, Freed landed the group a contract with Chance Records, a small Chicago outfit that was making a serious noise in blues and R&B, and already had the Flamingoes and the Spaniels under contract. For a year, they tried to chart with ballads—including a killer version of "Secret Love" with Lester singing lead—and jump numbers but saw little success at Chance, before they were dropped.

In October of 1954, the group moved to Chess Records, and their first session was one of the most productive in the history of the label, yielding 13 songs including one of the biggest hits in Chess' history, "Sincerely"—authored by Fuqua (with Freed taking half the royalties as "co-author," a common arrangement at the time for Freed and other managers), the Moonglows' recording charted in December of that year and bumped "Earth Angel" by the Penguins out of the number one R&B spot the following month, and later climbed to number 20 on the Hot 100 pop chart. The single rode the R&B listings for 20 weeks and sold over a quarter of a million copies, an extraordinary number for Chess in those days and all of it happening before R&B had fully crossed over to white listeners.

It was numbers like this that were delighting independent executives like Phil and Leonard Chess, and giving ulcers to executives at the major labels, who saw something happening in music that they'd somehow missed over the preceding year or two and were having trouble grasping even then. In the case of "Sincerely," it was such an attractive song that it begged to be covered by other artists in other styles—thus, the Moonglows became one of the earliest R&B groups to see an original of theirs picked up by a pop act, when the white sibling vocal trio the McGuire Sisters covered "Sincerely" in a pop style and got a number one pop hit and a million-selling single out of it. The success of the Moonglows' original version was the break they'd been waiting for, and they began playing some of the best gigs of their history, as part of Freed's huge package shows alongside acts like Joe Turner, the Clovers, and Lowell Fulson. In early 1955, the group's ranks expanded with the addition of Billy Johnson, a guitarist who'd previously played with Charles Brown. During the summer of 1955, the group was part of a package tour that included Muddy Waters, Sarah Vaughan, and Nappy Brown.

Alas, they found it difficult to repeat the crossover pop success of "Sincerely"—the group did produce such worthy efforts as "Most of All" (number five R&B), "Foolish Me," "Starlite," and "In My Diary." Then, in the middle and latter half of 1956, they succeeded anew with the ballad "We Go Together," which reached number nine on the R&B charts and attracted considerable interest from young white listeners in the bargain; and the rock & roll number "See Saw," which reached number nine R&B and got to number 25 on the pop charts. During this period, Chess also briefly attempted to double-up on the group's approach to the airwaves and radio play lists by taking some of the sides featuring Lester and Fuqua together on lead and issuing those under the name "the Moonlighters."

The group's status in the hierarchy of rock & roll—or, at least, that corner of it under the control of Freed—was confirmed when the Moonglows were included in the jukebox movie *Rock, Rock,*

Rock, working alongside Chuck Berry, the Flamingoes, LaVern Baker, the Johnny Burnette Trio, and Frankie Lymon & the Teenagers. Later that same year, they also began work on what was to have been their debut LP, and early in 1957 they made another screen appearance, in *Mr. Rock and Roll*, a second jukebox feature, sandwiched in between many of the same acts as the prior movie—this was to mark the last screen appearance of the original group, however.

During 1957, in the wake of their unfinished debut album, Lester receded from the lead vocal spot, yielding it to Fuqua, who already dominated the group as a producer, songwriter, and their de facto vocal arranger. "Please Send Me Someone to Love," which got to number five R&B and number 73 on the pop charts, featured Fuqua on lead vocals and reduced Lester to back-up. The friction between Lester and Fuqua continued through most of the year, and the latter's increasing control of the group's direction also caused friction with Barnes, Graves, and Johnson, who were more or less caught in the middle between the two most identifiable voices in the group. Complicating their strained internal dynamics were the changes in public taste that had taken place since 1955—they not only couldn't decide who ought to be leading them, or agree on who should sing lead, but also on which direction their music should go in, toward the more pop-oriented sound of the Platters, who were selling large numbers of records to white audiences, or toward the harder sound that seemed to be coming out of some quarters of the black community, and seemed to be where black listeners were moving.

Torn by these multiple schisms, the Moonglows' lineup collapsed under circumstances that are still a bit murky, in terms of who decided what and who exited. In late 1957, a pair of sides were recorded featuring Fuqua and possibly Johnson, and in early 1958, a new single appeared entitled "Ten Commandments of Love," featuring Fuqua as a speaker. It reached number nine as an R&B hit and number 22 as a pop single, the group's best pop performance in two years and one of their biggest sellers, except that it wasn't credited to the Moonglows—rather, it was also credited to Harvey & the Moonglows, and precisely who was singing on it behind Fuqua is still a matter of conjecture; some sources attribute the back-up to the original Moonglows, whereas others say with assurance that it was Fuqua's "new" Moonglows, actually formerly known as the Marquees, a Washington, D.C., outfit consisting of Marvin Gaye, Reese Palmer, James Knowland, and Chester Simmons. What is clear is that they accompanied Fuqua over the next year or so, credited as Harvey & the Moonglows. The group's ranks changed quickly—though he kept Gaye, who had sung lead on the group's recording of "Mama Loocie," with him—and eventually included a young Chuck Barksdale, from the Dells.

In addition to his work with the new group, Fuqua was featured on solo singles throughout 1958, including "Don't Be Afraid of Love," which he co-authored with Berry Gordy, Jr. and Billy Davis, and also turned up miming in the last (and best) of the Freed showcase films, *Go*

Johnny Go. Fuqua's professional association with Gordy had begun when they met, on the latter's visit to Chess to license the early sides of the Miracles; the two wrote songs together, and eventually Fuqua married Gordy's sister Gwen. He continued recording for several more years, including some legendary sides with Etta James, but increasingly concentrated on the purely creative rather than the performing side of music. After operating such independent labels as Tri-Phi (where he recorded not only his own and the later Harvey & the Moonglows stuff, but also the early Spinners, whom he discovered as the Domingoes, and with whom he sang as well), he joined Motown as the executive in charge of developing new talent, and became not only successful in that department but also as a producer and songwriter, and was collaborating successfully with Smokey Robinson in the 1990s.

Having had the group and the group name pulled out from under him, Lester went solo on the Chess label for a short time, before giving up performing for a decade. His name was well known enough and the recordings left behind with the group were good enough, however, so that as late as 1962 Chess saw the point in releasing a single credited to "Bobby Lester & the Moonglows," consisting of "Blue Velvet" and "Penny Arcade," the A-side culled from the group's abortive late 1956 album sessions—this may have been simply Chess's way of trying to amortize everything but the kitchen sink in their operation, but it is difficult to imagine any other artist of the era, apart from Elvis Presley or Clyde McPhatter (or deceased figures such as Buddy Holly or Eddie Cochran), getting their six-year-old recordings pushed as new releases.

Johnson passed through gigs backing Jackie Wilson and Brook Benton before joining Motown Records, and passed away in the late '80s. Walton put together a new Moonglows lineup in 1964 to cover some of the group's '50s sides, but this effort didn't last long, and Graves and Barnes left the music business, and the original Moonglows were consigned to history, apart from Chess' periodic attempts to continue selling sides left in the vaults. The label also released of a pair of LPs made up of the group's single sides, *Look, It's the Moonglows* (1959) and *The Best of Bobby Lester & the Moonglows* (1962). Chess kept several vestiges of the Moonglows sound alive more profitably when they signed the Dells, and the group's sound could also be heard in the early work of the Four Tops (who had also spent time on Chess) and the Temptations at Motown.

Lester tried reviving the group name twice, at the beginning and end of the '70s, and even recut "Sincerely" the first time around. That composition remained the jewel in Fuqua's songbag—in 1990, 36 years after the Moonglows cut their version and 35 years after the McGuire Sisters' pop hit, the Forester Sisters' country rendition of "Sincerely" earned a Grammy nomination; that same year, filmmaker Martin Scorsese (who is known to take a very deep interest in the music used in his movies) used the Moonglows' version of the song in the film *Goodfellas*. Between the original and the successful covers, "Sincerely" bids fair to remain a popular song well into the 21st century.

The Penguins

Formed 1954 in Los Angeles, CA

Best known for their hit single "Earth Angel," the doo wop quartet the Penguins were never able to replicate the success of their only Top 40 hit, but the song became a rock & roll classic. The Penguins formed in 1954, when the members—Cleveland Duncan (lead vocal), Curtis Williams (tenor vocal), Dexter Tisby (baritone vocal), and Bruce Tate (tenor vocal)—were all attending Fremont High School in Los Angeles, CA.

Although he wasn't the lead singer, Williams was the leader of the group. He learned "Earth Angel" from vocalist Jesse Belvin—some sources claim that Williams wrote the song alone, others say he co-wrote the song with Belvin, while others claim Gaynell Hodge, a member of the doo wop group the Turks, wrote the song with the duo (in fact, Hodge won a lawsuit filed in 1956 that gave him a co-writing credit)—and had the Penguins sing the song.

Around 1954, the Penguins signed with the local Los Angeles independent label Dootone Records. The group's first single was going to be the up-tempo "Hey Sinorita," and the ballad "Earth Angel" was going to be the B-side.

Upon the release of the single in the latter half of 1954, Los Angeles radio stations were receiving more requests for "Earth Angel" than "Hey Sinorita," and the song soon became the record's A-side. By the beginning of 1955, the single had scaled the national charts, spending three weeks at the top of the R&B charts and peaking at number eight on the pop charts.

For the next few years, the Penguins continued to record singles for Dootone Records. Shortly after the success of "Earth Angel," Tate left the group and Randolph Jones became their baritone vocalist. Around 1956, the Penguins left Dootone Records and signed with Mercury Records. After cutting some sides for Mercury, the group moved to Atlantic Records, where they had their second and final hit, "Pledge of Love," which climbed to number 15 on the R&B charts in the summer of 1957. That same year, the group released their only album, *The Cool, Cool Penguins*.

By 1959, the group had returned to their hometown of Los Angeles; shortly after their relocation, they broke up. Over the next four decades, Cleveland Duncan led various incarnations of the Penguins through reunion tours and re-recordings of their hits. In 1963, Duncan, Tisby, and two new members recorded "Memories of El Monte," a song future Mothers of Invention members Frank Zappa and Ray Collins wrote specifically for the group; the single failed to make any impact. Duncan went back to leading new incarnations of the Penguins, while Tisby briefly joined the Coasters.

Frankie Lymon

Born: Sept 30, 1942 in Harlem, NY
Died: Feb 20, 1968 in Harlem, NY

Frankie Lymon (1942–1968) & the Teenagers were a New York doo wop group consisting of Joe Negroni, Herman Santiago, Jimmy Merchant, and Sherman Garnes but centered around the extraordinary talents of their lead singer, 13-year-old Frankie Lymon. Lymon was credited with their first big hit, "Why Do Fools Fall in Love" (In the early '90s, a federal judge ruled after a lengthy trial that Lymon hadn't written "Why Do Fools Fall in Love" —another member of the Teenagers had). His wise-beyond-his-years vocal and performing abilities not only made the Teenagers a group several notches above the competition but made Lymon the first Black teenage pop star.

Though only together for a brief 18-month period, Lymon & the Teenagers exerted an enormous influence, spawning several "kid" vocal groups and providing initial inspiration to Berry Gordy to model his entire Motown production approach around Lymon's original vocal style. Inexplicably, the group split into two factions at the height of their success, and neither had a hit again. Lymon died from a drug overdose at age 26. Diana Ross, Smokey Robinson, Len Barry, and his principal protégé, Michael Jackson (whose early recordings with the Jackson 5 are virtual re-creations of the early Lymon sound, merely updated) all show the influence of Frankie Lymon & the Teenagers's groundbreaking work.

The Drifters

Formed May 1953 in New York, NY

The history of rhythm and blues is filled with vocal groups whose names—the Orioles, the Cadillacs, the Crows, the Flamingos, the Moonglows, the Coasters, the Penguins—are held in reverence by fanatics and devotees. The Drifters are part of an even more exclusive fraternity, as a group that managed to carve out a place for themselves in the R&B firmament and also define that music, not only at its inception as a national chart phenomenon in the early '50s but also in the decade that followed. Their place in history is as complex as their role in it, by virtue of the fact that there are two distinct phases to their music and the continuity of their membership, and their extraordinary longevity—only the Platters could claim as great a span of years as an active recording unit, though the latter group, due to major differences in the way they were organized, were far more stable in their membership and output. The Drifters can also claim a unique place in popular music history, as a major R&B group founded at the instigation of a record-label chief.

Their story began in early 1953, when Clyde McPhatter, the soaring high-tenor lead singer in the Dominoes, a vocal quintet formed by Billy Ward three years earlier, quit that group. The Dominoes were playing a scheduled gig at the New York club Birdland, one of their first performances without McPhatter, when one of the audience members present asked after the singer backstage. That fan was Ahmet Ertegun, a one-time record collector who had started Atlantic Records in the late '40s; as soon as he learned of McPhatter's having left the Dominoes, he contacted the singer and signed him to Atlantic.

It was Ertegun who gave McPhatter the impetus, as part of his contract, to start a group of his own, which came to be called the Drifters. The origins of the name and credit for thinking of it are obscure, although no one at Atlantic liked "the Drifters" at first, thinking it sounded too country & western—the explanation sometimes offered by those present was that the members simply drifted in from other groups.

The main source for McPhatter's backing singers was among the ranks of former members of the Mount Lebanon Singers, the gospel group with which McPhatter had sung in the '40s. He went through several attempts at assembling a group that would be acceptable to Ertegun and producer Jerry Wexler, going through as many as a dozen friends and acquaintances, a handful of whom actually made it to formal recording sessions. The initial, unsuccessful lineup, featuring William Anderson, David Baughn, Dave Baldwin (the brother of author James Baldwin), and James Johnson, recorded four songs on June 28, 1953, of which only "Lucille," a McPhatter-authored song, was ever released. In August, a second Drifters lineup was put together, with Gerhart Thrasher, Andrew Thrasher, two very experienced gospel singers on tenor and baritone, respectively, bass singer Willie Ferbee, and Walter Adams on the guitar. From the beginning, the group was unusual among R&B vocal ensembles in that a guitarist was part of their core lineup and the electric guitar central to their arrangements; Jimmy Oliver, who would soon take that spot as his own, also proved to be an important songwriter for the Drifters, especially for tenor Gerhart Thrasher. The new edition of the group cut five numbers on August 9, 1953, one of which was "Money Honey," written by arranger/pianist Jesse Stone. Released within a few weeks, it hit the number one spot on the R&B chart by mid-fall of that year, and it was occasionally cited in later years as the first rock & roll record, and later entered the repertory of Elvis Presley and dozens of lesser talents. The group's career was made after that, at least as long as Clyde McPhatter was singing lead with them.

This success didn't stop the regular lineup changes that would characterize the Drifters' history. By the time the Drifters were enjoying their breakthrough hit, a reconstituted lineup, with bass player Bill Pinkney and guitarist Jimmy Oliver joining Gerhart Thrasher and Andrew Thrasher, cut their first session. This was the lineup that lasted for the year that followed, and cut "Such a Night," a number two R&B hit, and a second R&B chart-topper with "Honey Love" in early 1954. By that time, the charts and radio play, along with audience sensibilities, had opened up and "Honey Love" also made number 21 on the pop charts late that spring. Not for the last time, it seemed as though the Drifters were headed for big things together, but a key member had developed other ideas by the fall of 1954.

Although he'd been assured of a considerable amount of musical control, McPhatter found that Ertegun and Wexler were, as the producers, always trying to push the group into directions of their own choosing. McPhatter didn't begrudge them their efforts at finding new sounds that might sell records to white as well as black audiences, but he didn't feel like participating. His goal was to cross over to pop audiences as a balladeer, and saw himself as having the potential to become another Nat "King" Cole, or perhaps a black answer to Frank Sinatra or Perry Como. By October of 1954, he had parted company with the group in favor of a solo career that would make him a success for the rest of the 1950s.

Rather than see the group in which they'd invested 18 months of their time go out of existence, Ertegun and Wexler were still interested in recording the Drifters, but that group's internal circumstances were vastly different once McPhatter was gone.

McPhatter had organized the Drifters under the auspices of his own business entity, Drifters Incorporated, so that he would have a share of their earnings, something that he'd been denied in the Dominoes; his own willingness to share those earnings with the other members has never been broached or questioned. He was half-owner of the group with his manager, George Treadwell, a former jazz musician who had masterminded the solo career of his first wife, Sarah Vaughan; when McPhatter left the group, rather than making a provision for the other members and his eventual successor to get his share, he sold out his interest in Drifters Incorporated to Treadwell.

This basically doomed the group to a permanent revolving-door lineup. From that day forward, all of the members of the Drifters were salaried employees, earning as little as $100 a week even into the early '60s, and getting no share of royalties from record sales, no benefits from the concert fees they commanded, nor any claim to the use of the name "the Drifters" if they left, no matter how successful the group became through their efforts. It thus became impossible for the group to hold on to anyone with serious talent or aspirations for a long-term career in music. This made the Drifters, for those present after McPhatter's exit, little more inviting than McPhatter's own tenure with the Dominoes, and he later regretted making the decision, recognizing not only what he had cheated himself of out by not hanging on to his share of the ownership but also what he had done to his fellow musicians.

The immediate problem facing all concerned in 1954, however, was finding a replacement for Clyde McPhatter, and some would argue that they never did. David Baughn, who had sung with a very early version of the Drifters, came in as a temporary replacement, singing at one recording session and serving as lead vocalist for six months' worth of live engagements (which was how the group generated most of its income). Baughn's singing was good enough, but the group sounded like an imitation of the McPhatter-era Drifters, and Atlantic declined to release any of these sides at the time, possibly due to their potential to interfere with McPhatter's solo releases, which were selling well. The label didn't know whether to shoot for an entirely new sound or to try to find a replacement who sounded like the former lead singer who, by 1956, was a major R&B star in his own right. Additionally, Baughn soon demonstrated an erratic personality, sufficiently unnerving to force Treadwell to recruit a second lead vocalist in Bobby Hendricks, who had previously sung with the Five Crowns and the Swallows. Attempts were made to record this lineup, and even bass singer Bill Pinkney was cut doing a lead vocal, but none of it was considered acceptable.

The lineup itself began to shift as Baughn quit, but the group soldiered on, drawing good crowds at their shows based on the quality of their earlier recordings. In 1955, however, they auditioned a young man who approached the group after a show in Cleveland. Johnny Moore had been a member of a group called the Hornets, who had done a little bit of recording without making any more than a local reputation for themselves. He sounded enough like McPhatter, however, with his pleasing high tenor, and was offered a spot in the Drifters the next day. Moore would prove to be a mainstay of the group in two different decades.

The Drifters resumed recording in September of 1955, with Nesuhi Ertegun and songwriter Jerry Leiber producing and with Moore singing lead. The result was a number one R&B chart single, "Adorable," which went a long way toward establishing their post-Clyde McPhatter reputation. This proved to be one of the very few major chart records they would enjoy during this era, however—the Drifters were still absent from the top of the pop charts, where the real money and huge sales figures lay. Their records during the late '50s were overlooked by most young white listeners, despite the presence of future rock & roll standards such as "Ruby Baby" in their output.

Dion would enjoy a much bigger hit with the latter song in the early '60s, but it was an important recording for the Drifters, marking their introduction to the talents of songwriters Jerry Leiber and Mike Stoller, who would later take over the job of producing the group. The Drifters' lineup was also stabilized for the first time in over a year. The original Drifters now entered their "silver age" behind Moore's cool high tenor, ably supported by the bass singing (and occasional lead spot) from Bill Pinkney and Bobby Hendricks' tenor. "I Gotta Get Myself a Woman," written by Jesse Stone and cut during the summer of 1956, brought the group a number 11 R&B hit and the group's fortunes once again seemed to be on a consistent upswing.

As it turned out, the black record-buying public wasn't prepared to fully accept a new Drifters, without McPhatter—black audiences practically worshipped the singer, who commanded a passionate loyalty that anticipated the future success of Sam Cooke. Additionally, the music was changing—white teenagers were now a much bigger part of the market than they had been in 1953–54, and Atlantic set its sights on that potentially much richer vein of listeners.

The end of 1956 saw the release of the first album by the group, entitled *Clyde McPhatter & the Drifters*. Such was the popularity of McPhatter at the time, and the tracks that he'd done with the Drifters, versus their recent work, that those 14 songs rated inclusion on an LP well over a year after his exit from the lineup in an effort to sell the music once more to his fans—in that regard, Atlantic was very forward-looking; very few labels in 1956 were releasing LPs aimed at black R&B listeners (apart from Elvis Presley's albums, very little white rock & roll made an impression on the album charts).

Late 1956 was also the point when the consequences of the Drifters' business organization caught up with the group. Their recent hits had led to more bookings than at any time since 1954, which was good for Treadwell and his partners, but difficult for the members, who were still working on straight salary and, by Bill Pinkney's estimation, very low salaries. He approached Treadwell for a new arrangement, or at least more money for the group members, and he was fired. His dismissal drove fellow founding member Andrew Thrasher out of the lineup as well, and out of music altogether. Pinkney and ex-Drifter Bobby Hendricks became the core of a new Atlantic group called the Flyers, who released one single that failed to attract much attention.

The new Drifters lineup was filled by bass singer Jimmy Ricks and then, more permanently, by Tom Evans, late of the Dominoes, and baritone Charlie Hughes. The group's fortunes now took a new turn as Jerry Leiber and Mike Stoller began producing their sessions in late 1956—unfortunately, their arrival on the scene coincided with Johnny Moore's receiving his draft notice in early 1957. The group was (no joke intended) adrift once again, in terms of its sound and lineup. Bobby Hendricks was brought back in, and Jimmy Millender took over the baritone chores, but there wasn't a lot of good material that came from those sessions. For a time, in the absence of an ability to create a successful Drifters sound, it seemed as though Atlantic was trying to turn them into another version of the Coasters, doing light-hearted versions of pop standards. In a way, this was understandable—black listeners held this era's Drifters at arm's length, while white teenagers were dominating the pop charts and they seemed, at least potentially, open to new records by anyone, so Atlantic decided to cater to them, hoping for a breakthrough.

By late 1958, Hendricks had announced his exit, and even guitarist Jimmy Oliver, who had managed to get several of his songs recorded during his four-year tenure with the group and was an unheralded mainstay of their sound, finally quit. The remaining members, such as they were, were working as hard as ever and wanted more money and, when Treadwell refused their request, they all walked out (or were fired *en masse*).

Treadwell was about to find himself without a group and faced with upcoming engagements to fulfill at the Apollo Theater in New York. He spotted his way out of this impasse at the Apollo, way down on a bill on May 30, 1958 on which the about-to-be-fired Drifters were headlining. The Five Crowns, or the Crowns, as they were then known, had been a fixture in Harlem for most of the 1950's, predating the Drifters without ever making a mark as a recording act, and enjoying precious little reputation as performers.

Treadwell approached their manager, Lover Patterson, explaining that he was dumping the existing Drifters and needed a new group to fulfill their performing obligations. Patterson agreed and the group followed suit, and all of the individual members' contracts, except for that of one of the group's two baritones, were sold to Treadwell. In later years, this kind of arrangement would become a little more familiar in the business—the Grass Roots essentially evolved this way, as did the performing version of the group Steam—but it was unusual in those days, and difficult to pull off, and mostly served to keep Treadwell from ending up in court.

The new Drifters lineup consisted of Charlie Thomas on lead, baritone Benjamin Earl Nelson, later known as Ben E. King, Dock Green (who had held the Crowns together) (baritone), and Elsbeary Hobbs singing bass. They did as they were required under the agreement and, for ten months, worked in the shadow of the old group, playing live gigs characterized by the awkwardness of performing the old songs as though they were their own, to mostly black audiences who knew that these weren't the Drifters. Atlantic still hoped to profit from the group, however, and a second Drifters LP, *Rockin' & Driftin'*, was released in late 1958, comprised entirely of single tracks recorded by the 1955–58 lineup. Ironically, in all of their 19-year history with Atlantic Records, the Drifters, in any incarnation, never recorded an actual "album" session; every one of their LPs was compiled from existing single tracks and B-sides and, except for the first album, all have a mix-and-match element to the memberships and, especially, the singers represented.

The group still had a recording contract with Atlantic Records and, despite the fact that the old Drifters' recent releases had done little business, the label decided to try once more with the new lineup and get a record out. On March 6, 1959, they went into the studio with Leiber & Stoller producing, to cut four songs. Charlie Thomas was supposed to sing lead but he developed mic-fright in the studio, and so Nelson was deputized for "There Goes My Baby," which he had co-written, along with "Hey Senorita," and "Oh My Love." "There Goes My Baby," co-written by Nelson and orchestrated by Stan Applebaum, was as much a landmark in the history of R&B and soul as "Money Honey" had been six years earlier. At the time, nobody present was sure of what they had because it sounded so chaotic, strange, and complicated—no one had ever used a string section, much less one recorded as prominently as this one was, on an R&B record, and no R&B record up until that time had ever dared sound so complex, overlaying Latin percussion, violins, and a fiercely passionate performance by the singer. It not only didn't sound anything like the old Drifters, but it didn't sound like anything else that had ever been heard on a commercial recording before. And it was a complete mess in the eyes of some observers, including Jerry Wexler, who said the song sounded like a radio picking up two different stations at once.

"There Goes My Baby" peaked at number two, their biggest hit to that date on the pop charts and their biggest seller up to that time, winning over both R&B and pop audiences and transforming the group and its image. Moreover, it marked the group's first impact on audiences overseas—the earlier Drifters, for all of their impact on rock & roll, never got a record released in Europe, but this new group and their sound would soon find a very important mass audience in England. The group seemed headed for a huge future when the problem of their business set-up came into play again. They'd cut other songs at that same session, including "Baltimore," which sounded like an update of the Cadillacs' "Speedo," but the strings-percussion-echo timbres of "There Goes My Baby," hung around long melodic lines, became the Drifters' trademark sound for the ten years that followed.

This seemed to be a new lease on life to the group, and then more troubles arose from within, owing to the way the Drifters were organized as a business. Ben Nelson wasn't happy working for $100 a week; not with the hundreds of miles of travel between some shows, and as many as six days of shows each week. He was so poor working for the group that he felt compelled to sell off his share of the songwriting on "There Goes My Baby." Accounts differ as to precisely what happened on this issue—some say that he sold the share off to Treadwell and his accountant, while Jerry Wexler claims that he accepted a document from the singer assigning him the copyright, in exchange for $200; Wexler held on to the document, and gave it back to the singer once the song was a hit so he could tear it up.

After approaching Treadwell for more money and being turned down, Nelson saw that there was no future as a member of the Drifters and announced his exit almost as soon as it came time to cut a follow-up. At the same moment, Lover Patterson played his trump card, a separate contract that he'd signed with the singer, as a solo artist, dated before Treadwell's offer. It all could have ended up in court but luckily for the singer and fans of the Drifters, cooler heads prevailed. He remained with Atlantic Records on their Atco subsidiary as a solo artist, and agreed to record with the group until a suitable replacement could be found, singing on "Dance With Me," "This Magic Moment," "I Count the Tears," and "Save the Last Dance for Me," the latter their only number one hit, among other songs, through the spring of 1960. By the time his exit had been arranged, Nelson had changed his name to the more memorable Ben E. King, which was how he emerged in his own right.

The post-1959 Drifters (which also included guitarist Billy Davis) are usually thought of as the "Ben E. King Drifters," but the reality was that King had left the group by the end of that same year. King's first successor was Johnny Williams, who exited suddenly in late 1960, but the Drifters quickly found a replacement in Rudy Lewis. An ex-member of the Clara Ward Singers, Lewis was the singer on "Some Kind of Wonderful," "Up on the Roof" (a Top Five hit), "Please Stay," "What to Do," and "On Broadway" (a Top Ten hit), among numerous other classic tracks by the group. Lewis, tragically, wasn't the longest lasting of the group's lead vocalists but his tenure with the group, following King's, arguably constituted the second half of a second golden age in their history.

Whoever was involved on a particular record, this lineup of the group was once again at a peak of influence in those years. "There Goes My Baby" anticipated the shift to a more pop-oriented brand of soul music, embraced by Sam Cooke and, even more so, by Berry Gordy at his fledgling Motown label. Indeed, the sound of "There Goes My Baby" was practically the prototype for Smokey Robinson & the Miracles' landmark single "Way Over There." Others also learned from them, most notably a young producer named Phil Spector, who was working at Atlantic as a session guitarist in the early '60s and ran with the sound he heard in Stan Applebaum's arrangements, expanding it into something new and turning it into his own trademark, imprinted on the work of a dozen top recording acts. And it was during the recording of his own "Please Stay" by the group that Burt Bacharach first encountered a vocalist named Dionne Warwick, who was part of the backing trio for the Drifters.

Between 1960 and 1964, the Drifters achieved a level of stability that was unprecedented in their history, and it was matched by their success. Not that they didn't make mistakes—they turned down "This Diamond Ring," and Atlantic never released their version of "Only in America," both of which became huge hits, in the hands of Gary Lewis & the Playboys and Jay & the Americans, respectively. Still, luck was with them even as essential personnel around them moved on—in late 1963, as Leiber & Stoller shifted their attention to their own record label, Red Bird, the Drifters got a new producer in Bert Berns, a songwriter with a feel for commercial soul music. "Vaya Con Dios," from their first session with the new producer (and which reflected his love of Latin themes), was a moderate pop chart hit. And in the spring of 1964, with Leiber & Stoller no longer writing the way they had been, the group was offered a new song by composers Art Resnick and Kenny Young, called "Under the Boardwalk."

It was scheduled for recording on May 21 of 1964. Then, on the night of May 20, just hours before the recording session, Rudy Lewis was found dead in his apartment under circumstances that are still in dispute—the police suspected a drug overdose, but people who knew Lewis insisted that his only vice was binge-eating, and that he had choked to death. Without any time to reschedule the session, Johnny Moore, who had rejoined the group as second tenor in early 1963, stepped into the breach. Moore, who had previously held the thankless task of leading the late-'50s Drifters, achieved a special magnificence at that session singing "Under the Boardwalk," which became the group's last Top Ten hit in 1964, peaking at number four. He became the longest lasting of the Drifters' various lead singers, lasting into the 1970s and beyond their time as a serious recording act.

By late 1964, Berns was moving on to other projects including the early releases of his new independent label, Bang Records, and the group found itself working with producer Tom Dowd in what were very unproductive sessions. They still had lots of bookings, and enough hits behind them to remain a thoroughly established act, but by that time the whole notion of soul music was changing around them, due in some measure to a vast array of other acts associated with Atlantic Records, including Wilson Pickett, Otis Redding, Sam & Dave, and Don Covay. The Drifters were never able to make the jump comfortably to this harder brand of soul music, and the loss of Berns as a producer after 1965 seemed to seal their fate. Their own sessions began to show a lack of urgency and organization, exemplified by the fact that one of the very best tracks of Moore's era, "In the Park," was left unfinished (without the group recorded behind him) and in the can for years. The death of George Treadwell in 1967 removed another layer of impetus behind the Drifters' continuation as a going concern.

They continued recording for Atlantic with a succession of producers until

1972. By that time, the company itself was part of a huge corporate conglomerate, far removed from its origins—Led Zeppelin, Yes, and Emerson, Lake & Palmer were the stars of the Atlantic roster then, and scarcely anyone at the company except Ertegun and Wexler likely even remembered who the Drifters were or how they'd started. Johnny Moore still sang lead, but there were no more hits after the mid-'60s. They tried altering their sound to mainstream adult pop, cutting old-style standards in an effort to capture older listeners. As the hits faded away and the bookings dried up, the group broke up yet again—in the end, Johnny Moore was the only recognizable Drifter and he did most of the singing on the records as well.

The 1970s saw a proliferation of acts trading on the Drifters name as the rock & roll revival suddenly made the group's classic repertory profitable again. Founding member Bill Pinkney led a group sometimes called "the Original Drifters" while Charlie Thomas led another version and Johnny Moore kept the fully authorized group under the auspices of Treadwell's widow Faye.

The result was a series of lawsuits that ultimately saw the various claimants divide different territories within the United States between them, while the Faye Treadwell-authorized group, led by Johnny Moore, moved to England, where they enjoyed a Top Ten hit in 1972 ("Come on Over to My Place"), falling under the influence of the Roger Cook/Roger Greenaway songwriting team. This incarnation of the group, no longer signed to Atlantic after 1972, was signed to Bell Records. The British-based version of the Drifters became a dance-disco outfit for a time in the late '70s, virtually irrelevant to the group's history, while Pinkney and Thomas maintained contact with the Drifters' roots, and even Jimmy Ricks, who was only in the group for a few months, turned up at some point leading a combo using the name. Ben E. King even returned to the lineup for a tour in the late '80s.

In the 1990s, after decades of conflicting and contradictory claims, a new court ruling determined that Faye Treadwell owned the trademark of the Drifters' name. The death of Johnny Moore in the 1990s brought the end of the era in the group's history, though Bill Pinkney—the last active original member from the early '50s—continued to front a group of Drifters at the end of the decade. The late '80s and early '90s also saw a full revival of the group's entire catalog; for decades, from the 1960s through the 1980s, fans and collectors in America had to content themselves with a single LP, the 1968 *Golden Hits* album, consisting of a selection of the group's early-'60s hits—none of the McPhatter-era cuts were around, nor were any other tracks from the '60s era. A pair of Rhino Records-inspired double-CD/LP sets helped break this logjam in the late '80s, and Rhino's 1996 triple-CD set *Rockin' & Driftin': The Drifters Box* opened the floodgates of their history. That same year, Sequel Records in England issued seven CDs devoted to the group's history, and more recently Collectables Records has been busy re-releasing the group's classic albums on CD.

The Platters

Formed 1953 in Los Angeles, CA

The Platters started out as a Los Angeles-based black doo wop group with little identity of their own to make them stand out from the pack. They started out making their first records for Federal, a subsidiary of Cincinnati's King Records. These early sides don't sound anything like the better-known sides that would eventually emerge from this group, instead merely aping the current R&B trends and styles of the day. What changed their fortunes can be reduced down to one very important name: their mentor, manager, producer, songwriter, and vocal coach, Buck Ram. Ram took what many would say were a run-of-the-mill R&B doo wop vocal group and turned them into stars and one of the most enduring and lucrative groups of all time. By 1954, Ram was already running a talent agency in Los Angeles, writing and arranging for publisher Mills Music, managing the Three Suns—a pop group with some success—and working with his protégés, the Penguins. The Platters seemed like a good addition to his stable.

After getting them out of their Federal contract, Ram placed them with the burgeoning national independent label Mercury Records (at the same time he brought over the Penguins following their success with "Earth Angel"), automatically getting them into pop markets through the label's distribution contacts alone. Then Ram started honing in on the group's strengths and weaknesses. The first thing he did was put the lead vocal status squarely on the shoulders of lead tenor Tony Williams. Williams' emoting power was turned up full blast with the group (now augmented with Zola Taylor from Shirley Gunter & the Queens) working as very well-structured vocal support framing his every note. With Ram's pop songwriting classics as their musical palette, the group quickly became a pop and R&B success, eventually earning the distinction of being the first black act of the era to top the pop charts. Considered the most romantic of all the doo wop groups (that is, the ultimate in "make out music"), hit after hit came tumbling forth in a seemingly effortless manner: "Only You," "The Great Pretender," "My Prayer," "Twilight Time," "Smoke Gets in Your Eyes," "Harbor Lights," all of them establishing the Platters as the classiest of all.

Williams struck out on his own in 1961 and, by the decade's end, the group had disbanded with various members starting up their own version of the Platters. This bit of franchising now extends into the present day, with an estimated 125 sanctioned versions of "the original Platters" out on the oldies circuit.

Sam Cooke

Born: Jan 22, 1931 in Clarksdale, MS
Died: Dec 11, 1964 in Los Angeles, CA

Sam Cooke was the most important soul singer in history—he was also the inventor of soul music, and its most popular and beloved performer in both the black and white communities. Equally important, he was among the first modern black performers and composers to attend to the

business side of the music business, and founded both a record label and a publishing company as an extension of his careers as a singer and composer. Yet, those business interests didn't prevent him from being engaged in topical issues, including the struggle over civil rights, the pitch and intensity of which followed an arc that paralleled Cooke's emergence as a star—his own career bridged gaps between black and white audiences that few had tried to surmount, much less succeeded at doing, and also between generations; where Chuck Berry or Little Richard brought black and white teenagers together, James Brown sold records to white teenagers and black listeners of all ages, and Muddy Waters got young white folkies and older black transplants from the South onto the same page, Cooke appealed to all of the above, and the parents of those white teenagers as well—yet he never lost his credibility with his core black audience.

In a sense, his appeal anticipated that of the Beatles, in breadth and depth. He was born Sam Cook in Clarksdale, MS, on January 22, 1931, one of eight children of a Baptist minister and his wife. Even as a young boy, he showed an extraordinary voice and frequently sang in the choir in his father's church. During the middle of the decade, the Cook family moved to Chicago's South Side, where the Reverend Charles Cook quickly established himself as a major figure in the religious community. Sam and three of his siblings also formed a group of their own, the Singing Children, in the 1930s. Although his own singing was confined to gospel music, he was aware and appreciative of the popular music of the period, particularly the melodious, harmony-based sounds of the Ink Spots, whose influence could later be heard in songs such as "You Send Me" and "For Sentimental Reasons." As a teenager, he was a member of the Teen Highway QCs, a gospel group that performed in churches and at religious gatherings. His membership in that group led to his introduction to the Soul Stirrers, one of the top gospel groups in the country, and in 1950 he joined them.

If Cooke had never recorded a note of music on his own, he would still be remembered today in gospel circles for his work with the Soul Stirrers. Over the next six years, his role within the group and his prominence within the black community rose to the point where he was already a star, with his own fiercely admiring and devoted audience, through his performances on songs like "Touch the Hem of His Garment," "Nearer to Thee," and "That's Heaven to Me." The group was one of the top acts on Art Rupe's Specialty Records label, and he might have gone on for years as their most popular singer, but Cooke's goal was to reach audiences beyond the religious community, and beyond the black population, with his voice. This was a tall order at the time, as the mere act of recording a popular song could alienate the gospel listenership in an instant; singing for God was regarded in those circles as a gift and a responsibility, and popular music, rock & roll, and R&B were to be abhorred, at least coming from the mouth of a gospel singer; the gap was so great that when a blues singer such as Blind Gary Davis became "sanctified" (that is, found religion) as the Rev. Gary Davis, he could still sing and play his old blues melodies, but had to devise new words, and he never sang the blues words again.

He tested the waters of popular music in 1956 with the single "Lovable," produced by Bumps Blackwell and credited under the name Dale Cooke so as not to attract too much attention from his existing audience. It was enough, however, to get Cooke dropped by the Soul Stirrers and their record label, but that freed him to record under his real name. The result was one of the biggest selling singles of the 1950s, a Cooke original entitled "You Send Me," which sold over two million copies on the tiny Keen Records label and hit number one on both the pop and R&B charts. Although it seems like a tame record today, "You Send Me" was a pioneering soul record in its time, melding elements of R&B, gospel, and pop into a sound that was new and still coalescing at the time.

Cooke was with Keen for the next two years, a period in which he delivered up some of the prettiest romantic ballads and teen pop singles of the era, including "For Sentimental Reasons," "Everybody Loves to Cha Cha Cha," "Only Sixteen," and "(What A) Wonderful World." These were extraordinarily beautiful records, and in between the singles came some early album efforts, most notably *Tribute to the Lady*, his album of songs associated with Billie Holiday. He was unhappy, however, with both the business arrangement that he had with Keen and the limitations inherent with recording for a small label—equally to the point, major labels were knocking on Cooke's door, including Atlantic and RCA Records; Atlantic, which was not yet the international conglomerate that it later became, was the top R&B-oriented label in the country and Cooke almost certainly would have signed there and found a happy home with the company, except that they wanted his publishing, and Cooke had seen the sales figures on his songs, as well as their popularity in cover versions by other artists, and was well aware of the importance of owning his copyrights.

Thus, he signed with RCA Records, then one of the three biggest labels in the world (the others being Columbia and Decca), even as he organized his own publishing company, Kags Music, and a record label, SAR, through which he would produce other artists' records—among those signed to SAR were the Soul Stirrers, Bobby Womack (late of the Valentinos, who were also signed to the label), former Soul Stirrers member Johnny Taylor, Billy Preston, Johnnie Morisette, and the Simms Twins.

Cooke's RCA sides were a strangely schizophrenic body of work, at least for the first two years. He broke new ground in pop and soul with the single "Chain Gang," a strange mix of sweet melodies and gritty, sweaty sensibilities that also introduced something of a social conscience to his work—a number two hit on both the pop and R&B charts, it was his biggest hit since "You Send Me" and heralded a bolder phase in his career. Singles like bluesy, romantic "Sad Mood," the idyllic romantic soul of "Cupid," and the straight-ahead dance tune "Twistin' the Night Away" (a pop Top Ten and a number one R&B hit), and "Bring It on Home to Me" all lived up to this promise, and also sold in huge numbers. But the first two albums that RCA had him do, *Hits of the Fifties* and *Cooke's Tour*, were among the lamest LPs ever recorded by any soul or R&B singer, comprised of washed-out pop tunes in arrangements that showed almost none of Cooke's gifts to their advantage.

In 1962, Cooke issued *Twistin' the Night Away*, a somewhat belated "twist" album that became one of his biggest-selling LPs. He didn't really hit his stride as an LP artist, however, until 1963 with the release of *Night Beat*, a beautifully self-contained, dark, moody assembly of blues-oriented songs that were among the best and most challenging numbers that Cooke had recorded up to that time. By the time of its release, he was mostly identified through his singles, which were among the best work of their era, and had developed two separate audiences, among white teen and post-teen listeners and black audiences of all ages. It was Cooke's hope to cross over to the white audience more thoroughly, and open up doors for black performers that, up to that time, had mostly been closed—he had tried playing the Copa in New York as early as 1957 and failed at the time, mostly owing to his inexperience, but in 1964 he returned to the club in triumph, an event that also yielded one of the most finely recorded live performances of its period. The problem with the Copa performance was that it didn't really represent what Sam Cooke was about in full—it was Cooke at his most genial and non-confrontational, doing his safest repertory for a largely middle-aged, middle-class white audience; they responded enthusiastically, to be sure, but only to Cooke's tamest persona.

In mid-1963, however, Cooke had done a show at the Harlem Square Club in Miami that had been recorded. Working in front of a black audience and doing his "real" show, he delivered a sweaty, spellbinding performance built on the same elements found in his singles and his best album tracks, combining achingly beautiful melodies and gritty soul sensibilities. The two live albums sum up the split in Cooke's career and the sheer range of his talent, the rewards of which he'd finally begun to realize more fully in 1963 and 1964.

The drowning death of his infant son in mid-1963 had made it impossible for Cooke to work in the studio until the end of that year. During that time, however, with Allen Klein now managing his business affairs, Cooke did achieve the financial and creative independence that he'd wanted, including more money than any black performer had ever been advanced before, and the eventual ownership of his recordings beginning in November of 1963—he had achieved creative control of his recordings as well, and seemed poised for a breakthrough. It came when he resumed making records, amid the musical ferment of the early '60s. Cooke was keenly aware of the music around him, and was particularly entranced by Bob Dylan's song "Blowin' in the Wind," its treatment of the plight of black Americans and other politically oppressed minorities, and its success in the hands of Peter, Paul & Mary—all of these factors convinced him that the time was right for songs that dealt with more than twisting the night away.

The result was "A Change Is Gonna Come," perhaps the greatest song to come out of the civil rights struggle, and one that seemed to close and seal the gap between the two directions of Cooke's career, from gospel to pop. Arguably his greatest and his most important song, it was an artistic apotheosis for Cooke. During this same period, he had also devised a newer, more advanced dance-oriented soul sound in the form of the song "Shake." These two recordings heralded a new era for Cooke and a new phase of his career, with seemingly the whole world open to him.

None of it was to be. Early in the day on December 11, 1964, while in Los Angeles, Cooke became involved in an altercation at a seedy motel, with a woman guest and the night manager, and was shot to death while allegedly trying to attack the manager. The case is still shrouded in doubt and mystery, and was never investigated the way the murder of a star of his stature would be today. Cooke's death shocked the black community and reverberated far beyond—his single "Shake" was a posthumous Top Ten hit, as were "A Change Is Gonna Come" and the *At the Copa* album, released in 1965. Otis Redding, Al Green, and Solomon Burke, among others, picked up key parts of Cooke's repertory, as did white performers, including the Animals and the Rolling Stones. Even the Supremes recorded a memorial album of his songs, which is now one of the most sought-after of their original recordings, in either LP or CD form.

His reputation survived, at least among those who were smart enough to look behind the songs—to hear Redding's performance of "Shake" at the Monterey Pop Festival, for example, and see where it came from. Cooke's own records were a little tougher to appreciate, however. Listeners who heard those first two, rather poor RCA albums, *Hits of the Fifties* and *Cooke's Tour*, could only wonder what the big deal was about, and several of the albums that followed were uneven enough to give potential fans pause. Meanwhile, the contractual situation surrounding Cooke's recordings greatly complicated the reissue of his work—Cooke's business manager, Allen Klein, exerted a good deal of control, especially over the songs cut during that last year of the singer's life. By the 1970s, there were some fairly poor, mostly budget-priced compilations available, consisting of the hits up through early 1963, and for a time there was even a television compilation out there, but that was it. The movie *National Lampoon's Animal House* made use of a pair of Cooke songs, "(What A) Wonderful World" and "Twistin' the Night Away," which greatly raised his profile among college students and younger baby-boomers, and Southside Johnny & the Asbury Jukes made almost a mini-career out of reviving Cooke's songs (most notably "Having a Party," and even part of "A Change Is Gonna Come") in concert. In 1984, *The Man and His Music* went some way to correcting the absence of all but the early hits in a career-spanning compilation, but since the mid-'90s, Cooke's final year's worth of releases have been separated from the earlier RCA and Keen material, and is in the hands of Klein's ABKCO label. Finally, in the late '90s and beyond, RCA, ABKCO, and even Specialty (which still owns Cooke's gospel sides with the Soul Stirrers) each issued comprehensive collections of their portions of Cooke's catalog.

The Coasters

**Formed Feb 1956 in Los Angeles, CA
Disbanded in 1972**

 The Coasters were one of the few artists in rock history to successfully straddle the line between music and comedy. Their undeniably funny lyrics and on-stage antics might have suggested a simple troupe of clowns, but Coasters records were no mere novelties—their material, supplied by the legendary team of Jerry Leiber and Mike Stoller, was too witty, their arrangements too well-crafted, and the group itself too musically proficient. That engaging and infectious combination made them one of the most popular early R&B/rock & roll acts, as well as one of the most consistently entertaining doo wop/vocal groups of all time.

The Coasters grew out of a successful Los Angeles doo wop group called the Robins, which had been recording since 1949 and working with Leiber & Stoller since 1953. Atlantic Records acquired the Robins in 1955, when the Leiber & Stoller composition "Smokey Joe's Cafe" was becoming too big a hit for their small Spark label to handle; its success scored the duo an independent contract with Atlantic as producers and composers. Amid uncertainties over their new major-label arrangement, the Robins split up that fall; lead tenor Carl Gardner (a more recent addition) and bass Bobby Nunn formed a new group, the Coasters (named for their West Coast base), which maintained the Leiber & Stoller association—an extremely wise move. The initial Coasters lineup was completed by baritone Billy Guy (a gifted comic vocalist) and second tenor Leon Hughes, with guitarist Adolph Jacobs figuring prominently on their recordings through 1959. Their first single, "Down in Mexico," became a Top Ten R&B hit in 1956, epitomizing the sort of humorous story-song Leiber & Stoller were perfecting. The Coasters hit again in 1957 with the double-sided smash "Young Blood"/"Searchin'," both sides of which reached the pop Top Ten. The follow-ups weren't as successful, and it was decided that both the group and Leiber & Stoller would move their operations to New York, where Atlantic was based. As a result, Nunn and Hughes left the group in late 1957, to be replaced respectively by bass Will "Dub" Jones (ex-Cadets, of "Stranded in the Jungle" fame) and second tenor Obie Jessie (for a very short period), then Cornell Gunter (ex-Flairs).

The Coasters' first recording in New York was 1958's "Yakety Yak," which featured King Curtis on tenor sax. Its witty, slice-of-life lyrics about a teenager being hassled by his parents struck a resounding chord, and "Yakety Yak" became the Coasters' first number-one pop hit that summer, topping the R&B charts as well. "Charlie Brown," which cast Jones in the title role of class clown (and immortalized him with the catch-phrase, "why's everybody always pickin' on me?"), hit number two on both the pop and R&B charts in 1959, firmly establishing the Coasters' widespread crossover appeal. More hits followed: the Western-themed "Along Came Jones," "Poison Ivy," "Shoppin' for Clothes," and the group's final Top 30 hit, 1961's burlesque-dancer tribute "Little Egypt."

Following "Little Egypt," Gunter departed, to be replaced by Earl "Speedo" Carroll (of the Cadillacs). Other personnel shifts ensued over the next few years, especially as the hits dried up; even more discouragingly, Leiber & Stoller left Atlantic in 1963. The Coasters parted ways with Atlantic in early 1966, signing with Columbia's Date subsidiary and reuniting with Leiber & Stoller for a time. Although they charted several times, no more hits were forthcoming, given the radically different musical climate; their last chart single was a 1971 cover of "Love Potion No. 9" (by which time Gardner was the only remaining original member), and their last new release came with a 1976 version of "If I Had a Hammer." Since then, numerous different Coasters line-ups have toured the oldies circuit; Gardner's holds the legal claim to legitimacy, but Gunter, Guy, Jones, Nunn, *and* Hughes all led differing lineups at one point or another. Nunn died of a heart attack in 1986, one year before the Coasters became the first vocal group inducted into the Rock and Roll Hall of Fame. Gunter was murdered in Las Vegas in 1990, and Jones passed away in early 2000.

Clyde McPhatter

Born: Nov 15, 1932 in Durham, NC
Died: Jun 13, 1972 in Teaneck, NJ

Clyde McPhatter was one of the most influential R&B singers of the '50s and early '60s. In his own time, his name and voice loomed so much larger than that of the group the Drifters, which he founded, that it took five years for them to recover from his departure. McPhatter was idolized by Black audiences as few singers before or since ever were, and for almost 15 years helped define rhythm & blues and its transformation into soul. In a way, he was the most improbable of R&B stars, a gentle high tenor who, superficially at least, seemed more suited to the angelic strains of gospel music. And his name gave some potential managers and agents pause—what kind of R&B singer, forget a star, was named Clyde? And Clyde McPhatter seemed like a backwoods burlesque of a Black American name. But when he sang, the doubts and the laughter all disappeared—even on his live album from the Apollo Theater, recorded during his declining years, when he describes physical lust in the hit "Ta Ta," he makes it feel urgent and real, and utterly convincing.

McPhatter was born in Durham, NC, on November 15, 1932, the fourth of six children of George and Beulah McPhatter. The family that was both musical and religious, George McPhatter preached at the Mount Calvary Baptist Church where Beulah McPhatter was the organist, and Clyde became a boy soprano in the church choir. The family moved to New Jersey in 1945 and McPhatter formed his first gospel group that year in high school. The McPhatters moved to New York City, and Clyde McPhatter joined the Mount Lebanon Singers, who were one of the most popular gospel groups on the East Coast, and sang with them in the second half of the '40s. In late 1950, McPhatter made the jump to secular music when he joined Billy Ward, a former boxer-turned-singer in the Dominoes. The group, usually known officially as Billy Ward & the Dominoes, signed with Syd Nathan's King Records label, and at the end of 1950 cut "Sixty Minute Man." That song went on to become the biggest R&B hit of 1951 and the first identifiable rock & roll record (though that phrase had not yet been coined for music) by a Black group to make the jump from the R&B to the pop charts. McPhatter stayed with Billy Ward & the Dominoes for three years, racking up a very respectable array of hits, including "Have Mercy Baby," "The Bells," "I'd Be Satisfied," and "These Foolish Things Remind Me of You," and playing as many engagements as they could handle. The problem for McPhatter was that Ward dominated the group's image and its finances—McPhatter's was the lead voice, and the voice that everyone identified; Ward had his name on the front end of the billing and collected all of the profits, while McPhatter, who was sometimes referred to as "Clyde Ward" by unknowing admirers, wasn't earning enough to live on from the meager salary that Ward paid him. Finally, in early 1953, McPhatter quit.

Ahmet Ertegun, the president and cofounder of Atlantic Records, was a fan of McPhatter's singing with the Dominoes and, on learning of his availability, approached him with a contract offer—to record his own group, if he could organize it. Thus were born the Drifters, originally organized by McPhatter in partnership with his manager George Treadwell. It was as the leader of the Drifters that McPhatter's career momentum picked up considerably—beginning with "Money Honey," which became the biggest R&B hit of 1954, he saw a year of notable chart activity and burgeoning popularity, around the singles "Such a Night," "Honey Love," "White Christmas," and "Whatch Gonna Do." McPhatter received his draft notice in 1954, but was lucky enough to be posted in America, which allowed him to continue to record with the group. He had already made a decision to leave the Drifters, however. He saw himself moving in a different direction from the group, toward a solo sound that would meld pop, R&B, and rock & roll all in one, and unlike a lot of other aspirants to that sort of stardom, McPhatter had what it took to pull it off. His high tenor was equally convincing on a slow ballad or a hard rock & roll number, and he saw no reason that he couldn't do both types of song his own way. He couldn't have known it at the time, but he was opening up a path that would later be followed by the likes of Elvis Presley and Sam Cooke, among many others.

Upon his discharge in 1955, McPhatter embarked on his official solo career, still recording for Atlantic Records. McPhatter first emerged in a duet with Ruth Brown on "Love Has Joined Us Together," which made number 8 on the R&B charts, and in August of that year he recorded "Seven Days," which became a number 2 R&B hit in early 1956. This was the first of McPhatter's attempts at a crossover record, complete with a softer pop orchestra and chorus behind his singing, but it was undercut on the pop charts by a variety of white cover versions, most notably by Dorothy Collins and the Crew Cuts. He fared better in the spring of 1956 with "Treasure of Love," which was not only his first solo R&B chart-topper, but also managed to make number 16 on the pop charts. "Just to Hold My Hand" kept him in the Top 10 on the R&B charts and the Top 30 in pop in the spring of 1957, and "Long Lonely Nights" topped out the R&B listings while just brushing the Top 50 for pop record compilers that summer. McPhatter was a big enough star that he was essentially the focus of two LP releases on Atlantic in the same year, unheard of for a Black artist in those days, when R&B albums (apart from Elvis' first RCA long-players, which were considered R&B) didn't sell in serious numbers. In 1956, Atlantic released *Clyde McPhatter & the Drifters* and followed it up with *Love Ballads* soon after—the latter revealed his and the label's strategy, with a cover depicting an audience of white teenage girls in tinted overlays, looking on toward the camera excitedly and longingly. His goal, and the hope of his label, was to follow the path opened previously by Nat "King" Cole had done starting from jazz, and Eddy Arnold had done from country, and cross over to pop audiences—he had aspirations of rivalling Frank Sinatra and Perry Como. McPhatter saw his biggest hit on Atlantic in 1958 with "A Lover's Question," co-authored by Brook Benton, which hit number 6 on the pop charts that fall while topping the R&B listings. He had three more charting singles in 1959, none of which broke the Top 10 in R&B, but saw another long-player released to his credit, entitled simply *Clyde*.

He left Atlantic that year after one last hit, "Lovey Dovey," closing out his career there with another Brook Benton song, "You Went Back on Your Word." McPhatter's contract was up, and he jumped to M-G-M Records, which was offering a large advance in its eagerness to grab hold of the R&B market. His relationship there lasted but a year, through four singles, of which only "Let's Try Again" matched his Atlantic hits, making the R&B Top 20. He also had some minor pop hits in "I Told Myself a Lie" and "Think Me a Kiss" in 1960. The early '60s were a tumultuous time for McPhatter, personally and musically. He jumped to Mercury Records as the new decade began, and his career seemed to pick up again with an R&B Top 10 single, "Ta Ta," which also made the pop charts. "I Never Knew" also did well, and was followed by a Top 10 pop single in 1962 with "Lover Please," written by Billy Swan. Behind the scenes, however, McPhatter was walking a tightrope of alcoholism and unreliability that was expending all of the capital that he'd built up in the music community and the Black community—he was a big enough name to still rate bookings at the Apollo Theater in Harlem, but hall managers and promoters, and his own backing bands, never knew what to expect from him, even in terms of repertory between rehearsals and showtime. Additionally, music was changing around him. McPhatter had served as a musical model for soul singers of two generations who followed him onto the charts—Ben E. King in the Drifters and solo, but also Jackie Wilson and Smokey Robinson, and they were all producing hit records in prodigious numbers between 1960 and 1965. Even his former group the Drifters, now reconstructed with an entirely new lineup and with a new sound, were enjoying massive radio play and record sales during this period around the voices of King, Rudy Lewis, and Johnny Moore. Additionally, Sam Cooke, who was of the same generation as McPhatter, and had made the same journey out of the deep south to the big city, and the cross-over from gospel to R&B and pop, was the dominant figure in soul music during the early '60s. All were good and were also reliable and professional, and there was just no room for McPhatter, who wasn't any of those things at the time.

Before leaving Mercury, McPhatter enjoyed slight success with "Deep in the Heart of Harlem," a song that seemed to emulate the soft soul sound of the Drifters of that era, and "Crying Won't Help You Now," and cut a good concert album, *Live at the Apollo*, in 1964, which featured a cross-section of his hits across his career dating back to the early '50s. He spent the next few years recording for smaller labels such as Amy Records, unable to get a hit or keep his performing career going. He must have appreciated the grim irony, that his one-time Drifters stablemate, bass singer Bill Pinkney, was leading a group of "Drifters" who sang McPhatter's repertory and had a viable concert career, especially in England. And then, in a maneuver that anticipated the career course of the latter day Drifters, McPhatter moved to England. McPhatter's Dominoes and Drifters records hadn't appeared in the U.K. at the time of their original release. In the early '60s, between the booming enthusiasm for American R&B and the release of his current solo records, and the groundwork laid by Pinkney in his performances, McPhatter achieved recognition there and found a fresh audience. He found work in British clubs for a few years, until the same personal problems caught up with him. He returned to America in the early '70s, signing with Decca Records at the time and releasing an album, *Welcome Home*. It failed to make any impact, and McPhatter himself denied having any audience or fans left, which was not the case. (Even this writer—as a neophyte R&B listener in the late '60s with a lot to learn, coming from a middle-class white neighborhood where Jimi Hendrix was the Black artist most often played, and in a time when not a single one of the early Drifters' songs was available on an album—knew who Clyde McPhatter was, or who he had been.)

It was too late for McPhatter, professionally and personally, however. Years of alcoholism and depression, and a failure to deal with his problems ended with a fatal heart attack in New York in 1972. It took years for Atlantic, where he'd been signed for what were probably the six most optimistic years of his career, to begin to make his music available in the United States (though their British division made some efforts overseas). In the CD era, in addition to its own best of compilation *Deep Sea Ball*, the label has licensed different parts of his legacy to Collectables and Sequel. There is no definitive compilation of his music, or biography of this seminal R&B and soul star.

Jackie Wilson

Born: Jun 9, 1934 in Detroit, MI
Died: Jan 21, 1984

 Jackie Wilson was one of the most important agents of black pop's transition from R&B into soul. In terms of vocal power (especially in the upper register), few could outdo him; he was also an electrifying on-stage showman.

He was a consistent hitmaker from the mid-'50s through the early '70s, although never a crossover superstar. His reputation isn't quite on par with Ray Charles, James Brown, or Sam Cooke, however, because his records did not always reflect his artistic genius. Indeed, there is a consensus of sorts among critics that Wilson was something of an underachiever in the studio, due to the sometimes inappropriately pop-based material and arrangements that he used.

Wilson was well-known on the R&B scene before he went solo in the late '50s. In 1953 he replaced Clyde McPhatter in Billy Ward & the Dominoes, one of the top R&B vocal groups of the '50s. Although McPhatter was himself a big star, Wilson was as good as or better than the man whose shoes he filled. Commercially, however, things took a downturn for the Dominoes in the Wilson years, although they did manage a Top 20 hit with "St. Therese of the Roses" in 1956. Elvis Presley was one of those who was mightily impressed by Wilson in the mid-'50s; he can be heard praising Jackie's on-stage cover of "Don't Be Cruel" in between-song banter during the *Million Dollar Quartet* session in late 1956.

Wilson would score his first big R&B (and small pop) hit in late 1956 with the brassy, stuttering "Reet Petite," which was co-written by an emerging Detroit songwriter named Berry Gordy Jr. Gordy would also help write a few other hits for Jackie in the late '50s, "To Be Loved," "Lonely Teardrops," "That's Why (I Love You So)," and "I'll Be Satisfied"; they also crossed over to the pop charts, "Lonely Teardrops" making the Top Ten. Most of these were upbeat, creatively arranged marriages of pop and R&B that, in retrospect, helped set the stage both for '60s soul and for Gordy's own huge pop success at Motown. The early Gordy-Wilson association has led some historians to speculate how much differently (and better) Jackie's career might have turned out had he been on Motown's roster instead of the Brunswick label.

In the early '60s, Wilson maintained his pop stardom with regular hit singles that often used horn arrangements and female choruses that have dated somewhat badly, especially in comparison with the more creative work by peers such as Charles and Brown from this era. Wilson also sometimes went into out-and-out operatic pop, as on "Danny Boy" and one of his biggest hits, "Night" (1960). At the same time, he remained capable of unleashing a sweaty, up-tempo, gospel-soaked number: "Baby Workout," which fit that description to a T, was a number five hit for him in 1963. It's true that you have to be pretty selective in targeting the worthwhile Wilson records from this era; 1962's *At the Copa*, for instance, has Jackie trying to combine soul and all-around entertainment, and not wholly succeeding with either strategy. Yet some of his early Brunswick material is also fine uptown soul; not quite as earthy as some of his fans would have liked him to sound, no doubt, but worth hearing.

Wilson was shot and seriously wounded by a female fan in 1961, though he made a recovery. His career was more seriously endangered by his inability to keep up with changing soul and rock trends. Not everything he did in the mid-'60s is totally dismissible; "No Pity (In the Naked City)," for instance, is something like *West Side Story* done uptown soul style. In 1966, his career was briefly revived when he teamed up with Chicago soul producer Carl Davis, who had been instrumental in the success of Windy City performers like Gene Chandler, Major Lance, and Jerry Butler. Davis successfully updated Wilson's sound with horn-heavy arrangements, getting near the Top Ten with "Whispers," and then making number six in 1967 with "Higher and Higher." And that was really the close of Wilson's career as either a significant artist or commercial force, although he had some minor chart entries through the early '70s.

While playing a Dick Clark oldies show at the Latin Casino in New Jersey in September 1975, Wilson suffered an onstage heart attack while singing "Lonely Teardrops." He lapsed into a coma, suffering major brain damage, and was hospitalized until his death in early 1984.

James Brown

Born May 5, 1933 in Macon, GA

"Soul Brother Number One," "the Godfather of Soul," "the Hardest Working Man in Show Business," "Mr. Dynamite"—those are mighty titles, but no one can question that James Brown has earned them more than any other performer. Other singers were more popular, others were equally skilled, but few other African-American musicians have been so influential on the course of popular music. And no other musician, pop or otherwise, put on a more exciting, exhilarating stage show—Brown's performances were marvels of athletic stamina and split-second timing.

Through the gospel-impassioned fury of his vocals and the complex polyrhythms of his beats, Brown was a crucial midwife in not just one, but two revolutions in American black music. He was one of the figures most responsible for turning R&B into soul; he was, most would agree, *the* figure most responsible for turning soul music into the funk of the late '60s and early '70s. Since the mid-'70s, he's done little more than tread water artistically; his financial and drug problems eventually got him a controversial prison sentence. Yet in a sense his music is now more influential than ever, as his voice and rhythms were sampled on innumerable rap and hip-hop recordings, and critics have belatedly hailed his innovations as among the most important in all of rock or soul.

Brown's rags-to-riches-to-rags story has heroic and tragic dimensions of mythic resonance. Born into poverty in the South, he ran afoul of the law by the late '40s on an armed robbery conviction. With the help of singer Bobby Byrd's family, Brown gained parole, and started a gospel group with Byrd, changing their focus to R&B as the rock revolution gained steam. The Flames, as the Georgian group were known in the mid-'50s, were signed by Federal/King, and had a huge R&B hit right off the bat with the wrenching, churchy ballad "Please, Please, Please." By now the Flames had become James Brown & the Famous Flames, the charisma, energy, and talent of Brown making him the natural star attraction.

All of Brown's singles over the next two years flopped, as he sought to establish his own style, recording material that was obviously derivative of heroes like Roy Brown, Hank Ballard, Little Richard, and Ray Charles. In retrospect, it can be seen that Brown was in the same position as dozens of other R&B one-shots—talented singers in need of better songs, or not fully on the road to a truly original sound. What made Brown succeed where hundreds of others failed was his superhuman determination, working the chitlin circuit to death, sharpening his band, and keeping an eye on new trends. He was on the verge of being dropped from King in late 1958 when his perseverance finally paid off, as "Try Me" became a number-one R&B (and small pop) hit, and several follow-ups established him as a regular visitor to the R&B charts.

Brown's style of R&B got harder as the '60s began, as he added more complex, Latin- and jazz-influenced rhythms on hits like "Good Good Lovin'," "I'll Go Crazy," "Think," and "Night Train," alternating these with torturous ballads that featured some of the most frayed screaming to be heard outside of the church. Black audiences already knew that Brown had the most exciting live act around, but he truly started to become a phenomenon with the release of *Live at the Apollo* in 1963. Capturing a James Brown concert in all its whirling-dervish energy and calculated spontaneity, it reached number two in the album charts, an unprecedented feat for a hardcore R&B LP.

Live at the Apollo was recorded and released against the wishes of the King label. It was these kinds of artistic stand-offs that led Brown to seek better opportunities elsewhere. In 1964, he ignored his King contract to record "Out of Sight" for Smash, igniting a lengthy legal battle that prevented him from issuing vocal recordings for about a year. When he finally resumed recording for King in 1965, he had a new contract that granted him far more artistic control over his releases.

Brown's new era had truly begun, however, with "Out of Sight," which topped the R&B charts and made the pop Top 40. For some time, Brown had been moving toward more elemental lyrics which threw in as many chants and screams as words, and more intricate beats and horn charts that took some of their cues from the ensemble work of jazz outfits. "Out of Sight" wasn't called funk when it came out, but it had most of the essential ingredients. These were amplified and perfected on 1965's "Papa's Got a Brand New Bag," a monster that finally broke Brown to the white audience, reaching the Top Ten. The even more adventurous follow-up, "I Got You (I Feel Good)," did even better, making number three.

These hits kicked off Brown's period of greatest commercial success and public visibility. From 1965 to the end of the decade, he was rarely off the R&B charts, often on the pop listings, and all over the concert circuit and national television, even meeting with Vice President Hubert Humphrey and other important politicians as a representative of the black community. His music became even bolder and funkier, as melody was dispensed with almost altogether in favor of chunky rhythms and magnetic interplay between his vocals, horns, drums, and scratching electric guitar (heard to best advantage on hits like "Cold Sweat," "I Got the Feelin'," and "There Was a Time"). The lyrics were now not so much words as chanted, stream-of-consciousness slogans, often aligning themselves with black pride as well as good old-fashioned (or new-fashioned) sex. Much of the credit for the sound he devised belonged to (and has now been belatedly attributed) his top-notch supporting musicians, such as saxophonists Maceo Parker, St. Clair Pinckney, and Pee Wee Ellis; guitarist Jimmy Nolen; backup singer and longtime loyal associate Bobby Byrd; and drummer Clyde Stubblefield.

Brown was both a brilliant bandleader and a stern taskmaster, leading his band to walk out on him in late 1969. Amazingly, he turned the crisis to his advantage by recruiting a young Cincinnati outfit called the Pacemakers, featuring guitarist Catfish Collins and bassist Bootsy Collins. Although they only stayed with him for about a year, they were crucial to Brown's evolution into even harder funk, emphasizing the rhythm and the bottom even more. The Collins brothers, for their part, put their apprenticeship to good use, helping define '70s funk as members of the Parliament/Funkadelic axis.

In the early '70s, many of the most important members of Brown's late-'60s band returned to the fold, to be billed as the J.B's (they also made records on their own). Brown continued to score heavily on the R&B charts throughout the first half of the 1970s, the music becoming even more and more elemental and beat-driven. At the same time, he was retreating from the white audience he had cultivated during the mid- to late '60s; records like "Make It Funky," "Hot Pants," "Get on the Good Foot," and "The Payback" were huge soul sellers, but only modest pop ones. Critics charged, with some justification, that the Godfather was starting to repeat and recycle himself too many times. It must be remembered, though, that these songs were made for the singles-radio-jukebox market and not meant to be played one after the other on CD compilations (as they are today).

By the mid-'70s, Brown was beginning to burn out artistically. He seemed shorn of new ideas, was being out-gunned on the charts by disco, and was running into problems with the IRS and his financial empire. There were sporadic hits, and he could always count on enthusiastic live audiences, but by the 1980s, he didn't have a label. With the explosion of rap, however, which frequently sampled vintage JB records, Brown was now hipper than ever. He collaborated with Afrika Bambaataa on the critical smash single "Unity," and re-entered the Top Ten in 1986 with "Living in America." Rock critics, who had always ranked Brown considerably below Otis Redding and Aretha Franklin in the soul canon, began to re-evaluate his output, particularly his funk years, sometimes anointing him not just as Soul Brother Number One, but as *the* most important black musician of the rock era.

In 1988, Brown's personal life came crashing down in a well-publicized incident in which he was accused by his wife of assault and battery. After a year skirting hazy legal and personal troubles, he led the police on an interstate car chase after allegedly threatening people with a handgun. The episode ended in a six-year prison sentence that many felt excessive; he was paroled after serving two years.

It's probably safe to assume that Brown will not make any more important recordings, although he continues to perform and release new material like 1998's *I'm Back*. Yet his music is probably more popular in the American mainstream today than it has been since the 1970s, and not just among young rappers and samplers. For a long time his cumbersome, byzantine discography was mostly out of print, with pieces available only on skimpy greatest-hits collections. A series of exceptionally well-packaged reissues on PolyGram has changed the situation; the *Star Time* box set is the best overview, with other superb compilations devoted to specific phases of his lengthy career, from '50s R&B to '70s funk.

The Marcels

Formed in Pittsburgh, PA

This Pittsburgh ensemble deserved a much better fate than being known primarily for a novelty-tinged cover of "Blue Moon." Baritone vocalist Richard F. Knauss teamed with Fred Johnson, Gene J. Bricker, Ron Mundy, and lead vocalist Cornelius Harp, an integrated ensemble. They named themselves after Harp's hairstyle, the marcel. The group did a string of covers as demo tapes that were sent to Colpix. The label's A&R director had them cut several oldies at RCA's New York studios in 1961, one of them being "Blue Moon." They used the bass intro arrangement from the Cadillacs' "Zoom" and the results were a huge hit. It eventually topped both the pop and R&B charts, and also was an international smash. The group eventually appeared in the film *Twist Around the Clock* with Dion and Chubby Checker. They eventually recorded an 18-cut LP for Colpix. Alan Johnson and Walt Maddox later replaced Knauss and Gene Bricker, making them an all-black unit. The group did score another Top Ten pop single with "Heartaches," another cover of a pre-rock single. This peaked at number seven pop and number 19 R&B in 1961. They continued recording on Kyra, Queen Bee, St. Clair, Rocky, and Monogram with varying lineups, but never again equaled their past success.

The Shirelles

Formed 1958 in Passaic, NJ

The Shirelles were the first major female vocal group of the rock era, defining the so-called girl group sound with their soft, sweet harmonies and yearning innocence. Their music was a blend of pop/rock and R&B—especially doo wop and smooth uptown soul—that appealed to listeners across the board, before Motown ever became a crossover phenomenon with white audiences. Even if the Shirelles were not technically the first of their kind, their success was unprecedented, paving the way for legions of imitators; their inviting musical blueprint had an enduring influence not just on their immediate followers, but on future generations of female pop singers, who often updated the style with a more modern sensibility. What was more, they provided some of the earliest hits for important Brill Building songwriters like Gerry Goffin & Carole King, Burt Bacharach & Hal David, and Van McCoy.

The Shirelles were originally formed in 1958 in Passaic, NJ, by four high school friends: Doris Coley (later Doris Kenner-Jackson), Addie "Micki" Harris, Shirley Owens (later Shirley Alston), and Beverly Lee. Christening themselves the Poquellos, the girls wrote a song called "I Met Him on a Sunday" and entered their school talent show with it. A school friend had them audition for her mother, Florence Greenberg, who ran a small record label; she was impressed enough to become the group's manager, and changed their name to the Shirelles by combining frequent lead singer Owens' first name with doo woppers the Chantels. The Shirelles' recording of "I Met Him on a Sunday" was licensed by Decca and climbed into the national Top 50 in 1958. Two more singles flopped, however, and Decca passed on further releases. Greenberg instead signed them to her new label, Scepter Records, and brought in producer Luther Dixon, whose imaginative, sometimes string-heavy arrangements would help shape the group's signature sound.

"Dedicated to the One I Love" (1959) and "Tonight's the Night" (1960) both failed to make much of an impact on the pop charts, although the latter was a Top 20 R&B hit. However, they broke big time with the Goffin-King composition "Will You Love Me Tomorrow"; released in late 1960, it went all the way to number one pop, making them the first all-female group of the rock era to accomplish that feat; it also peaked at number two R&B. Its success helped send a re-release of "Dedicated to the One I Love" into the Top Five on both the pop and R&B charts in 1961, and "Mama Said" did the same; a more R&B-flavored outing, "Big John," also went to number two that year. 1962 continued their run of success, most notably with "Soldier Boy," a Luther Dixon/Florence Greenberg tune that became their second pop number one; they also had a Top Ten pop and R&B hit with "Baby It's You." Unfortunately, Dixon subsequently left the label; the Shirelles managed to score one more pop/R&B Top Ten with 1963's "Foolish Little Girl," but found it difficult to maintain their previous level of success.

The group went on to record material for the film *It's a Mad, Mad, Mad, Mad World*, headlined the first integrated concert show in Alabama, and helped a young Dionne Warwick get some of her first exposure (subbing for Owens and Coley when each took a leave of absence to get married). A money dispute with Scepter tied up their recording schedule for a while in 1964, and although it was eventually settled, the Shirelles were still bound to a label where their run was essentially over. Of course, this was also because of the British Invasion, whose bands were among the first to cover their songs; not only their hits, but lesser-known items like "Boys" (the Beatles) and "Sha La La" (a hit for Manfred Mann). The Shirelles scraped the lower reaches of the charts a few more times, making their last appearance, ironically, with 1967's "Last Minute Miracle." Doris Kenner left the group the following year to concentrate on raising her family, and the remaining Shirelles continued as a trio, cutting singles for Bell, United Artists, and RCA through 1971. The group continued to tour the oldies circuit, however, and appeared in the 1973 documentary *Let the Good*

Times Roll. Shirley Alston left for a solo career in 1975, upon which point Doris Kenner-Jackson returned. Micki Harris died of a heart attack during a performance in Atlanta on June 10, 1982, upon which point the group went into what turned out to be a temporary retirement; the three remaining charter members recorded together for the last time on a 1983 Dionne Warwick record. Different Shirelles lineups toured the oldies circuit in the '90s, though Beverly Lee eventually secured the official trademark. They were officially inducted into the Rock and Roll Hall of Fame in 1996. Doris Kenner-Jackson passed away after a bout with breast cancer in Sacramento on February 4, 2000.

Barrett Strong

Born Feb 5, 1941 in Westpoint, MS

A pivotal figure in Motown's formative years, singer/composer Barrett Strong was a key associate and friend of Berry Gordy. It was his hit "Money (That's What I Want)" for Anna Records in 1960 that provided vital capital for Gordy to expand his operation. The song gave Strong his only major hit as a vocalist, reaching number two on the R&B charts and barely missing the pop Top 20.

During the late '60s and early '70s, Strong collaborated with Norman Whitfield on some historic songs that included Marvin Gaye's "I Heard It Through the Grapevine" and "Too Busy Thinking About My Baby," the Temptations' "Papa Was a Rolling Stone" and "Ball of Confusion," Edwin Starr's "War," and "Take Me in Your Arms and Love Me" for Gladys Knight & the Pips, which he also co-wrote. Strong left Motown when the label moved to Los Angeles in 1972, and he signed with Epic. After one failed single, Strong moved to Capitol, where he had the LP *Stronghold* released in 1975 and later *Live & Love* in 1976. Though it wasn't a hit, his song "Man up in the Sky" was a '70s soul gem. Johnny Bristol later re-recorded it. Strong continued into the '80s, recording "Rock It Easy" for an independent label and writing and arranging "You Can Depend on Me," which was included on the Dells' *The Second Time* LP in 1988.

Smokey Robinson & the Miracles

If you're looking for the all-time number-one purveyor of mainstream romantic soul, Smokey Robinson may well be the man, in the face of some towering competition. With the Miracles in the 1960s, he paced dozens of tuneful Motown hits with his beautiful high tenor. As a solo performer from the 1970s onward, he was one of the staples of urban contemporary music. But his singing gifts, as notable as they are, comprise only one of his hats: he's also one of pop's best and most prolific songwriters. As a songwriter and producer, he was the most important musical component to Motown's early success, not only on the hits by the Miracles, but for numerous other acts as well (especially Mary Wells and the Temptations).

Robinson first crossed paths with Motown founder Berry Gordy, Jr. in the late '50s in Detroit. In retrospect, this may have been the most important meeting in both men's lives. Robinson needed a mentor and an outlet for his budding talents as a singer and songwriter; the ambitious Gordy needed someone with multi-faceted musical vision. Gordy encouraged and polished Robinson's songwriting in particular in the early days, in which the Miracles were one of many acts bridging the doo-wop and early soul eras.

Before solidifying their relationship with the embryonic Motown operation, the Miracles issued a few singles on the End and Chess labels, the most successful of which was "Got a Job." There was no national action for the Miracles until "Shop Around" in late 1960. Gordy withdrew the original single in favor of a faster, more fully produced version of the song; it made number two, doing much not only to establish the Miracles, but to establish the Motown label itself. The song also heralded many of the important elements of the Motown sound, with its gospel-ish interplay between lead and backup vocals, its rhythmic groove, and its blend of R&B and pop.

While Robinson is most often thought of as a romantic balladeer, the Miracles were also capable of grinding out some excellent up-tempo party tunes, particularly in their early days. "Mickey's Monkey" (which the group gave an athletically electrifying performance of in the 1964 *T.A.M.I. Show* movie), a 1963 Top Ten hit, is the most famous of these; there was also "Going to a Go-Go" and smaller hits like "I Gotta Dance to Keep From Crying." The 1962 Top Ten hit "You've Really Got a Hold on Me," however, was the key cut in forming Robinson's romantic persona, with its pleading, soaring vocals, exquisite melody, and carefully crafted lyrics. Bob Dylan was impressed enough by Robinson's facility for imaginative wordplay to dub him "America's greatest living poet" (a phrase which has possibly become the most quoted example of one rock giant praising another).

Surveying Robinson's achievements during the 1960s, one wonders if the man ever slept. While the Miracles were never Motown's biggest act at any given time, they were one of its very most consistent, entering the Top 40 25 times over the course of the decade. "I Second That Emotion," "The Love I Saw in You Was Just a Mirage," "The Tracks of My Tears," "Ooo Baby Baby," and "Baby, Baby Don't Cry" were some of their biggest singles, and usually represented Motown at its most sophisticated and urbane. Robinson also was extremely active at Motown as a songwriter and producer for other acts. The number one singles "My Guy" (Mary Wells) and "My Girl" (Temptations) were each Robinson songs and productions (the latter with fellow Miracle Ronnie White), and Robinson also did some excellent work with the Marvelettes and Marvin Gaye. He also toured with the Miracles, and started a family with the Miracles' female singer, Claudette Rogers, whom he married in 1964. Rogers stopped touring with the group in the mid-'60s, although she continued to sing on their records.

Starting in 1967, the billing on Miracles releases was changed to Smokey Robinson & the Miracles, presaging Robinson's solo career. The group continued to spin out hits until the early '70s, however, getting their only number one in 1970 with the upbeat "The Tears of a

Clown" (which had actually been recorded back in 1966). Robinson left the group to go on his own in 1972; the Miracles continued without him with limited success, although they had a number one hit in 1976 with "Love Machine, Pt. 1."

Robinson had been made a vice president at Motown near the beginning of his career in 1961. He recorded frequently as a solo artist for Motown in the '70s and '80s, in a considerably mellower vein than his Miracles work, in keeping with the general shift of Motown and soul toward urban contemporary. Robinson, in fact, provided that genre with one of its catch phrases with the title of his 1975 album, *A Quiet Storm*. "Cruisin'" (1979) and "Being With You" (1981) were his biggest solo hits, although artistically and commercially his solo era wasn't nearly as successful as his music with the Miracles.

Maurice Williams

Born in Lancaster, SC

Maurice Williams is one of the most extraordinarily durable figures in the history of classic R&B and rock & roll, despite the fact that, as a performer, he only ever racked up one major national hit on the pop charts. That song, "Stay," became one of the classic singles in the history of rock 'n roll and R&B—a number one hit upon its release in 1960 on Al Silver's Herald label, and a popular favorite for decades since, revived in 1987 with its prominent use in the movie *Dirty Dancing*. Maurice Williams & the Zodiacs recorded only two more minor pop hits before they disappeared from the charts, but Williams has remained active as a performer and, periodically, as a recording artist and songwriter ever since.

Williams was born in Lancaster, SC, in 1940 (one source indicates Apr 26, 1938), and showed himself musically inclined from a very early age—he started learning the piano from his older sister in the late 1940s, practicing daily so that by the time he was ten years old he was having friends from elementary school over for informal jam sessions at his house. Williams had sung in church, but his interest lay more in popular music, and in 1953, he and his friends were ready to form a group that they called the Royal Charms. The group's original membership, in addition to Williams, included Earl Gainey (tenor, guitar), Willie Jones (baritone), William Massey (tenor, baritone, trumpet), and Norman Wade (bass). They played school events and talent shows, winning several and acquiring a local following, before they finally got a paying gig at the local Veterans of Foreign Wars post. The year they'd started out, 1953, Williams had also written two songs that were to have a pivotal effect on his life and career, and the group's history: "Little Darling" and "Stay."

The Royal Charms loved performing, and were popular locally, but working the area around Lancaster, they found their prospects limited. The group's first real break took place in 1956 when a Nashville disc jockey hooked them up with Ernie Young, the head of Excello Records—Williams, then only 16, bluffed his way into an audition over the phone and then had to raise money from friends and local merchants in Lancaster to make the trip to Nashville in December of 1956.

"Little Darling" impressed Young, although he altered it somewhat, giving the song a calypso beat that it didn't originally have. He also insisted on the group changing its name—it seemed as though every R&B vocal group (the word "doo wop" hadn't been invented yet) had either "Royal" or "Charms" in its name, and bird-named groups were too common as well. Young happened to like flowers, and selected the name the Gladiolas.

"Little Darling" by the Gladiolas was released by Excello in January of 1957 and was a hit on the R&B charts, rising to number 11 in a four-week run in the early spring of that year. It had a more muted presence on the pop charts, lingering there for 11 weeks but never getting higher than number 41.

What happened next is a matter of interpretation. In some historians' eyes, the Gladiolas' version of the song was undercut by a competing rendition, recorded for Mercury by a white Canadian group called the Diamonds, which rose to number one on the pop charts and sold more than a million copies, even becoming a definitive "doo wop"-type single. On the other hand, some listeners, comparing the two versions, say that the Diamonds' version is more fully realized than that by the Gladiolas, not only with a more ambitious arrangement and greater vocal virtuosity, but a better sound; the Gladiolas' single, by contrast, almost seems like a demo, only partly realized in technical terms.

Regardless of the virtues of either, Williams, for his part, never minded the Diamonds' version, because Young—in an example of honesty all too rare in the record business in those days—told him that, as writer of the song, all he should care about is that it sells and gets played, not whose version sells. Young had also left him with full rights as songwriter, rather than trying to buy them away from him, which Williams admits he could've done for practically no money at all in those days. It was a decision that was to earn Williams a vast amount of money at the age of 17 and beyond, and educated him painlessly and well about the business side of the music business.

Williams was a serious high school student, and he earned a music scholarship to Allen University in Columbia, SC, that he had to turn down—he was simply doing too much in music to interrupt his career, tempting as it was. The Gladiolas kept performing, touring the West once before returning to South Carolina, where they became a heavy favorite among fraternities, especially at the University of South Carolina. At the end of 1958, the group decided against re-signing with Excello, which meant they had to give up their name, which Young owned. This could have been a disaster, forcing them to re-establish themselves in a new incarnation, but a name and a song, courtesy of Williams, made that easy. According to Williams, it was group member Bobby Gore who saw a German car called a Zodiac, and immediately seized on the name—Maurice Williams & the Zodiacs became the group's new identity.

Over the next year, the original Zodiacs' lineup expanded to nine members, including two saxmen (Calvin McKinnie, Harold Alexander). In 1960, the band hooked up with Al Silver of Herald Records in New York, by way of producers Phil Gernhardt and Al McCullough.

The group was supposed to provide demos, and Williams retrieved a song he'd written back in 1953—strangely enough, to the same girl for whom he'd written "Little Darling"—called "Stay" and presented it to Silver.

The group signed with Herald and "Stay," sparked by a stunning falsetto performance by Shane Gaston, became their debut on the label during the summer of 1960. It hit number one that fall and easily topped a million sales at the time, also becoming the biggest hit in the history of Herald Records. Williams & the Zodiacs never had another record nearly as big as "Stay," which came out at just the right moment and seemed to sell in subsequent years at the drop of a hat, as a romantic and nostalgia favorite—by some estimates, their record has topped ten million sales internationally. Additionally, other artists, including the Four Seasons, Jackson Browne, and Rufus & Chaka Khan, all made the Top 20 or better with their respective versions of the song, and the Hollies cut it as a single at the outset of their career.

The Zodiacs didn't fare as well as the song. "I Remember," also released on Herald, never made it past number 86 on the pop charts and didn't appear on the R&B charts at all. Neither did "Come Along," which was released in the spring of 1961 and only climbed to number 83 on the pop charts. During the mid-'60s, the group hooked up with the New Orleans-based production team of Marshall Sehorn and Allen Toussaint. With their guidance, the group cut a passionate, soulful recording of Williams' "May I," a dazzlingly beautiful song that held a lot of promise. Unfortunately, they chose to license it to Vee Jay, which was then the most successful black-owned record company in the world. But Vee Jay went into bankruptcy within days of the record's national release, and "May I" never recovered—the record did get out on the Dee Su label in New Orleans, which rescued it physically from oblivion, and it found an audience on the radio. It has been certified a million-seller by the RIAA, despite never managing to appear on either the pop or R&B charts. Five years later, it became a modest Top 40 hit in a smoother version by Bill Deal & the Rhondels, a white dance-rock and R&B-based band from the Virginia-Carolinas area who'd been doing it on stage for years. The group subsequently released records on Atlantic, Sea-Horn, and Scepter, including a fine single, "Return," with Gladys Knight & the Pips singing behind them. Williams saw minimal chart action from any of this, but remained active—Maurice Williams & the Zodiacs were still a major draw in the South, especially in their native state, and in 1965 cut a live album at Myrtle Beach, SC.

Throughout the 1970s and 1980s, Williams led various incarnations of the Zodiacs on oldies tours, primarily on the beach music circuit on the U.S. East Coast. In the wake of *Dirty Dancing*, which yielded sales of another eight million copies of "Stay," he re-emerged as a recording artist on the Ripete label, based in Columbia, SC, which specializes in beach music (they've also got a best-of the Swinging Medallions out on CD). Ripete has since released the impossible-to-find 1965 live album on CD, and an excellent career anthology of Maurice Williams & the Zodiacs.

Chuck Jackson

Born Jun 22, 1937 in Latta, SC

He's relatively forgotten today, and his brand of "uptown" soul is dismissed by the relatively vocal clique of critics who prefer their soul deep and down-home. But Chuck Jackson was a regular visitor to the R&B charts (and an occasional one to the pop listings) in the early '60s with such early pop-soul concoctions as "I Don't Want to Cry," "Any Day Now," and "Tell Him I'm Not Home." His records were very much of a piece with New York pop-rock-soul production, with cheeky brass, sweeping strings, and female backup vocalists. Those production trills make his work sound dated to some listeners, and his hoarse, emotional vocals weren't as subtle or commanding as peers like Ben E. King or Wilson Pickett. On its own terms, though, his best work is quite good, whether you prefer pop to soul or vice versa.

Jackson sang with one of the best doo wop groups, the Dell-Vikings, for a while in the late '50s (although he doesn't appear on their hit singles). Spotted by Scepter Records while performing with Jackie Wilson's Revue, he started recording for the label in 1961. As was the case with labelmates Dionne Warwick and the Shirelles, Jackson's early-'60s arrangements blended pop, R&B, and New York-session professionalism. Like Warwick, Jackson was one of the first singers to successfully record Bacharach-David material; one of his best singles, "I Keep Forgettin'" (1962), was written and produced by Leiber-Stoller. Jackson had some success with some duets with Maxine Brown in the mid-'60s, but he left Wand in 1967 for Motown, at the urging of Smokey Robinson. Jackson was (perhaps understandably) lost in the shuffle during his four years at Motown, and he's barely been heard from since, although he remains a favorite on England's "Northern soul" scene.

Maxine Brown

Born Apr 27, 1932 in Kingstree, SC

Although she never had many hits, Maxine Brown was one of the most underrated soul and R&B vocalists of the '60s. During the '60s she released a series of singles for Nomar and Wand, with only a couple of songs—"All in My Mind," "Funny," "Something You Got," "Oh No Not My Baby"—managing to become either pop or R&B hits. Despite her lack of hits, Brown is acknowledged as one of the finest R&B vocalists of her time, capable of delivering soul, jazz, and pop with equal aplomb.

Born in Kingstree, South Carolina, Brown began singing as a child, singing with two New York-based gospel groups when she was a teenager. In 1960, she signed with the small Nomar label, who released the smooth soul ballad "All in My Mind" late in the year. The single became a hit, climbing to number two on the R&B charts (number 19 pop), and it was quickly followed by "Funny," which peaked at number three. Brown was poised to become a star, and she moved to ABC-Paramount in 1962, but she left the label within a year without scoring any hits. She signed to the New York-based, uptown soul label Wand in 1963.

Brown recorded her best work at Wand, having a string of moderate hits for the label over the next three years. Among these were the Carole King/David Goffin song "Oh No Not My Baby," which reached number 24 on the pop charts; "It's Gonna Be Alright" and the Chuck Jackson duets "Something You Got," "Hold On I'm Coming," and "Daddy's Home." Part of the reason Brown didn't receive much exposure is that the label focused much of their attention on Dionne Warwick, leaving Maxine Brown to toil in semi-obscurity. In 1969, she left Wand and signed with Commonwealth United, where she had the minor hits "We'll Cry Together" and "I Can't Get Along Without You." In 1971, she moved to Avco Records, but all of her recordings for the label went ignored and she faded away over the course of the decade.

Ben E. King

Born Sep 23, 1938 in Henderson, NC

From the groundbreaking orchestrated productions of the Drifters to his own solo hits, Ben E. King was the definition of R&B elegance. King's plaintive baritone had all the passion of gospel, but the settings in which it was displayed were tailored more for his honey smooth phrasing and crisp enunciation, proving for perhaps the first time that R&B could be sophisticated and accessible to straight pop audiences. King's approach influenced countless smooth soul singers in his wake and his records were key forerunners of the Motown sound.

King was born Benjamin Earl Nelson in Henderson, NC, in 1938, and sang with his church choir before the family moved to Harlem in 1947. In junior high, he began performing with a street corner doo wop group called the Four B's, which won second place in an Apollo Theater talent contest. While still in high school, he was offered a chance to join the Moonglows, but was simply too young and inexperienced to stick. He subsequently worked at his father's restaurant as a singing waiter, which led to an invitation to become the baritone singer in a doo wop outfit called the Five Crowns in 1958. The Five Crowns performed several gigs at the Apollo Theater along with the Drifters, whose career had begun to flounder in the years since original lead singer Clyde McPhatter departed. Drifters manager George Treadwell, dissatisfied with the group members' unreliability and lack of success, fired them all in the summer of 1958 and hired the Five Crowns to assume the name of the Drifters (which he owned).

The new Drifters toured for about a year, playing to often hostile audiences who knew they were a completely different group. In early 1959, they went into the studio with producers Jerry Leiber and Mike Stoller to cut their first records. A song Nelson (still performing under his given name) co-wrote called "There Goes My Baby" became his first lead vocal and the lush backing arrangement made highly unorthodox (in fact, virtually unheard-of) use of a string section. "There Goes My Baby" became a massive hit, laying the groundwork for virtually every smooth/uptown soul production that followed. Over the next two years, Nelson sang lead on several other Drifters classics, including "Dance With Me," "This Magic Moment," "Save the Last Dance for Me," and "I Count the Tears."

In 1960, Nelson approached Treadwell about a salary increase and a fairer share of the group's royalties. Treadwell rebuffed him and Nelson quit the group, at this point assuming the more memorable stage name Ben E. King in preparation for a solo career. Remaining on Atlantic, King scored his first solo hit with the stylish, Latin-tinged ballad "Spanish Harlem," a Jerry Leiber/Phil Spector composition that hit the Top Ten in early 1961. The follow-up, "Stand By Me," a heartfelt ode to friendship and devotion co-written by King, became his signature song and an enduring R&B classic; it was also his biggest hit, topping the R&B charts and reaching the pop Top Five. King scored a few more chart singles through 1963, including velvety smooth pop-soul productions like "Amor," "Don't Play That Song (You Lied)," and the Italian tune "I (Who Have Nothing)." In the post-British Invasion years, King had a rough go of it on the pop charts but continued to score R&B hits. 1967's Southern-fried "What Is Soul?" was one of his last singles for Atco; seeking to revive his commercial fortunes, King departed in 1969.

A 1970 album on Maxwell, *Rough Edges*, failed to generate much attention, and King was forced to make a living touring the oldies circuit. In 1975, Atlantic president Ahmet Ertegun caught King's act in a Miami lounge and invited him to re-sign with the label. King scored an unlikely comeback smash with the disco track "Supernatural Thing, Part I," which returned him to the top of the R&B charts in 1975 and also reached the pop Top Five. While he was unable to duplicate that single's success, King recorded several more albums for Atlantic up through 1981, and also collaborated with the Average White Band in 1977 on the album *Benny & Us*. After leaving Atlantic a second time, King toured in a version of the Drifters beginning in 1982. In 1986, "Stand By Me" was prominently featured in the Rob Reiner film of the same name; re-released as a single, it climbed into the Top Ten all over again. In its wake, King returned to solo recording, issuing a new album every few years all the way up through the '90s. He also guested on recordings by Heaven 17 and Mark Knopfler, among others. King's 1999 album *Shades of Blue* (on Half Note Records) found him branching out into jazz territory, performing with a big band and guests like Milt Jackson and David "Fathead" Newman.

The Marvelettes

Formed 1960 in Inkster, MI

Probably the most pop-oriented of Motown's major female acts, the Marvelettes didn't project as strong an identity as the Supremes, Mary Wells, or Martha Reeves, but recorded quite a few hits, including Motown's first number one single, "Please Mr. Postman" (1961). "Postman," as well as other chirpy early-'60s hits like "Playboy," "Twistin' Postman," and "Beechwood 4-5789," were the label's purest girl group efforts. Featuring two strong lead singers, Gladys Horton and Wanda Young, the Marvelettes went through five different

lineups, but maintained a high standard on their recordings. After a few years, they moved from girl group sounds to up-tempo and mid-tempo numbers that were more characteristic of Motown's production line. They received no small help from Smokey Robinson, who produced and wrote many of their singles; Holland-Dozier-Holland, Berry Gordy, Mickey Stevenson, Marvin Gaye, and Ashford-Simpson also got involved with the songwriting and production at various points. After the mid-'60s Wanda Young assumed most of the lead vocal duties; Gladys Horton departed from the group in the late '60s. While the Marvelettes didn't cut as many monster smashes as most of their Motown peers after the early '60s, they did periodically surface with classic hits like "Too Many Fish in the Sea," "Don't Mess With Bill," and "The Hunter Gets Captured by the Game." There were also plenty of fine minor hits and misses, like 1965's "I'll Keep Holding On," which is just as memorable as the well-known Motown chart-toppers of the era. The group quietly disbanded in the early '70s after several years without a major hit.

The Mar-Keys

Formed 1958 in Memphis, TN

Despite scoring only one national hit, the 1961 instrumental smash "Last Night," the Mar-Keys remain one of the most important groups ever to emerge from the Memphis music scene. As the first house band for the legendary Stax label, they appeared on some of the greatest records in soul history, with their ranks also producing such renowned musicians as guitarist Steve Cropper and bassist Donald "Duck" Dunn. The Mar-Keys formed in 1958 and included drummer Terry Johnson, pianist Jerry Lee "Smoochie" Smith, saxophonists Don Nix and Charles Axton, and trumpeter Wayne Jackson in addition to Cropper and Dunn. Originally dubbed the Royal Spades, in 1960 the group joined the staff at Axton's mother Estelle's Satellite label, backing artists that included Rufus Thomas and his daughter Carla. A year later, the Mar-Keys headlined the Chips Moman-penned "Last Night," which reached the number three spot in the summer of 1961. When Satellite changed its name to Stax, the Mar-Keys remained on board, laying the foundation for the classic Memphis soul sound with their funky, sophisticated grooves; concurrently they recorded a series of singles including "Pop-Eye Stroll," "The Morning After," and "Philly Dog," although none repeated the commercial success of "Last Night." In 1962 Cropper and Dunn left the lineup to co-found the famed Booker T. and the MG's. Other personnel changes followed, although the Mar-Keys continued on for several more years before the name was eventually dropped. Jackson then formed another top-notch session group, the Memphis Horns, while Axton led the Packers, scoring a 1965 hit with "Hole in the Wall." Nix, meanwhile, mounted a solo career, also producing records for artists including Freddie King, Jeff Beck, and Furry Lewis.

Solomon Burke

Born 1936 in Philadelphia, PA

 While Solomon Burke never made a major impact upon the pop audience—he never, in fact, had a Top 20 hit—he was an important early soul pioneer. On his '60s singles for Atlantic, he brought a country influence into R&B with emotional phrasing and intricately constructed, melodic ballads and mid-tempo songs. At the same time, he was surrounded with sophisticated "uptown" arrangements and provided with much of his material by his producers, particularly Bert Berns. The combination of gospel, pop, country, and production polish was basic to the recipe of early soul. While Burke wasn't the only one pursuing this path, not many others did so as successfully. And he, like Otis Redding and Wilson Pickett, was an important influence upon the Rolling Stones, who covered Burke's "Cry to Me" and "Everybody Needs Somebody to Love" on their early albums.

Burke came by his gospel roots even more deeply than most soul stars. He was preaching at his family's Philadelphia church, and hosting his own gospel radio show, even before he'd reached his teens. He began recording gospel and R&B sides for Apollo in the mid- to late '50s. Like several former gospel singers (Aretha Franklin, Wilson Pickett), he was molded into a more secular direction when he signed with Atlantic in the 1960s.

Burke had a wealth of high-charting R&B hits in the early half of the '60s, which crossed over to the pop listings in a mild fashion as well. "Just Out of Reach," "Cry to Me," "If You Need Me," "Got to Get You Off My Mind," "Tonight's the Night," and "Goodbye Baby (Baby Goodbye)" were the most successful of these, although unlike Franklin or Pickett, he wasn't able to expand his R&B base into a huge pop following as well. He left Atlantic in the late '60s, and spent the next decade hopping between various labels, getting his biggest hit with a cover of Creedence Clearwater Revival's "Proud Mary" in 1969, and recording an album in the late '70s with cult soulster Swamp Dogg as producer.

In the 1980s and 1990s, Burke became one of the most visible living exponents of classic soul music, continuing to tour and record albums in a rootsy, at times gospelish style. Although these were critically well received, their stylistic purity also ensured that their market was primarily confined to roots music enthusiasts, rather than a pop audience. His live and later recorded work, however, is a favorite of those who want to experience a soul legend with his talents and stylistic purity relatively intact. Burke's 2002 release *Don't Give Up on Me* was hailed as a major comeback for the legendary soul man. Great songwriters like Elvis Costello, Dan Penn, Nick Lowe, and Tom Waits contributed songs and Joe Henry produced the album, which has been compared to Johnny Cash's landmark album *American Recordings*. After the critical success of *Don't Give Up On Me* reaffirmed Burke's status as one of the greatest living exponents of classic soul, the singer teamed up with producer Don Was for *Make Do With What You Got*, a updated variation on his classic style which was released in the spring of 2005.

Gene Chandler

Born: Jul 6, 1937 in Chicago, IL

 Gene Chandler is remembered by the rock & roll audience almost solely for the classic novelty and doo wop-tinged soul ballad "Duke of Earl"; the unforgettable opening chant of the title leading the way, the song was a number one hit in 1962. He's esteemed by soul fans as one of the leading exponents of the '60s Chicago soul scene, along with Curtis Mayfield and Jerry Butler. Born Eugene Dixon, he was a member of the doo wop group the Dukays and "Duke of Earl" was actually a Dukays recording; Dixon was renamed Gene Chandler and the single bore his credit as a solo singer. Chandler never approached the massive pop success of that chart-topper (although he occasionally entered the Top 20), but he was a big star with the R&B audience with straightforward mid-tempo and ballad soul numbers in the mid-'60s, many of which were written by Curtis Mayfield and produced by Carl Davis. Chandler's success became more fitful after Mayfield stopped penning material for him, although he enjoyed some late-'60s hits and had a monster pop and soul smash in 1970 with "Groovy Situation." His last successes were the far less distinguished disco- and dance-influenced R&B hits "Get Down" (1978) and "Does She Have a Friend?" (1980).

Eddie Holland

Born: Oct 30, 1939 in Detroit, MI

 One-third of an amazing songwriting and production trio, Eddie Holland hasn't been as successful on his own as when teamed with brother Brian Holland and Lamont Dozier. The trio wrote numerous hits for Motown acts through the '60s before departing in 1968. They formed their own label in 1970, Hot Wax/Invictus, and had success for a while with such acts as The Chairmen Of The Board, Laura Lee, and the Honey Cone. Eddie Holland scored his biggest hit as a solo artist back in 1962, with "Jamie" reaching number six on the R&B charts and peaking at #30 pop. He recorded three more songs for Motown in the mid-'60s, but none of them were hits, and he then concentrated on songwriting and production.

Mary Wells

Born: May 13, 1943 in Detroit, MI
Died: Jul 26, 1992 in Los Angeles, CA

 Time and legions of other soul superstars have obscured the fact that for a brief moment, Mary Wells was Motown's biggest star. She came to the attention of Berry Gordy as a 17-year-old, hawking a song she'd written for Jackie Wilson; that song, "Bye Bye Baby," became her first Motown hit in 1961. The full-throated approach of that single was quickly toned down in favor of a pop-soul sound. Few other soul singers managed to be as shy and sexy at the same time as Wells (Bar-

bara Lewis is the only other that springs to mind), and the soft-voiced singer found a perfect match with the emerging Motown production team, especially Smokey Robinson. Robinson wrote and produced her biggest Motown hits; "Two Lovers," "You Beat Me to the Punch," and "The One Who Really Loves You" all made the Top Ten in the early '60s, and "My Guy" hit the number one spot in mid-1964, at the very height of Beatlemania.

Mary turned 21 years old as "My Guy" was rising to the top of the charts, and left Motown almost immediately afterward for a reported advance of several hundred thousand dollars from 20th Century Fox. The circumstances remain cloudy years later, but Wells and her husband-manager felt Motown wasn't coming through with enough money for their new superstar; she was also lured by the prospect of movie roles through 20th Century Fox (which never materialized). It's been rumored that Wells was being groomed for the sort of plans that were subsequently lavished upon Diana Ross; more nefariously, it's also been rumored that Motown quietly discouraged radio stations from playing Wells' subsequent releases. What is certain is that Wells never remotely approached the success of her Motown years, entering the pop Top 40 only once (although she had some R&B hits). Motown, for their part, took care throughout the rest of the '60s not to lose their big stars to larger labels.

Wells' departure from Motown was so dramatic and unsuccessful that it has tended to overshadow the quality of her later work, which has almost always been dismissed as trivial by critics. True, it didn't match the quality of her Motown recordings—Smokey Robinson could not be replaced. But her '60s singles for 20th Century Fox (whom she ended up leaving after only a year), Atco, and Jubilee were solid pop-soul on which her vocal talents remained undiminished. She wrote and produced a lot of her late-'60s and early-'70s sessions with her second husband, guitarist Cecil Womack (brother of Bobby), and these found her exploring a somewhat earthier groove than her more widely known pop efforts. She had trouble landing recording deals in the '70s and '80s, and succumbed to throat cancer in 1992.

Marvin Gaye

Born: Apr 2, 1939 in Washington, D.C.
Died: Apr 1, 1984 in Los Angeles, CA

 One of the most gifted, visionary, and enduring talents ever launched into orbit by the Motown hit machine, Marvin Gaye blazed the trail for the continued evolution of popular black music. Moving from lean, powerful R&B to stylish, sophisticated soul to finally arrive at an intensely political and personal form of artistic self-expression, his work not only redefined soul music as a creative force but also expanded its impact as an agent for social change.

Marvin Pentz Gay, Jr. (in the style of his hero Sam Cooke, he added the "e" to his surname as an adult) was born April 2, 1939, in Washington, D.C. The second of three children born to the Reverend Marvin Gay, Sr., an ordained minister in the House of God—a conservative Christian sect that fuses elements of orthodox Judaism and Pentecostalism, imposes strict codes of conduct, and observes no holidays—he began singing in church at the age of three, quickly becoming a soloist in the choir. Gaye later took up piano and drums, and music became his escape from the nightmarish realities of his home life—throughout his childhood, his father beat him on an almost daily basis.

After graduating from high school, Gaye enlisted in the U.S. Air Force; upon his discharge, he returned to Washington and began singing in a number of street-corner doo wop groups, eventually joining the Rainbows, a top local attraction. With the help of mentor Bo Diddley, the Rainbows cut "Wyatt Earp," a single for the OKeh label that brought them to the attention of singer Harvey Fuqua, who in 1958 recruited the group to become the latest edition of his backing ensemble, the Moonglows. After relocating to Chicago, the Moonglows recorded a series of singles for Chess, including 1959's "Mama Loocie." While touring the Midwest, the group performed in Detroit, where Gaye's graceful tenor and three-octave vocal range won the interest of fledgling impresario Berry Gordy, Jr., who signed him to the Motown label in 1961.

While first working at Motown as a session drummer and playing on early hits by Smokey Robinson & the Miracles, he met Gordy's sister Anna, and married her in late 1961. Upon mounting a solo career, Gaye struggled to find his voice, and early singles failed. Finally, his fourth effort, "Stubborn Kind of Fellow," became a minor hit in 1962, and his next two singles—the 1963 dance efforts "Hitch Hike" and "Can I Get a Witness"—both reached the Top 30. With 1963's "Pride and Joy," Gaye scored his first Top Ten smash, but often found his role as a hitmaker stifling—his desire to become a crooner of lush romantic ballads ran in direct opposition to Motown's all-important emphasis on chart success, and the ongoing battle between his artistic ambitions and the label's demands for commercial product continued throughout Gaye's long tenure with the company.

With 1964's *Together*, a collection of duets with Mary Wells, Gaye scored his first charting album; the duo also notched a number of hit singles together, including "Once Upon a Time" and "What's the Matter With You, Baby?" As a solo performer, Gaye continued to enjoy great success, scoring three superb Top Ten hits—"Ain't That Peculiar," "I'll Be Doggone," and "How Sweet It Is (To Be Loved by You)"—in 1965. In total, he scored some 39 Top 40 singles for Motown, many of which he also wrote and arranged. With Kim Weston, the second of his crucial vocal partners, he also established himself as one of the era's dominant duet singers with the stunning "It Takes Two."

However, Gaye's greatest duets were with Tammi Terrell, with whom he scored a series of massive hits penned by the team of Nickolas Ashford and Valerie Simpson, including 1967's "Ain't No Mountain High Enough" and "Your Precious Love," followed by 1968's "Ain't Nothing Like the Real Thing" and "You're All I Need to Get By." The team's success was tragically cut short in 1967 when, during a concert appearance in Virginia, Terrell collapsed into Gaye's arms on-stage, the first evidence of a brain tumor that abruptly ended her performing career and finally killed her on March 16, 1970. Her illness and eventual loss left Gaye deeply shaken, marring the chart-topping 1968 success of "I Heard It Through the Grapevine," his biggest hit and arguably the pinnacle of the Motown sound.

At the same time, Gaye was forced to cope with a number of other personal problems, not the least of which was his crumbling marriage. He also found the material he recorded for Motown to be increasingly irrelevant in the face of the tremendous social changes sweeping the nation, and after scoring a pair of 1969 Top Ten hits with "Too Busy Thinking About My Baby" and "That's the Way Love Is," he spent the majority of 1970 in seclusion, resurfacing early the next year with the self-produced *What's Going On*, a landmark effort heralding a dramatic shift in both content and style that forever altered the face of black music. A highly percussive album that incorporated jazz and classical elements to forge a remarkably sophisticated and fluid soul sound, *What's Going On* was a conceptual masterpiece that brought Gaye's deeply held spiritual beliefs to the fore to explore issues ranging from poverty and discrimination to the environment, drug abuse, and political corruption; chief among the record's concerns was the conflict in Vietnam, as Gaye structured the songs around the point of view of his brother Frankie, himself a soldier recently returned from combat.

The ambitions and complexity of *What's Going On* baffled Berry Gordy, who initially refused to release the LP; he finally relented, although he maintained that he never understood the record's full scope. Gaye was vindicated when the majestic title track reached the number two spot in 1971, and both of the follow-ups, "Mercy Mercy Me (The Ecology)" and "Inner City Blues (Make Me Wanna Holler)," also reached the Top Ten. The album's success guaranteed Gaye continued artistic control over his work and helped loosen the reins for other Motown artists, most notably Stevie Wonder, to also take command of their own destinies. Consequently, in 1972, Gaye changed directions again, agreeing to score the blaxploitation thriller *Trouble Man*; the resulting soundtrack was a primarily instrumental effort showcasing his increasing interest in jazz, although a vocal turn on the moody, minimalist title track scored another Top Ten smash.

The long-simmering eroticism implicit in much of Gaye's work reached its boiling point with 1973's *Let's Get It On*, one of the most sexually charged albums ever recorded; a work of intense lust and longing, it became the most commercially successful effort of his career, and the title cut became his second number one hit. *Let's Get It On* also marked another significant shift in Gaye's lyrical outlook, moving him from the political arena to a deeply personal, even insular stance that continued to define his subsequent work. After teaming with Diana Ross for the 1973 duet collection *Marvin and Diana*, he returned to work on his next solo effort, *I Want You*; however, the record's completion was delayed by his 1975 divorce from Anna Gordy. The dissolution of his marriage threw Gaye into a tailspin, and he spent much of the mid-'70s in divorce court. To combat Gaye's absence from the studio, Motown released the 1977 stopgap *Live at the London Palladium*, which spawned the single "Got to Give It Up, Pt. 1," his final number one hit.

As a result of a 1976 court settlement, Gaye was ordered to make good on missed alimony payments by recording a new album, with the intention that all royalties earned from its sales would then be awarded to his ex-wife. The 1978 record, a two-LP set sardonically titled *Here, My Dear*, bitterly explored the couple's relationship in such intimate detail that Anna Gordy briefly considered suing Gaye for invasion of privacy. In the interim, he had remarried and begun work on another album, *Lover Man*, but scrapped the project when the "Ego Tripping Out" lead single—a telling personal commentary presented as a duet between the spiritual and sexual halves of his identity, which biographer David Ritz later dubbed the singer's "divided soul"—failed to chart. As his drug problems increased and his marriage to new wife Janis also began to fail, he relocated to Hawaii in an attempt to sort out his personal affairs.

In 1981, longstanding tax difficulties and renewed pressures from the IRS forced Gaye to flee to Europe, where he began work on the ambitious *In Our Lifetime*, a deeply philosophical record that ultimately severed his longstanding relationship with Motown after he claimed the label had remixed and edited the album without his consent. Additionally, Gaye stated that the finished artwork parodied his original intent, and that even the title had been changed to drop an all-important question mark. Upon signing with Columbia in 1982, he battled stories of erratic behavior and a consuming addiction to cocaine to emerge triumphant with *Midnight Love*, an assured comeback highlighted by the luminous Top Three hit "Sexual Healing." The record made Gaye a star yet again, and in 1983 he made peace with Berry Gordy by appearing on a television special celebrating Motown's silver anniversary. That same year, he also sang a soulful and idiosyncratic rendition of "The Star-Spangled Banner" at the NBA All-Star Game; it instantly became one of the most controversial and legendary interpretations of the anthem ever performed. And it was to be his final public appearance.

Gaye's career resurgence brought with it an increased reliance on cocaine; finally, his personal demons forced him back to the U.S., where he moved in with his parents in an attempt to regain control of his life. Tragically, the return home only exacerbated his spiral into depression; he and his father quarrelled bitterly, and Gaye threatened suicide on a number of occasions. Finally, on the afternoon of April 1, 1984—one day before his 45th birthday—Gaye was shot and killed by Marvin Sr. in the aftermath of a heated argument. In the wake of his death, Motown and Columbia teamed up to issue two 1985 collections of outtakes, *Dream of a Lifetime*—a compilation of erotic funk workouts teamed with spiritual ballads—and the big band-inspired *Romantically Yours*. (*Vulnerable*, a collection of ballads that took over 12 years to complete, finally saw release in 1996.) With Gaye's death also came a critical reevaluation of his work, which deemed *What's Going On* to be one of the landmark albums in pop history, and his 1987 induction into the Rock & Roll Hall of Fame permanently enshrined him among the pantheon of musical greats.

The Contours

Formed 1958 in Detroit, MI

 The Contours are widely remembered for their 1962 smash "Do You Love Me?," one of the early hits that helped put Motown on the map. Yet they aren't always associated with their contribution to the label; they were one of the roughest, hardest R&B groups Berry Gordy ever signed, and their sound simply didn't resemble the smooth, sophisticated blueprint that later became Motown's trademark. Nor did their stage presence; in contrast to the slick choreography and wardrobe of Motown's signature artists, the Contours were all wild, irrepressible energy, leaping and sliding all over the stage and even doing the splits. As a result, they fell out of favor once Motown got its crossover-friendly hit factory up and running, and never duplicated the success of their first hit.

Formed in Detroit in 1958, the Contours originally began life as a quartet called the Blenders. Lead singer Billy Gordon, Billy Hogg, Sylvester Potts, and Joe Billinglea were soon joined by Hubert Johnson, a cousin of the legendary Jackie Wilson, as well as guitarist Huey Davis. Changing their name to the Contours, the group landed an audition with Berry Gordy's fledgling Motown label. Gordy was not impressed and told them to try again in a year, and they enlisted Jackie Wilson's aid in honing their act. Wilson personally recommended the group to Gordy, who finally relented and signed them up in 1961. The Contours' first single "Whole Lotta Woman" sank without a trace, and Gordy nearly dropped them until Wilson once again interceded on their behalf. The move paid off handsomely when Gordy offered them a chance to cut "Do You Love Me?," a song originally intended for the Temptations, who couldn't quite nail down the rough and rowdy feel Gordy wanted. Released in 1962, "Do You Love Me?" zoomed straight to the top of the R&B charts in just a few short weeks, peaking at number three on the pop side.

Although the Contours were riding high thanks to their hit and their exciting live act, they found the momentum difficult to maintain. They were able to score a follow-up hit, "Shake Sherrie," in 1963, and ran off a string of R&B Top 40 singles over 1965–1966: "Can You Jerk Like Me?," the Top Ten "The Day When She Needed Me," the Smokey Robinson-penned "First I Look at the Purse," and "Just a Little Misunderstanding." Despite the often high quality of those singles, the Contours simply weren't getting the attention—either from the label or the public—that Motown's top stars were, and their sound was more of an anomaly at Hitsville than ever. By this time, the original quintet was no longer intact; new members included Joe Stubbs, brother of the Four Tops' Levi Stubbs, and Dennis Edwards, who went on to replace David Ruffin in the Temptations.

The Contours had their last charting single in 1967 with "It's So Hard Being a Loser"; Billinglea and Potts subsequently led versions of the group on the oldies circuit during the '70s and '80s. Sadly, Johnson committed suicide in 1981, and wasn't around to witness the 1988 revival of "Do You Love Me?" thanks to the wildly popular film *Dirty Dancing*. Billingslea, Potts, and their new cohorts hit the oldies circuit with renewed vigor, and also cut the album *Running in Circles* for U.K. Motown revivalist Ian Levine's Motorcity label in 1990. Stubbs passed away in 1998, and guitarist Davis did likewise in 2002.

Booker T. & the MG's

Formed 1962 in Memphis, TN
Disbanded in 1968

As the house band at Stax Records in Memphis, Booker T. & the MG's may have been the single greatest factor in the lasting value of that label's soul music—not to mention Southern soul as a whole. Their tight, impeccable grooves can be heard on classic hits by Otis Redding, Wilson Pickett, Carla Thomas, Albert King, and Sam & Dave, just to name the very most prominent examples. For that reason alone, they would deserve their spot in rock & roll's hall of fame. But in addition to their formidable skills as a house band, on their own they were one of the top instrumental outfits of the rock era, cutting classics like "Green Onions," "Time Is Tight," and "Hang 'em High."

The anchors of the Booker T. sound were Steve Cropper, whose slicing, economic riffs influenced tons of other guitar players, and Booker T. Jones himself, who provided much of the groove with his floating organ lines. In 1960, Jones started working as a session man for Stax, where he met Cropper. Cropper had been in the Mar-Keys, famous for the 1961 instrumental hit "Last Night," which laid out the prototype for much of the MG's (and indeed Memphis soul's) sound with its organ-sax-guitar combo. With the addition of drummer Al Jackson and bassist Lewis Steinberg, they became Booker T. & the MG's. In a couple years or so, Steinberg would be replaced permanently by Donald "Duck" Dunn, who, like Cropper, had also played with the Mar-Keys.

The band's first and biggest hit, "Green Onions" (number three, 1962), came about by accident. Jamming in the studio while fruitlessly waiting for Billy Lee Riley to show up for a session, they came up with a classic minor-key, bluesy soul instrumental, distinguished by its nervous organ bounce and ferocious bursts of guitar. For the next five years, they'd have trouble recapturing its commercial success, though the standard of their records remained fairly high, and Stax's dependence upon them as the house band ensured a decent living.

In the late '60s, the MG's really hit their stride with "Hip Hug-Her," "Groovin'," "Soul-Limbo," "Hang 'em High," and "Time Is Tight," all of which were Top 40 charters between 1967 and 1969. As a band that featured two blacks and two whites playing as tightly together as possible, they also set a somewhat under-appreciated example of both how integrated, self-contained bands could succeed, and how both black and white musicians could play funky soul music. As is the case with most instrumental rock bands, their singles contained their best material, and they're best appreciated via anthologies. But their albums were not inconsequential, and occasionally ambitious (they did an entire instrumental version of the Beatles' *Abbey Road*, which they titled *McLemore Avenue* in honor of the location of Stax's studios).

Though they'd become established stars by the end of the decade, the group began finding it difficult to work together, not so much because of personnel problems, but because of logistical difficulties. Cropper was often playing sessions in Los Angeles, and Jones was often absent from Memphis while he finished his music studies at Indiana University. The band decided to break up in 1971, but were working on a reunion album in 1975 when Al Jackson was tragically shot and killed in his Memphis home by a burglar. The remaining members have been active as recording artists and session musicians since, Cropper and Dunn joining the Blues Brothers for a while in the late '70s.

The MG's got back into the spotlight in early 1992 when they were the house band for an extravagant Bob Dylan tribute at Madison Square Garden. More significantly, in 1993 they served as the backup band for a Neil Young tour, one which brought both them and Young high critical marks. The following year, they released a comeback album, arranged in much the style of their vintage '60s sides, which proved that their instrumental skills were still intact. Like most such efforts, though, it ultimately failed to recreate the spark and spontaneity it so obviously wanted to achieve.

Martha & the Vandellas

Formed 1963 in Detroit, MI
Disbanded in 1972

Along with the Supremes, Martha & the Vandellas defined the distaff side of the Motown sound in the 1960s; their biggest hits, including "Heat Wave," "Dancing in the Street," and "Nowhere to Run," remain among the most potent and enduring dance records of the era. The vocal group was led by Martha Reeves who, along with fellow Detroit natives Annette Sterling Beard, Gloria Williams, and Rosalind Ashford, founded the Del-Phis in 1960. After Reeves landed a secretarial position at the offices of Motown Records, the Del-Phis were tapped to record a one-off single for the label's Melody imprint, which they cut under the name the Vels.

The single fizzled, and Williams exited, reducing the group to a trio. After backing Marvin Gaye on the superb 1962 record "Stubborn Kind of Fellow," they were renamed Martha & the Vandellas, taking inspiration from Detroit's Van Dyke Street and Reeves' heroine Della Reese. When singer Mary Wells failed to show up for a recording date, musicians' union rules demanded that a vocalist be found to fulfill contractual obligations; as a result, Reeves was yanked from the secretarial pool and laid down what would become Martha & the Vandellas' first record, 1963's "I'll Have to Let Him Go."

The Top 30 success of the ballad "Come and Get These Memories" brought the group the attention of Motown's hit-making production team Holland-Dozier-

Holland, who crafted their next smash, the galvanizing Top Five classic "Heat Wave," which perfected the mix of impassioned call-and-response vocals, pulsing rhythms, and full-bodied horns that became the trio's trademark. Following another Top Ten hit, "Quicksand," Beard retired, and was replaced by former Velvelette Betty Kelly. After singer Kim Weston turned down the Marvin Gaye/Ivy Jo Hunter/Mickey Stevenson composition "Dancing in the Street," the song was shuttled to Martha & the Vandellas; refashioned by Holland-Dozier-Holland to fit the group's formula, the anthem became their biggest hit and definitive statement, reaching number two in the summer of 1964. A year later, they returned with another smash, the savage "Nowhere to Run," followed by "I'm Ready for Love."

In 1967, Kelly exited, and was replaced by Reeves' younger sister Lois; on subsequent releases, the group was billed as Martha Reeves & the Vandellas. 1967's "Jimmy Mack" and "Honey Chile" were the last records overseen by the Holland-Dozier-Holland team before their defection from Motown, and were also the final significant Vandellas hits; in 1968, Martha Reeves fell seriously ill, and in 1969 Ashford departed, with another former Velvelette, Sandra Tilley, assuming her position. The trio continued unsuccessfully for a few more years before breaking up in the wake of a December, 1972, farewell performance at Detroit's Cobo Hall. After Motown relocated its corporate offices to Los Angeles (a move Reeves denied she was privy to), the singer, who had begun a solo career, sued to have her contract with the label annulled; in her 1994 autobiography, *Dancing in the Street*, she charged that the Vandellas' career, though highly successful in its own right, could have been even greater had Motown founder Berry Gordy, Jr. given their music the same obsessive attention he afforded to Diana Ross & the Supremes.

Reeves recorded her debut solo effort, *Martha Reeves: Produced by Richard Perry*, for MCA in 1974; though a few more LPs followed, including 1976's *The Rest of My Life* and 1978's *We Meet Again*, she received little notice on her own, and eventually suffered a pair of nervous breakdowns that led to a brief period of institutionalization. Lois Reeves, meanwhile, went on to work with Al Green, while Sandra Tilley retired from music; she died in 1982 following surgery on a brain tumor. In 1989, Martha Reeves, Annette Beard, and Rosalind Ashford successfully sued Motown for back royalties, and occasionally reunited for performances in the 1990s. Reeves also continued as a solo artist, and in addition performed with a Vandellas unit consisting of Lois and a third sister, Delphine.

Stevie Wonder
AKA Steveland Morris

Born May 13, 1950 in Saginaw, MI

Stevie Wonder is a much-beloved American icon and an indisputable genius not only of R&B but popular music in general. Blind virtually since birth, Wonder's heightened awareness of sound helped him create vibrant, colorful music teeming with life and ambition. Nearly everything he recorded bore the stamp of his

sunny, joyous positivity; even when he addressed serious racial, social, and spiritual issues (which he did quite often in his prime), or sang about heartbreak and romantic uncertainty, an underlying sense of optimism and hope always seemed to emerge. Much like his inspiration, Ray Charles, Wonder had a voracious appetite for many different kinds of music, and refused to confine himself to any one sound or style. His best records were a richly eclectic brew of soul, funk, rock & roll, sophisticated Broadway/Tin Pan Alley-style pop, jazz, reggae, and African elements—and they weren't just stylistic exercises; Wonder took it all and forged it into his own personal form of expression. His range helped account for his broad-based appeal, but so did his unique, elastic voice, his peerless melodic facility, his gift for complex arrangements, and his taste for lovely, often sentimental ballads. Additionally, Wonder's pioneering use of synthesizers during the '70s changed the face of R&B; he employed a kaleidoscope of contrasting textures and voices that made him a virtual one-man band, all the while evoking a surprisingly organic warmth. Along with Marvin Gaye and Isaac Hayes, Wonder brought R&B into the album age, crafting his LPs as cohesive, consistent statements with compositions that often took time to make their point. All of this made Wonder perhaps R&B's greatest individual auteur, rivaled only by Gaye or, in later days, Prince. Originally, Wonder was a child prodigy who started out in the general Motown mold, but he took control of his vision in the '70s, spinning off a series of incredible albums that were as popular as they were acclaimed; most of his reputation rests on these works, which most prominently include *Talking Book*, *Innervisions*, and *Songs in the Key of Life*. His output since then has been inconsistent, marred by excesses of sentimentality and less of the progressive imagination of his best work, but it's hardly lessened the reverence in which he's long been held.

Wonder was born Steveland Hardaway Judkins in Saginaw, MI, on May 13, 1950 (he later altered his name to Steveland Morris when his mother married). A premature infant, he was put on oxygen treatment in an incubator; likely it was an excess of oxygen that exacerbated a visual condition known as retinopathy of prematurity, causing his blindness. In 1954, his family moved to Detroit, where the already musically inclined Stevie began singing in his church's choir; from there he blossomed into a genuine prodigy, learning piano, drums, and harmonica all by the age of nine. While performing for some of his friends in 1961, Stevie was discovered by Ronnie White of the Miracles, who helped arrange an audition with Berry Gordy at Motown. Gordy signed the youngster immediately and teamed him with producer/songwriter Clarence Paul, under the new name Little Stevie Wonder. Stevie released his first two albums in 1962: *A Tribute to Uncle Ray*, which featured covers of Stevie's hero Ray Charles, and *The Jazz Soul of Little Stevie*, an orchestral jazz album spotlighting his instrumental skills on piano, harmonica, and assorted percussion. Neither sold very well, but that all changed in 1963 with the live album *The 12 Year Old Genius*, which featured a new extended version of the harmonica instrumental "Fingertips." Edited for release as a single, "Fingertips, Pt.

2" rocketed to the top of both the pop and R&B charts, thanks to Wonder's irresistible, youthful exuberance; meanwhile, *The 12 Year Old Genius* became Motown's first chart-topping LP.

Wonder charted a few more singles over the next year, but none on the level of "Fingertips, Pt. 2." As his voice changed, his recording career was temporarily put on hold, and he studied classical piano at the Michigan School for the Blind in the meantime. He dropped the "Little" portion of his stage name in 1964, and re-emerged the following year with the infectious, typically Motown-sounding dance tune "Uptight (Everything's Alright)," a number one R&B/Top Five pop smash. Not only did he co-write the song for his first original hit, but it also reinvented him as a more mature vocalist in the public's mind, making the similar follow-up "Nothing's Too Good for My Baby" another success. The first signs of Wonder's social activism appeared in 1966 via his hit cover of Bob Dylan's "Blowin' in the Wind" and its follow-up, "A Place in the Sun," but as Motown still had the final say on Wonder's choice of material, this new direction would not yet become a major facet of his work.

By this time, Wonder was, however, beginning to take more of a hand in his own career. He co-wrote his next several hits, all of which made the R&B Top Ten—"Hey Love," "I Was Made to Love Her" (an R&B number one that went to number two pop in 1967), and "For Once in My Life" (another smash that reached number two pop and R&B). Wonder's 1968 album *For Once in My Life* signaled his budding ambition; he co-wrote about half of the material and, for the first time, co-produced several tracks. The record also contained three more singles in the R&B chart-topper "Shoo-Be-Doo-Be-Doo-Da-Day," "You Met Your Match," and "I Don't Know Why." Wonder scored again in 1969 with the pop and R&B Top Five hit "My Cherie Amour" (which he'd actually recorded three years prior) and the Top Ten "Yester-Me, Yester-You, Yesterday." In 1970, Wonder received his first-ever co-production credit for the album *Signed, Sealed & Delivered*; he co-wrote the R&B chart-topper "Signed, Sealed, Delivered I'm Yours" with singer Syreeta Wright, whom he married later that year, and also scored hits with "Heaven Help Us All" and a rearrangement of the Beatles' "We Can Work It Out." In addition, two other Motown artists had major success with Wonder co-writes: the Spinners' "It's a Shame" and the Miracles' only pop number one, "Tears of a Clown."

1971 brought a turning point in Wonder's career. On his 21st birthday, his contract with Motown expired, and the royalties set aside in his trust fund became available to him. A month before his birthday, Wonder released *Where I'm Coming From*, his first entirely self-produced album, which also marked the first time he wrote or co-wrote every song on an LP (usually in tandem with Wright) and the first time his keyboard and synthesizer work dominated his arrangements. Gordy was reportedly not fond of the work, and it wasn't a major commercial success, producing only the Top Ten hit "If You Really Love Me" (plus a classic B-side in "Never Dreamed You'd Leave in Summer"). Nonetheless, it was clearly an ambitious attempt at making a unified album-length artistic statement, and served notice that Wonder was no longer content to release albums composed of hit singles and assorted filler. Accordingly, Wonder did not immediately renew his contract with Motown, as the label had expected; instead, he used proceeds from his trust fund to build his own recording studio and to enroll in music theory classes at USC. He negotiated a new deal with Motown that dramatically increased his royalty rate and established his own publishing company, Black Bull Music, which allowed him to retain the rights to his music; most importantly, he wrested full artistic control over his recordings, as Gaye had just done with the landmark *What's Going On*.

Freed from the dictates of Motown's hit-factory mindset, Wonder had already begun following a more personal and idiosyncratic muse. One of his negotiating chips had been a full album completed at his new studio; Wonder had produced, played nearly all the instruments, and written all the material (with Wright contributing to several tracks). Released under Wonder's new deal in early 1972, *Music of My Mind* heralded his arrival as a major, self-contained talent with an original vision that pushed the boundaries of R&B. The album produced a hit single in the spacy, synth-driven ballad "Superwoman (Where Were You When I Needed You)," but like contemporary work by Hayes and Gaye, *Music of My Mind* worked as a smoothly flowing song suite unto itself. Around the same time it was released, Wonder's marriage to Wright broke up; the two remained friends, however, and Wonder produced and wrote several songs for her debut album. The same year, Wonder toured with the Rolling Stones, bringing his music to a large white audience as well.

For the follow-up to *Music of My Mind*, Wonder refined his approach, tightening up his songcraft while addressing his romance with Wright. The result, *Talking Book*, was released in late 1972 and made him a superstar. Song for song one of the strongest R&B albums ever released, *Talking Book* also perfected Wonder's spacy, futuristic experiments with electronics, and was hailed as a magnificently realized masterpiece. Wonder topped the charts with the gutsy, driving funk classic "Superstition" and the mellow, jazzy ballad "You Are the Sunshine of My Life," which went on to become a pop standard; those two songs went on to win three Grammys between them. Amazingly, Wonder only upped the ante with his next album, 1973's *Innervisions*, a concept album about the state of contemporary society that ranks with Gaye's *What's Going On* as a pinnacle of socially conscious R&B. The ghetto chronicle "Living for the City" and the intense spiritual self-examination "Higher Ground" both went to number one on the R&B charts and the pop Top Ten, and *Innervisions* took home a Grammy for Album of the Year. Wonder was lucky to be alive to enjoy the success; while being driven to a concert in North Carolina, a large timber fell on Wonder's car. He sustained serious head injuries and lapsed into a coma, but fortunately made a full recovery.

Wonder's next record, 1974's *Fulfillingness' First Finale*, was slightly more insular and less accessible than its immediate predecessors, and unsurprisingly imbued with a sense of mortality. The hits, however, were the upbeat "Boogie On, Reggae Woman" (a number one R&B and Top Five pop hit) and the venomous Richard Nixon critique "You Haven't Done Nothin'" (number one on both sides). It won him a second straight Album of the Year Grammy, by which time he'd been heavily involved as a producer and writer on Syreeta's second album, *Stevie Wonder Presents Syreeta*. Wonder subsequently retired to his studio and spent two years crafting a large-scale project that would stand as his magnum opus. Finally released in 1976, *Songs in the Key of Life* was a sprawling two-LP-plus-one-EP set that found Wonder at his most ambitious and expansive. Some critics called it brilliant but prone to excess and indulgence, while others hailed it as his greatest masterpiece and the culmination of his career; in the end, they were probably both right. "Sir Duke," an ebullient tribute to music in general and Duke Ellington in particular, and the funky "I Wish" both went to number one pop and R&B; the hit "Isn't She Lovely," a paean to Wonder's daughter, became something of a standard, and "Pastime Paradise" was later sampled for the backbone of Coolio's rap smash "Gangsta's Paradise." Not surprisingly, *Songs in the Key of Life* won a Grammy for Album of the Year; in hindsight, though, it marked the end of a remarkable explosion of creativity and of Wonder's artistic prime.

Having poured a tremendous amount of energy into *Songs in the Key of Life*, Wonder released nothing for the next three years. When he finally returned in 1979, it was with the mostly instrumental *Journey Through the Secret Life of Plants*, ostensibly the soundtrack to a never-released documentary. Although it contained a few pop songs, including the hit "Send One Your Love," its symphonic flirtations befuddled most listeners and critics. It still made the Top Ten on the LP chart on Wonder's momentum alone—one of the stranger releases to do so. To counteract possible speculation that he'd gone off the deep end, Wonder rushed out the straightforward pop album *Hotter Than July* in 1980. The reggae-flavored "Master Blaster (Jammin')" returned him to the top of the R&B charts and the pop Top Five, and "Happy Birthday" was part of the ultimately successful campaign to make Martin Luther King's birthday a national holiday (Wonder being one of the cause's most active champions). Artistically speaking, *Hotter Than July* was a cut below his classic '70s output, but it was still a solid outing; fans were so grateful to have the old Wonder back that they made it his first platinum-selling LP.

In 1981, Wonder began work on a follow-up album that was plagued by delays, suggesting that he might not be able to return to the visionary heights of old. He kept busy in the meantime, though; in 1982, his racial-harmony duet with Paul McCartney, "Ebony and Ivory," hit number one, and he released a greatest-hits set covering 1972–1982 called *Original Musiquarium I*. It featured four new songs, of which "That Girl" (number one R&B, Top Five pop) and the lengthy, jazzy "Do I Do" (featuring Dizzy Gillespie; number two R&B) were significant hits. In 1984, still not having completed the official follow-up to *Hotter Than July*, he recorded the soundtrack to the Gene Wilder comedy *The Woman in Red*, which wasn't quite a full-fledged Stevie Wonder album but did feature a number of new songs, including "I Just Called to Say I Love You." Adored by the public (it was his biggest-selling single ever) and loathed by critics (who derided it as sappy and simple-minded), "I Just Called to Say I Love You" was an across-the-board number one smash, and won an Oscar for Best Song.

Wonder finally completed the official album he'd been working on for nearly five years, and released *In Square Circle* in 1985. Paced by the number one hit "Part Time Lover"—his last solo pop chart-topper—and several other strong songs, *In Square Circle* went platinum, even if Wonder's synthesizer arrangements now sounded standard rather than groundbreaking. He performed on the number one charity singles "We Are the World" by USA for Africa and "That's What Friends Are For" by Dionne Warwick & Friends, and returned quickly with a new album, *Characters*, in 1987. While *Characters* found Wonder's commercial clout on the pop charts slipping away, it was a hit on the R&B side, topping the album charts and producing a number one hit in "Skeletons." It would be his final release of the '80s; he didn't return until 1991, with the soundtrack to the Spike Lee film *Jungle Fever*. His next full album of new material, 1995's *Conversation Peace*, was a commercial disappointment, despite winning two Grammys for the single "For Your Love." That same year, Coolio revived "Pastime Paradise" in his own brooding rap smash "Gangsta's Paradise," which became the year's biggest hit. Wonder capitalized on the renewed notoriety by cutting a hit duet with Babyface, "How Come, How Long," in 1996. Since then, Motown has released a number of remasters and compilations attempting to define and repackage Wonder's vast legacy. His far-reaching influence was felt in the neo-soul movement that came to prominence in the late '90s, and he also remained a composer of choice for jazz artists looking to incorporate harmonically sophisticated pop/R&B tunes into their repertoires. That only scratches the surface of Wonder's impact on contemporary popular music, which is why he was inducted into the Rock 'n' Roll Hall of Fame in 1989, and remains a living legend regardless of whatever else he does.

Wilson Pickett

Born Mar 18, 1941 in Prattville, AL

Of the major '60s soul stars, Wilson Pickett was one of the roughest and sweatiest, working up some of the decade's hottest dancefloor grooves on hits like "In the Midnight Hour," "Land of 1000 Dances," "Mustang Sally," and "Funky Broadway." Although he tends to be held in somewhat lower esteem than more versatile talents like Otis Redding and Aretha Franklin, he is often a preferred alternative of fans who like their soul on the rawer side. He also did a good deal to establish the sound of Southern soul with his early hits, which were often written and recorded with the cream of the session musicians in Memphis and Muscle Shoals.

Before establishing himself as a solo artist, Pickett sang with the Falcons, who had a Top Ten R&B hit in 1962 with "I Found a Love." "If You Need Me" (covered by the Rolling Stones) and "It's Too Late" were R&B hits for the singer before he hooked up with Atlantic Records, who sent him to record at Stax in Memphis in 1965. One early result was "In the Midnight Hour," whose chugging horn line, loping funky beats, and impassioned vocals combined into a key transitional performance that brought R&B into the soul age. It was an R&B chart-topper and a substantial pop hit (number 21), though its influence was stronger than that respectable position might indicate: thousands of bands, black and white, covered "In the Midnight Hour" on stage and record in the 1960s.

Pickett had a flurry of other galvanizing soul hits over the next few years, including "634-5789," "Mustang Sally," and "Funky Broadway," all of which, like "In the Midnight Hour," were frequently adapted by other bands as dance-ready numbers. The king of that hill, though, had to be "Land of 1000 Dances," Pickett's biggest pop hit (number six), a soul anthem of sorts with its roll call of popular dances, and covered by almost as many acts as "Midnight Hour" was.

Pickett didn't confine himself to the environs of Stax for long; soon he was also cutting tracks at Muscle Shoals. He recorded several early songs by Bobby Womack. He used Duane Allman as a session guitarist on a hit cover of the Beatles' "Hey Jude." He cut some hits in Philadelphia with Gamble-Huff productions in the early '70s. He even did a hit version of the Archies' "Sugar, Sugar." The hits kept rolling through the early '70s, including "Don't Knock My Love" and "Get Me Back on Time, Engine Number 9."

One of the corollaries of '60s soul is that if a performer rose to fame with Motown or Atlantic, he or she would produce little of note after leaving the label. Pickett, unfortunately, did not prove an exception to the rule. His last big hit was "Fire and Water," in 1972. He continued to be active on the tour circuit; his most essential music, all from the 1960s and early '70s, was assembled for the superb Rhino double-CD anthology *A Man and a Half*. *It's Harder Now*, his first new material in over a decade, followed in 1999.

The Impressions

Formed 1958 in Chicago, IL
Disbanded in 1983

The quintessential Chicago soul group, the Impressions' place in R&B history would be secure if they'd done nothing but launch the careers of soul legends Jerry Butler and Curtis Mayfield. But far more than that, the Impressions recorded some of the most distinctive vocal-group R&B of the '60s under Mayfield's guidance. Their style was marked by airy, feather-light harmonies and Mayfield's influentially sparse guitar work, plus, at times, understated Latin rhythms. If their sound was sweet and lilting, it remained richly soulful thanks to the group's firm grounding in gospel tradition; they popularized the three-part vocal trade-offs common in gospel but rare in R&B at the time, and recorded their fair share of songs with spiritual themes, both subtle and overt. Furthermore, Mayfield's interest in the civil rights movement led to some of the first socially conscious R&B songs ever recorded, and his messages grew more explicit as the '60s wore on, culminating in the streak of brilliance that was his early-'70s solo work. The Impressions carried on without Mayfield, but only matched their earlier achievements in isolated instances, and finally disbanded in the early '80s.

The Impressions were formed in Chicago in 1957 as a doo wop group called the Roosters, a group of Chattanooga, TN, transplants that included vocalists Sam Gooden and brothers Richard and Arthur Brooks. Lead singer Jerry Butler joined up and soon brought in his friend Curtis Mayfield as guitarist; the two had previously sung together in a church choir and a couple of local gospel groups as youths. Renamed the Impressions by their manager, the group scored a major hit in 1958 with the classic ballad "For Your Precious Love," which hit the pop Top 20 and the R&B Top Five. Butler's gospel-inflected lead vocal was a departure from the norm, and the fact that the single billed him in front of the rest of the group foreshadowed his quick exit for a solo career, after just one more single ("Come Back My Love"). With new vocalist Fred Cash in tow, Mayfield took over the lead tenor role, eventually becoming the group's chief composer as well. First, though, he hit the road as guitarist and musical director for Butler's backing band, and also co-wrote some of Butler's earliest singles, including the R&B number one "He Will Break Your Heart" in late 1960.

Mayfield's success as a songwriter encouraged him to form his own publishing company. With the money he earned by working with Butler, he reconvened the Impressions and brought them to New York to record for ABC-Paramount in 1961. Their first single, the Latin-inflected "Gypsy Woman," was a number two R&B smash, also reaching the pop Top 20. Several follow-ups failed to duplicate its chart success, and the Brooks brothers left the group in 1962; now down to a trio, the Impressions returned to Chicago and began recording with arranger Johnny Pate, whose horn and string embellishments added a bit more heft to their sound. They struck gold in 1963 with "It's All Right," whose gospel-style lead-swapping helped make it not only their first R&B number one, but their biggest pop hit as well, with a peak of number four. The same year, they issued their eponymous first LP, which many critics still consider one of their finest. 1964 brought the hit single "Keep on Pushing," the first of Mayfield's numerous black pride anthems (though at this stage, his sentiments were much less explicit than they would later become). The album of the same name also featured a marching-beat cover of the gospel standard "Amen," inspired by the song's inclusion in the Sidney Poitier film *Lilies of the Field*. Gospel also informed what became perhaps the best-known Impressions hit, 1965's "People Get Ready"; if its lyrics weren't overtly political, Mayfield's intent was clear, as the song became an anthem of transcendence for the civil rights movement and an oft-covered soul standard.

The mid-'60s saw Mayfield trying to keep pace with the Motown hit factory by incorporating elements of its style into his own writing. The group recorded prolifically in 1965, but their commercial fortunes dropped off over the next couple of years. When the Impressions returned to the upper reaches of the R&B charts, it was with 1968's "We're a Winner," the most straightforward celebration of black pride Mayfield had yet composed. That summer, the group left ABC to record for Mayfield's newly formed Curtom imprint, which allowed them greater freedom in terms of the lyrical content Mayfield wanted to pursue. More aggressive message tracks like "This Is My Country," "Choice of Colors," and "Check Out Your Mind" followed over the next couple of years, as did some of the group's most consistent albums, particularly *The Young Mods' Forgotten Story* (1969). 1970's *Check Out Your Mind* was Mayfield's final album with the Impressions, but the group remained on Curtom after his departure, and he continued to write and produce some of their material.

Mayfield was replaced on lead vocals by Leroy Hutson, who debuted on LP with 1972's *Times Have Changed*. At this point, the Impressions were still overshadowed by their ex-leader, who was riding high with brilliant works like *Superfly*. But Mayfield's solo momentum cooled down a bit, and after Hutson departed in 1973, new singers Ralph Johnson and Reggie Torian joined Cash and Gooden for the R&B chart-topper "Finally Got Myself Together (I'm a Changed Man)," cut with ex-Motown producer Ed Townsend in 1974. Townsend continued to work with the group for the next couple of years with some success, but in 1976 Johnson left to join the unsuccessful Mystique. Around that point, the Impressions parted ways with Curtom; Nate Evans replaced Johnson, and the group recorded for Cotillion and 20th Century/Chi-Sound with little chart success. Evans eventually departed, leaving the group a trio again. They recorded their final album, *Fan the Fire*, in 1981; Gooden and Cash occasionally reunited with Mayfield and sometimes Butler for touring commitments. Mayfield was paralyzed in a heartbreaking stage accident in 1990, when a lighting scaffold toppled over on him; he passed away in 1999.

Rufus Thomas

Born Mar 26, 1917 in Cayce, MS

Few of rock & roll's founding figures are as likable as Rufus Thomas. From the 1940s onward, he has personified Memphis music; his small but witty cameo role in Jim Jarmusch's *Mystery Train*, a film which satirizes and enshrines the city's role in popular culture, was entirely appropriate. As a recording artist, he wasn't a major innovator, but he could always be depended upon for some good, silly, and/or outrageous fun with his soul dance tunes. He was one of the few rock or soul stars to reach his commercial and artistic peak in middle age, and was a crucial mentor to many important Memphis blues, rock, and soul musicians.

Thomas was already a professional entertainer in the mid-'30s, when he was a comedian with the Rabbit Foot Minstrels. He recorded music as early as 1941, but really made his mark on the Memphis music scene as a deejay on WDIA, one of the few black-owned stations of the era. He also ran talent shows on Memphis' famous Beale Street that helped showcase the emerging skills of such influential figures as B.B. King, Bobby Bland, Junior Parker, Ike Turner, and Roscoe Gordon.

Thomas had his first success as a recording artist in 1953 with "Bear Cat," a funny answer record to Big Mama Thornton's "Hound Dog." It made number three on the R&B charts, giving Sun Records its first national hit, though some of the sweetness went out of the triumph after Sun owner Sam Phillips lost a lawsuit for plagiarizing the original Jerry Leiber/Mike Stoller tune. Thomas, strangely, would make only one other record for Sun, and recorded only sporadically throughout the rest of the 1950s.

Thomas and his daughter Carla would become the first stars for the Stax label, for whom they recorded a duet in 1959, "'Cause I Love You" (when the company was still known as Satellite). In the '60s, Carla would become one of Stax's biggest stars. On his own, Rufus wasn't as successful as his daughter, but issued a steady stream of decent dance/novelty singles.

These were not deep or emotional statements, or meant to be. Vaguely prefiguring elements of funk, the accent was on the stripped-down groove and Rufus' good-time vocals, which didn't take himself or anything seriously. The biggest by far was "Walking the Dog," which made the Top Ten in 1963, and was covered by the Rolling Stones on their first album.

Thomas hit his commercial peak in the early '70s, when "Do the Funky Chicken," "(Do The) Push and Pull," and "The Breakdown" all made the R&B Top Five. As the song titles themselves make clear, funk was now driving his sound rather than blues or soul. Thomas drew upon his vaudeville background to put them over on-stage with fancy footwork that displayed remarkable agility for a man well into his 50s. The collapse of the Stax label in the mid-'70s meant the end of his career, basically, as it did for many other artists with the company. In 2001, Rufus Thomas was inducted into the Blues Hall of Fame. Later that year, on December 15, he died at St. Francis Hospital in Memphis, TN.

Carla Thomas

Born Dec 21, 1942 in Memphis, TN

In the glorious decade and a half of sound that was Stax in the '60s and early '70s, Carla Thomas was the Queen of Memphis Soul. She was born in Memphis in 1942, and 18 years later she recorded a duet with her father Rufus Thomas, giving the fledgling Satellite label its first taste of success with the regional hit "Cause I Love You." As her 18th birthday drew nigh, she cut her first solo single, the teen ballad "Gee Whiz (Look at His Eyes)." Written a few years earlier and rejected by Vee-Jay in Chicago, it gave Satellite its first national hit, breaking the Top Ten mark on both the R&B and pop charts. Shortly thereafter Satellite became Stax, and Carla proceeded to claw her way onto the national charts another 22 times with such immortal slices of soul as her answer song to Sam Cooke, "I'll Bring It on Home to You," as well as "Let Me Be Good to You," "B-A-B-Y," "Tramp" (with Otis Redding), and "I Like What You're Doing to Me." Carla released six solo albums and, with Redding, one duet album on Stax between 1961 and 1971.

Doris Troy

Born Jan 16, 1937 in New York, NY

 Surely one of the most talented one-hit wonders of the rock era, Doris Troy hit the Top Ten with "Just One Look" in 1963, but also recorded many other fine pop-soul sides for Atlantic between 1963 and 1965. Unlike many soul performers of the time, Troy wrote most of her own material (under the pseudonym Payne), and had already written for other artists and sung backup with Dionne and Dee Dee Warwick and Cissy Houston on New York soul records before striking out on her own. More melodically ambitious and stylistically eclectic than many of her peers, her Atlantic sides blend elements of gospel, girl group, blues, and pop into a rich New York soul sound. Troy never reached the charts again after "Just One Look," but was more appreciated in England, where she toured occasionally and where the Hollies covered her "What'cha Gonna Do About It" on their first album. Moving to Britain, she recorded an album for Apple in 1970 with assistance from George Harrison and Billy Preston. In the early '70s, she sang backup vocals for British rock groups, most notably the Rolling Stones and Pink Floyd, in addition to recording a couple more albums. In the '80s she starred in Mama I Want to Sing, a musical based on her life story. The musical became a touring success, one which Troy remained involved with until 1998. She continued to perform in Las Vegas until her death from emphysema on February 17, 2004.

The Temptations

Formed 1960 in Detroit, MI

 Thanks to their fine-tuned choreography—and even finer harmonies—the Temptations became the definitive male vocal group of the 1960s; one of Motown's most elastic acts, they tackled both lush pop and politically charged funk with equal flair, and weathered a steady stream of changes in personnel and consumer tastes with rare dignity and grace. The Temptations' initial five-man lineup formed in Detroit in 1961 as a merger of two local vocal groups, the Primes and the Distants. Baritone Otis Williams, Elbridge (aka El, or Al) Bryant, and bass vocalist Melvin Franklin were longtime veterans of the Detroit music scene when they joined together in the Distants, who in 1959 recorded the single "Come On" for the local Northern label. Around the same time, the Primes, a trio comprised of tenor Eddie Kendricks, Paul Williams (no relation to Otis), and Kell Osborne, relocated to the Motor City from their native Alabama; they quickly found success locally, and their manager even put together a girl group counterpart dubbed the Primettes. (Later, three of the Primettes—Diana Ross, Mary Wilson and Florence Ballard—formed the Supremes).

In 1961, the Primes disbanded, but not before Otis Williams saw them perform live, where he was impressed both by Kendricks' vocal prowess and Paul Williams' choreography skills. Soon, Otis Williams, Paul Williams, Bryant, Franklin, and Kendricks joined together as the Elgins; after a name change to the Temptations, they signed to the Motown subsidiary Miracle, where they released a handful of singles over the ensuing months. Only one, the 1962 effort "Dream Come True," achieved any commercial success, however, and in 1963, Bryant either resigned or was fired after physically attacking Paul Williams. The Tempts' fortunes changed dramatically in 1964 when they recruited tenor David Ruffin to replace Bryant; after entering the studio with writer/producer Smokey Robinson, they emerged with the pop smash "The Way You Do the Things You Do," the first in a series of 37 career Top Ten hits. With Robinson again at the helm, they returned in 1965 with their signature song, "My Girl," a number one pop and R&B hit; other Top 20 hits that year included "It's Growing," "Since I Lost My Baby," "Don't Look Back," and "My Baby."

In 1966, the Tempts recorded another Robinson hit, "Get Ready," before forgoing his smooth popcraft for the harder-edged soul of producers Norman Whitfield and Brian Holland. After spotlighting Kendricks on the smash "Ain't Too Proud to Beg," the group allowed Ruffin to take control over a string of hits including "Beauty's Only Skin Deep" and "(I Know) I'm Losing You." Beginning around 1967, Whitfield assumed full production control, and their records became ever rougher and more muscular, as typified by the 1968 success "I Wish It Would Rain." After Ruffin failed to appear at a 1968 live performance, the other four Tempts fired him; he was replaced by ex-Contour Dennis Edwards, whose less polished voice adapted perfectly to the psychedelic-influenced soul period the group entered following the success of the single "Cloud Nine." As the times changed, so did the group, and as the 1960s drew to a close, the Temptations' music became overtly political; in the wake of "Cloud Nine"—its title a thinly veiled drug allegory—came records like "Run Away Child, Running Wild," "Psychedelic Shack," and "Ball of Confusion (That's What the World Is Today)."

After the chart-topping success of the gossamer ballad "Just My Imagination (Running Away With Me)" in 1971, Kendricks exited for a solo career. Soon, Paul Williams left the group as well; long plagued by alcoholism and other personal demons, he was eventually discovered dead from a self-inflected gunshot on August 17, 1973, at the age of 34. In their stead the remaining trio recruited tenors Damon Harris and Richard Street; after the 1971 hit "Superstar (Remember How You Got Where You Are)," they returned in 1972 with the brilliant number one single "Papa Was a Rolling Stone." While the Tempts hit the charts regularly throughout 1973 with "Masterpiece," "Let Your Hair Down," and "The Plastic Man," their success as a pop act gradually dwindled as the 1970s wore on. After Harris exited in 1975 (replaced by tenor Glenn Leonard), the group cut 1976's *The Temptations Do the Temptations*, their final album for Motown. With Louis Price taking over for Edwards, they signed to Atlantic, and attempted to reach the disco market with the LPs *Bare Back* and *Hear to Tempt You*.

After Edwards returned to the fold (resulting in Price's hasty exit), the Temptations re-entered the Motown stable, and scored a 1980 hit with "Power." In 1982, Ruffin and Kendricks returned for *Re-*

union, which also included all five of the current Tempts; a tour followed, but problems with Motown, as well as personal differences, cut Ruffin's and Kendricks' tenures short. In the years that followed, the Temptations continued touring and recording, although by the 1990s they were essentially an oldies act; only Otis Williams, who published his autobiography in 1988, remained from the original lineup. The intervening years were marked by tragedy: after touring in the late '80s with Kendricks and Edwards as a member of the "Tribute to the Temptations" package tour, Ruffin died on June 1, 1991, after overdosing on cocaine; he was 50 years old. On October 5, 1992, Kendricks died at the age of 52 of lung cancer, and on February 23, 1995, 52-year-old Franklin passed away after suffering a brain seizure. In 1998, the Temptations returned with *Phoenix Rising*; that same year, their story was also the subject of a well-received NBC television miniseries. *Ear-Resistable* followed in the spring of 2000.

Isaac Hayes

Born Aug 20, 1942 in Covington, TN

Few figures exerted greater influence over the music of the 1960s and 1970s than Isaac Hayes; after laying the groundwork for the Memphis soul sound through his work with Stax-Volt Records, Hayes began a highly successful solo career which predated not only the disco movement but also the evolution of rap.

Hayes was born on August 20, 1942, in Covington, TN; his parents died during his infancy, and he was raised by his grandparents. After making his public debut singing in church at the age of five, he taught himself piano, organ and saxophone before moving to Memphis to perform on the city's club circuit in a series of short-lived groups like Sir Isaac and the Doo-Dads, the Teen Tones, and Sir Calvin and His Swinging Cats. In 1962, he began his recording career, cutting sides for a variety of local labels.

Two years later, Hayes began playing sax with the Mar-Keys, which resulted in the beginning of his long association with Stax Records. After playing on several sessions for Otis Redding, Hayes was tapped to play keyboards in the Stax house band, and eventually established a partnership with songwriter David Porter. Under the name the Soul Children, the Hayes-Porter duo composed some 200 songs, reeling off a string of hits for Stax luminaries like Sam & Dave (the brilliant "When Something Is Wrong With My Baby," "Soul Man," and "Hold On, I'm Comin'"), Carla Thomas ("B-A-B-Y,") and Johnnie Taylor ("I Got to Love Somebody's Baby," "I Had a Dream").

In 1967, Hayes issued his debut solo LP *Presenting Isaac Hayes*, a loose, jazz-flavored effort recorded in the early-morning hours following a raucous Stax party. With the release of 1969's landmark *Hot Buttered Soul*, he made his commercial breakthrough; the record's adventuresome structure (comprising four lengthy songs), ornate arrangements, and sensual grooves—combined with the imposing figure cut by his shaven head, omnipresent sunglasses, and fondness for gold jewelry—made Hayes one of the most distinctive figures in music.

After a pair of 1970 releases, *The Isaac Hayes Movement* and *To Be Continued*, he reached his commercial zenith in 1971 with the release of *Shaft*, the score from the Gordon Parks film of the same name. Not only did the album win Hayes an Academy Award for Best Score (the first African-American composer to garner such an honor), but the single "Theme From 'Shaft,'" a masterful blend of prime funk and pre-rap monologues, became a number one hit.

After 1971's superb *Black Moses* and 1973's *Joy*, Hayes composed two 1974 soundtracks, *Tough Guys* and *Truck Turner* (in which he also starred). By 1975, relations with Stax had disintegrated following a battle over royalties, and soon he severed his ties with the label to form his own Hot Buttered Soul imprint. Although both 1975's *Chocolate Chip* and 1976's *Groove-a-Thon* went gold, his records of the period attracted considerably less attention than prior efforts; combined with poor management and business associations, Hayes had no choice but to file for bankruptcy in 1976.

After the 1977 double-LP *A Man and a Woman*, recorded with Dionne Warwick, Hayes began a comeback on the strength of the hit singles "Zeke the Freak," "Don't Let Go" and "Do You Wanna Make Love." Following the success of his 1979 collection of duets with Millie Jackson titled *Royal Rappins*, he issued a pair of solo records, 1980's *And Once Again* and 1981's *Lifetime Thing* before retiring from music for five years. After returning in 1986 with the LP *U Turn* and the Top Ten R&B hit "Ike's Rap," Hayes surfaced two years later with *Love Attack* before again dropping out of music to focus on acting.

In 1995, fully enshrined as one of the forefathers of hip-hop and newly converted to Scientology, Hayes emerged with two concurrent releases, the vocal *Branded* and instrumental *Raw and Refined*. Under the official name Nene Katey Ocansey I, he also served as a member of the royal family of the African nation of Ghana while continuing simultaneous careers as an actor, composer, and humanitarian. In 1997, Hayes provided the voice of what was slated to be a one-time character on the animated series *South Park*—Jerome "Chef" McElroy, the main characters' favorite school cafeteria worker. Hayes was an instant hit, and Chef became a regular character on the show, lending advice and, oftentimes, breaking into songs that gently sent up Hayes' image as one of R&B's ultimate love men.

South Park made Hayes more visible than ever and cemented his status as an icon with a whole new generation. He contributed the infamous "Chocolate Salty Balls" to the *South Park* tie-in album *Chef Aid*, and naturally appeared in the film *South Park: Bigger, Longer, Uncut*. In 2000, Hayes revisited his biggest triumph of the past by appearing in the remake of *Shaft* starring Samuel L. Jackson. The following year, he supported Alicia Keys as a musician and arranger on her acclaimed debut *Songs in A Minor*.

David Porter

Born Nov 21, 1941 in Memphis, TN

David Porter is most famous as the songwriting partner of Isaac Hayes during the 1960s. Functioning as house composers for Stax, they penned most of Sam & Dave's hits, including such classics as "Soul Man" and "Hold On! I'm Coming"; they also wrote material for other acts on the roster, such as Carla Thomas, Johnnie Taylor, and the Soul Children. Starting in the late '60s, Hayes became increasingly involved in his own recording career, eventually leading to the end of the partnership. Many soul fans remain unaware that Porter also began to record his own albums for Stax. In fact, in the '60s he had released a few singles for Savoy and Hi under the pseudonyms of Little David and Kenny Cain, and had done a single for Stax itself in 1965, "Can't See You When I Want To." A remake of "Can't See You When I Want To" became a Top 30 R&B hit for Porter, and he cut several albums for Stax in the early '70s, including an ambitious concept LP, *Victim of the Joke?* which connected conventional pop/soul tunes with dialog. By this time he had teamed up with a different songwriting partner, Ronnie Williams, but as a solo artist he ultimately made little impact.

The Four Tops

Formed 1956 in Detroit, MI

The Four Tops' story is one of longevity and togetherness: these Motown legends teamed up in high school and spent over four decades without a single personnel change. In between, they became one of the top-tier acts on a label with no shortage of talent, ranking with the Temptations and the Supremes as Motown's most consistent hitmakers. Where many other R&B vocal groups spotlighted a tenor-range lead singer, the Four Tops were fronted by deep-voiced Levi Stubbs, who never cut a solo record outside of the group. Stubbs had all the grit of a pleading, wailing, gospel-trained soul belter, but at the same time, the Tops' creamy harmonies were smooth enough for Motown's radio-friendly pop-soul productions. From 1964–1967, the Four Tops recorded some of the Holland-Dozier-Holland team's greatest compositions, including "Reach Out, I'll Be There," "I Can't Help Myself (Sugar Pie, Honey Bunch)," "Standing in the Shadows of Love," "Bernadette," and "Baby I Need Your Loving." The group's fortunes took a downturn when their chief source of material left the label, but they enjoyed a renaissance in the early '70s, which saw them switching to the ABC-Dunhill imprint. Regardless of commercial fortunes, they kept on performing and touring, scoring the occasional comeback hit.

The Four Tops began life in 1953 (some accounts say 1954), when all of the members were attending Detroit-area high schools. Levi Stubbs and Abdul "Duke" Fakir went to Pershing, and met Northern students Renaldo "Obie" Benson and Lawrence Payton at a friend's birthday party, where the quartet first sang together. Sensing an immediate chemistry, they began rehearsing together and dubbed themselves the Four Aims. Payton's cousin Roquel Davis, a budding songwriter who sometimes sang with the group during its early days, helped them get an audition with Chess Records in 1956. Although Chess was more interested in Davis, who went on to become Berry Gordy's songwriting partner, they also signed the Four Aims, who became the

Four Tops to avoid confusion with the Ames Brothers. The Four Tops' lone Chess single, "Kiss Me Baby," was an unequivocal flop, and the group moved on to similarly brief stints at Red Top and Riverside. They signed with Columbia in 1960 and were steered in a more upscale supperclub direction, singing jazz and pop standards. This too failed to break them, although they did tour with Billy Eckstine during this period.

In 1963, the Four Tops signed with longtime friend Berry Gordy's new label, specifically the jazz-oriented Workshop subsidiary. They completed a debut LP, to be called *Breaking Through*, but Gordy scrapped it and switched their style back to R&B, placing them on Motown with the Holland-Dozier-Holland songwriting team. After a full decade in existence, the Four Tops finally notched their first hit in 1964 with "Baby I Need Your Loving," which just missed the pop Top Ten. Early 1965 brought the follow-up ballad hit "Ask the Lonely," and from then on there was no stopping them. "I Can't Help Myself (Sugar Pie, Honey Bunch)" went all the way to number one that spring, and the follow-up "It's the Same Old Song" reached the Top Five. The hits continued into 1966, with "Something About You" "Shake Me, Wake Me (When It's Over)," and "Loving You Is Sweeter Than Ever" all coming in succession. The fall of 1966 brought the group's masterpiece in the form of the virtual soul symphony "Reach Out, I'll Be There"; not only did it become their second number one pop hit, it also wound up ranking as the creative peak of the group's career and one of Motown's finest singles ever. During this period, the Tops also earned a reputation as one of Motown's best live acts, having previously honed their performances for years before hitting the big time.

The Four Tops kicked off 1967 with the dramatic Top Ten smash "Standing in the Shadows of Love," which was followed by the Top Five "Bernadette." "7-Rooms of Gloom" and "You Keep Running Away" reached the Top 20, but toward the end of the year, Holland-Dozier-Holland left Motown over a financial dispute, which didn't bode well for the Four Tops' impressive hit streak. Their next two hits, 1968's "Walk Away Renee" and "If I Were a Carpenter," were both covers of well-known recent songs (by the Left Banke and Tim Hardin, respectively), and while both made the Top 20, they heralded a rough couple of years where top-drawer material was in short supply. They enjoyed a resurgence in 1970 under producer Frank Wilson, who helmed a hit cover of the Tommy Edwards pop standard "It's All in the Game" and a ballad co-written by Smokey Robinson, "Still Water (Love)." The Tops also recorded with the post-Diana Ross Supremes, scoring a duet hit with a cover of "River Deep-Mountain High" in 1971.

When Motown moved its headquarters to Los Angeles in 1972, the Four Tops parted ways with the company, choosing to remain in their hometown of Detroit. They signed with ABC-Dunhill and were teamed with producers/songwriters Dennis Lambert and Brian Potter, who did their best to re-create the group's trademark Motown sound. The immediate result was "Keeper of the Castle," the Four Tops' first Top Ten hit in several years. They followed it in early 1973 with "Ain't No Woman (Like the One I've Got)," a gold-selling smash that proved to be their final Top Five pop hit. That year they also recorded the theme song to the film *Shaft in Africa*, "Are You Man Enough." Several more R&B chart hits followed over the next few years, with the last being 1976's "Catfish"; after a final ABC album in 1978, the Tops largely disappeared from sight before resurfacing on Casablanca in 1981. Incredibly, their first single, "When She Was My Girl," went all the way to number one on the R&B charts, just missing the pop Top Ten. The accompanying album, *Tonight!*, became their last to hit the Top 40.

The Four Tops rejoined Motown in 1983, the year of the company's 25th anniversary, and toured extensively with the Temptations. They also recorded a couple albums of new material that failed to sell well, and wound up leaving Motown amid confusion over proper musical direction. Meanwhile, Levi Stubbs provided the voice for Audrey the man-eating plant in the film version of *Little Shop of Horrors*. The Four Tops next caught on with Arista, where in 1988 they scored their last Top 40 pop hit, the aptly titled "Indestructible." The Four Tops were inducted into the Rock and Roll Hall of Fame in 1990, and continued to tour the oldies circuit. In 1997, Lawrence Payton passed away due to cancer of the liver, which proved to be the only thing that could break up the Four Tops. After some consideration, the remaining members hired Theo Peoples to take Payton's place on tour.

The Supremes

Formed 1961 in Detroit, MI

The most successful black performers of the 1960s, the Supremes for a time rivaled even the Beatles in terms of red-hot commercial appeal, reeling off five number-one singles in a row at one point. Critical revisionism has tended to undervalue the Supremes' accomplishments, categorizing their work as more lightweight than the best soul stars' (or even the best Motown stars'), and viewing them as a tool for Berry Gordy's crossover aspirations. There's no question that there was about as much pop as soul in the Supremes' hits, that even some of their biggest hits could sound formulaic, and that they were probably the black performers who were most successful at infiltrating the tastes and televisions of middle America. This shouldn't diminish either their extraordinary achievements or their fine music, the best of which renders the pop vs. soul question moot with its excellence.

The Supremes were not an overnight success story, although it might have seemed that way when they began topping the charts with sure-fire regularity. The trio that would become famous as the Supremes—Diana Ross, Mary Wilson, and Florence Ballard—met in the late '50s in Detroit's Brewster housing project. Originally known as the Primettes, they were a quartet (Barbara Martin was the fourth member) when they made their first single for the Lupine label in 1960. By the time they debuted for Motown in 1961, they had been renamed the Supremes;

Barbara Martin reduced them to a trio when she left after their first single.

The Supremes' first Motown recordings were much more girl group-oriented than their later hits. Additionally, not all of them featured Diana Ross on lead vocals; Flo Ballard, considered to have as good or better a voice, also sang lead. Through a lengthy series of flops, Berry Gordy remained confident that the group would eventually prove to be one of Motown's biggest. By the time they finally did get their first Top 40 hit, "When the Lovelight Starts Shining Through His Eyes," in late 1963, Ross had taken over the lead singing for good.

Ross was not the most talented female singer at Motown; Martha Reeves and Gladys Knight in particular had superior talents. What she did have, however, was the most purely pop appeal. Gordy's patience and attention paid off in mid-1964, when "Where Did Our Love Go" went to number one. Written by Holland-Dozier-Holland, it established the prototype for their run of five consecutive number-one hits in 1964–1965 (also including "Baby Love," "Stop! In the Name of Love," "Come See About Me," and "Back in My Arms Again"). Ross' cooing vocals would front the Supremes' decorative backup vocals, put over on television and live performance with highly stylized choreography and visual style. Holland-Dozier-Holland would write and produce all of the Supremes' hits through the end of 1967.

Not all of the Supremes' singles went to number one after 1965, but they usually did awfully well, and were written and produced with enough variety (but enough of a characteric sound) to ensure continual interest. The chart-topping (and uncharacteristically tough) "You Keep Me Hangin' On" was the best of their mid-period hits. Behind the scenes, there were some problems brewing, although these only came to light long after the event. Other Motown stars (most notably Martha Reeves) resented what they perceived as the inordinate attention lavished upon Ross by Gordy, at the expense of other artists on the label. The other Supremes themselves felt increasingly pushed to the background. In mid-1967, as a result of what was deemed increasingly unprofessional behavior, Ballard was replaced by Cindy Birdsong (from Patti LaBelle and the Bluebelles). Ballard become one of rock's greatest tragedies, eventually ending up on welfare, and dying in 1976.

After Ballard's exit, the group would be billed as Diana Ross & the Supremes, fueling speculation that Ross was being groomed for a solo career. The Supremes had a big year in 1967, even incorporating some mild psychedelic influences into "Reflections." Holland-Dozier-Holland, however, left Motown around this time, and the quality of the Supremes' records suffered accordingly (as did the Motown organization as a whole). The Supremes were still superstars, but as a unit, they were disintegrating; it's been reported that Wilson and Birdsong didn't even sing on their final hits, a couple of which ("Love Child" and "Someday We'll Be Together") were among their best.

In November 1969, Ross' imminent departure for a solo career was announced, although she played a few more dates with them, the last in Las Vegas in January 1970. Jean Terrell replaced Ross, and the group continued through 1977, with some more personnel changes (although Mary Wilson was always involved). Some of the early Ross-less singles were fine records, particularly "Stoned Love," "Nathan Jones," and the Supremes-Four Tops duet "River Deep—Mountain High." Few groups have been able to rise to the occasion after the loss of their figurehead, though, and the Supremes proved no exception, rarely making the charts after 1972. It is the Diana Ross-led era of the 1960s for which they'll be remembered.

Junior Walker & the All-Stars

Formed 1964 in Detroit, MI

Motown's skilled but mostly anonymous instrumentalists very rarely stepped out on their own. The lone exception to the rule was tenor saxman Junior Walker, whose rough-and-ready, old-school R&B was a marked contrast with the label's typically smooth, polished product. Walker's squealing gutbucket style was inspired by jump blues and early R&B, particularly players like Louis Jordan, Earl Bostic, and Illinois Jacquet. Possessed of a raspy, untrained voice, Walker's singing nonetheless complemented the energy of his sax playing, and he cut a wealth of danceable, party hearty R&B for Motown during his heyday in the second half of the '60s.

Walker was born Autry DeWalt II on June 14, 1931 (even though Motown gave his birth date as 1942), in Blytheville, AR. (Some accounts list his birth name as Oscar G. Mixon, which was then changed at some point during his early childhood.) DeWalt grew up in South Bend, IN, and began playing the saxophone in high school; he was soon performing in local jazz and R&B clubs with his first band, the Jumping Jacks, under the name Junior Walker. He next joined a trio led by drummer Billy "Stix" Nicks, which also featured organist Fred Patton; they soon added backing vocalist and guitarist Willie Woods, and played around northern Indiana and southern Michigan. Walker took over the group after Nicks joined the Army; in the late '50s, he relocated to Battle Creek, MI, and formed a band billed as Junior Walker & the All-Stars. Initially, they featured Patton, Woods, and drummer Tony Washington; Patton was later replaced by Victor Thomas, and Washington by Jack Douglas and, finally, James Graves. The All-Stars continued to play around the area, and took up a residency in Battle Creek's El Grotto club. There they were discovered by singer Johnny Bristol, who recommended them to his friend, ex-Moonglow Harvey Fuqua. Fuqua signed the group to his Harvey label in 1961; they made their first recordings in 1962, and the following year Fuqua's labels were absorbed by Motown.

Walker & the All-Stars ended up on their Soul subsidiary, debuting for the label in 1964. In early 1965, they scored their first big hit with the dance tune "Shotgun," which marked Walker's vocal debut; in fact, the only reason he sang the song was that the vocalist he'd hired didn't show up for the session, and he was somewhat flabbergasted by the label's decision to leave his vocal intact. Berry Gordy's instincts proved right, however, when "Shotgun" topped the R&B charts and hit the pop Top Five. A steady stream of mostly instrumental R&B chart hits followed, including "Do the Boomerang," "Shake and Fingerpop," and "How Sweet It Is (To Be Loved by You)" (Walker was, naturally, encouraged to record instrumental versions of Motown hits). In 1966, Graves left and was replaced by old cohort Billy "Stix" Nicks, and Walker's hits continued apace with tunes like "I'm a Road Runner" and "Pucker Up Buttercup." Toward the end of the '60s, seeking to diversify their approach, the All-Stars began recording more ballad material, complete with string arrangements and Walker vocals. That approach resulted in the group's second Top Five pop hit, the R&B number one "What Does It Take (To Win Your Love)," which helped refuel Walker's career. He landed several more R&B Top Ten hits over the next few years, with the last coming in 1972.

Walker resurfaced as a solo artist during the disco era, working with producer Brian Holland beginning in 1976 with the single "Hot Shot"; a pair of albums followed. In 1979, Walker joined up with another former Motown mainstay in 1979, signing with producer Norman Whitfield's Whitfield label, though without much success. Walker returned to the spotlight in 1981 with a well-publicized (and well-executed) guest solo on Foreigner's Top Five hit "Urgent." Two years later, he resigned with Motown and recorded *Blow the House Down*; by that time, his melodic style was being absorbed into a new generation of R&B-flavored jazz instrumentalists. Walker continued to tour through the '80s and '90s, sometimes with his son Autry DeWalt III playing drums. Unfortunately, in 1993 his activities were severely curtailed by cancer, which claimed his life on November 23, 1995. In the wake of his death, Billy "Stix" Nicks continued to tour with a version of the All-Stars.

Brenda Holloway

Born Jun 21, 1946 in Atascadero, CA

One of the sexiest singers on the Motown label, Brenda Holloway was also one of its grittiest, with a strong gospel influence more typical of Southern soul than the company's usual polish. Best known for her ballad hit "Every Little Bit Hurts," Holloway also recorded (and co-wrote) the original version of "You've Made Me So Very Happy," which soon became a hit for jazz-rockers Blood Sweat & Tears.

Holloway was born in Atascadero, CA, in 1946 and grew up in the Watts section of Los Angeles; as a child, she learned violin and began singing in church with her younger sister Patrice (who later became a prominent session singer and contributed vocals to Josie & the Pussycats). After singing with the group that later became the Whispers, Holloway's first professional recording was made at age 14, backing 12-year-old Patrice on a locally released single. Brenda herself soon began cutting records on several different L.A. labels, and she and her sister also found work as session vocalists.

In 1964, Holloway performed a rendition of Mary Wells' "My Guy" at a DJ convention in Los Angeles. Motown founder Berry Gordy happened to be there, and he was so struck by the power of her vocals (not to mention her physical form) that he made Holloway his first West Coast signing, placing her on the

Tamla subsidiary. Her debut single, "Every Little Bit Hurts," was an R&B smash that also reached number 12 on the pop charts, and was covered by British R&B aficionados like the Spencer Davis Group and the Small Faces; it became the title track of her first album, also released in 1964. Holloway also found fans in the Beatles, who gave her an opening slot on their 1965 American tour.

She scored several more R&B hits through 1965—"I'll Always Love You" and the Smokey Robinson-penned tracks "When I'm Gone" and "Operator." However, Tamla scrapped a follow-up album, which would have been called *Hurtin' and Cryin'*, and Holloway began to feel that she was getting the short end of the stick. She frequently traveled from her home in Los Angeles to record in Detroit, and began to feel that the material she was given wasn't always up to snuff, perhaps because of her distance. She began to work more on her own writing, often in partnership with her sister, and with a bit of outside help they co-wrote "You've Made Me So Very Happy" in 1968. Holloway's version was a minor R&B hit, but Blood Sweat & Tears turned it into a major pop hit the following year.

Holloway's second album, *The Artistry of Brenda Holloway*, was finally released in 1968, but that year she announced her retirement from the music business, citing her disillusionment with Motown and her fears of being drawn into the stereotypical hedonistic lifestyle (which conflicted with her still-deep religious convictions). She later married a minister and raised three daughters, returning to music in 1980 with the gospel album *Brand New*. Holloway's records remained popular on England's so-called "Northern soul" scene, and in 1987 she traveled to the U.K. to record several Motown-style singles for producer Ian Levine's Motorcity label. In 1995, motivated by the death of Mary Wells, she returned to live performance around the L.A. area, often in tandem with fellow soul veteran Brenton Wood. She performed in the U.K. as well, and in 1999 she signed with the revived Volt label to record *It's a Woman's World*, which took a more contemporary urban approach.

Joe Tex

Born: Aug 8, 1933 in Rogers, TX
Died: Aug 13, 1982 in Navasota, TX

Joe Tex made the first Southern soul record that also hit on the pop charts ("Hold What You've Got," in 1965, made number five in Billboard). His raspy-voiced, jackleg preacher style also laid some of the most important parts of rap's foundation. He is, arguably, the most underrated of all the '60s soul performers associated with Atlantic Records, although his records were more likely than those of most soul stars to become crossover hits.

Tex was born Joseph Arrington in Rogers, TX, in 1933, and displayed his vocal talent quickly, first in gospel, then in R&B. By 1954, he'd won a local talent contest and come to New York, where he recorded a variety of derivative (and endlessly repackaged) singles for King, some as a ballad singer, some as a Little Richard-style rocker.

Tex's career didn't take off until he began his association with Nashville song publisher Buddy Killen, after Tex wrote James Brown's 1961 song "Baby You're Right." In 1965, Killen took him to Muscle Shoals, not yet a fashionable recording center, and they came up with "Hold What You've Got," which is about as close to a straight R&B ballad as Tex ever came. It was followed by a herd more, most of which made the R&B charts, a few cracking the pop Top 40.

Tex made his mark by preaching over tough hard soul tracks, clowning at some points, swooping into a croon at others. He was perhaps the most rustic and back-country of the soul stars, a role he played to the hilt by using turns of phrase that might have been heard on any ghetto street corner, "One Monkey Don't Stop No Show" the prototype. In 1966, his "I Believe I'm Gonna Make It," an imaginary letter home from Vietnam, became the first big hit directly associated with that war. His biggest hit was "Skinny Legs and All," from a 1967 live album, his rapping pure hokum over deeply funky riffs. "Skinny Legs" might have served as a template for all the raucous, ribald hip-hop hits of pop's future.

After "Skinny Legs," Tex had nothing but minor hits for five years until "I Gotcha" took off, a grittier twist on the funk that was becoming disco. He was too down-home for the slickness of the disco era, or so it would have seemed, yet in 1977, he adapted a dance craze, the Bump, and came up with the hilarious "Ain't Gonna Bump No More (With No Big Fat Woman)," his last Top Ten R&B hit, which also crossed over to number 12 on the pop chart.

In the early '70s, Tex converted to Islam and in 1972 changed his offstage name to Joseph Hazziez. He spent much of the time after "Ain't Gonna Bump" on his Texas farm, although he did join together with Wilson Pickett, Ben E. King, and Don Covay for a reformed version of the Soul Clan in 1980. He died of a heart attack in 1982, only 49 years old. Killen, King, Covay, Pickett, and the great songwriter Percy Mayfield served as pallbearers.

Otis Redding

Born: Sep 9, 1941 in Dawson, GA
Died: Dec 10, 1967 in Madison, WI

One of the most influential soul singers of the 1960s, Otis Redding exemplified to many listeners the power of Southern "deep soul"—hoarse, gritty vocals, brassy arrangements, and an emotional way with both party tunes and aching ballads. He was also the most consistent exponent of the Stax sound, cutting his records at the Memphis label/studios that did much to update R&B into modern soul. His death at the age of 26 was tragic not just because he seemed on the verge of breaking through to a wide pop audience (which he would indeed do with his posthumous number one single, "[Sittin' On] The Dock of the Bay"). It was also unfortunate because, as "Dock of the Bay" demonstrated, he was also at a point of artistic breakthrough in terms of the expression and sophistication of his songwriting and singing.

Although Redding at his peak was viewed as a consummate, versatile showman, he began his recording career in the early '60s as a Little Richard-styled shouter. The Georgian was working in the band of guitarist Johnny Jenkins at the time, and in 1962 he took advantage of an opportunity to record the ballad "These Arms of Mine" at a Jenkins session. When it became an R&B hit, Redding's solo career was truly on its way, though the hits didn't really start to fly until 1965 and 1966, when "Mr. Pitiful," "I've Been Loving You Too Long," "I Can't Turn You Loose," a cover of the Rolling Stones' "Satisfaction," and "Respect" (later turned into a huge pop smash by Aretha Franklin) were all big sellers.

Redding wrote much of his own material, sometimes with the assistance of Booker T. & the MG's guitarist Steve Cropper. Yet at the time, Redding's success was primarily confined to the soul market; his singles charted only mildly on the pop listings. He was nonetheless tremendously respected by many white groups, particularly the Rolling Stones, who covered Redding's "That's How Strong My Love Is" and "Pain in My Heart." (Redding also returned the favor with "Satisfaction.")

One of Redding's biggest hits was a duet with fellow Stax star Carla Thomas, "Tramp," in 1967. That was the same year he began to show signs of making major inroads into the white audience, particularly with a well-received performance at the Monterey Pop Festival (also issued on record). Redding's biggest triumph, however, came just days before his death, when he recorded the wistful "(Sittin' On) The Dock of the Bay," which represented a significant leap as far as examination of more intensely personal emotions. Also highlighted by crisp Cropper guitar leads and dignified horns, it rose to the top of the pop charts in early 1968.

Redding, however, had perished in a plane crash in Wisconsin on December 10, 1967, in an accident that also took the lives of four members from his backup band, the Bar-Kays. A few other singles became posthumous hits, and a good amount of other unreleased material was issued in the wake of his death. These releases weren't purely exploitative in nature, in fact containing some pretty interesting music, and little that could be considered embarrassing. What Redding might have achieved, or what directions he might have explored, are among the countless tantalizing "what if" questions in rock & roll history. As it is, he did record a considerable wealth of music at Stax, which is now available on thoughtfully archived reissues.

Barbara Lewis

Born Feb 9, 1943 in South Lyon, MI

Pop-soul doesn't get much better than Barbara Lewis, whose seductive, emotive croon took "Hello Stranger" to number three in 1963. The Michigan native had been writing songs since the age of nine, and began recording as a teenager with producer Ollie McLaughlin, who'd also had a hand in the careers of Del Shannon, the Capitols, and Deon Jackson. Lewis wrote all of the songs on her debut LP (including "Hello Stranger"), and confidently handled harmony soul numbers (some with backing by the Dells) and more pop-savvy tunes, some of which, like "Hello Stranger," were driven by an organ and a bossa nova-like beat. Follow-ups to "Hello Stranger" didn't sell nearly as well (although one of her singles, "Someday We're Gonna Love Again," was covered by the Searchers for a British Invasion hit). In the mid-'60s, she began doing some recordings in New York City, with assistance from producers like Bert Berns and Jerry Wexler, that employed more orchestral arrangements and pop-conscious material. The approach clicked, both commercially and artistically: "Baby I'm Yours" and "Make Me Your Baby" were both big hits, and both among the best mid-'60s girl group style productions.

Lewis cut an album in the late '60s for Stax (on the Enterprise subsidiary) that, as one would expect, gave her sound a grittier approach, without compromising the smooth and poppy elements integral to the singer's appeal. It passed mostly unnoticed, though, and Lewis withdrew from the music business after a few other singles. The "beach music" scene of the Carolinas remains a bastion of appreciation for Lewis' records, which continue to enjoy popularity and airplay there decades after their original release.

Isley Brothers

Formed 1954 in Cincinnati, OH

First formed in the early '50s, the Isley Brothers enjoyed one of the longest, most influential, and most diverse careers in the pantheon of popular music—over the course of nearly a half century of performing, the group's distinguished history spanned not only two generations of Isley siblings but also massive cultural shifts which heralded their music's transformation from gritty R&B to Motown soul to blistering funk. The first generation of Isley siblings was born and raised in Cincinnati, OH, where they were encouraged to begin a singing career by their father, himself a professional vocalist, and their mother, a church pianist who provided musical accompaniment at their early performances. Initially a gospel quartet, the group was comprised of Ronald, Rudolph, O'Kelly, and Vernon Isley; after Vernon's 1955 death in a bicycling accident, tenor Ronald was tapped as the remaining trio's lead vocalist. In 1957, the brothers went to New York City to record a string of failed doo wop singles; while performing a spirited reading of the song "Lonely Teardrops" in Washington, D.C., two years later, they interjected the line "You know you make me want to shout," which inspired frenzied audience feedback. An RCA executive in the audience saw the concert, and when he signed the Isleys soon after, he instructed that their first single be constructed around their crowd-pleasing catch phrase; while the call-and-response classic "Shout" failed to reach the pop Top 40 on its initial release, it eventually became a frequently covered classic.

Still, success eluded the Isleys, and only after they left RCA in 1962 did they again have another hit, this time with their seminal cover of the Top Notes' "Twist and Shout." Like so many of the brothers' early R&B records, "Twist and Shout" earned greater commercial success when later rendered by a white group—in this case, the Beatles; other acts who notched hits by closely following the Isleys' blueprint were the Yardbirds ("Respectable," also covered by the Outsiders), the Human Beinz ("Nobody but Me"), and Lulu ("Shout"). During a 1964 tour, they recruited a young guitarist named Jimmy James to play in their backing band; James—who later shot to fame under his given name, Jimi Hendrix—made his first recordings with the Isleys, including the single "Testify," issued on the brothers' own T-Neck label. They signed to the Motown subsidiary Tamla in 1965, where they joined forces with the famed Holland-Dozier-Holland writing and production team. Their first single, the shimmering "This Old Heart of Mine (Is Weak for You)," was their finest moment yet, and barely missed the pop Top Ten.

"This Old Heart of Mine" was their only hit on Motown, however, and when the song hit number three in Britain in 1967, the Isleys relocated to England in order to sustain their flagging career; after years of writing their own material, they felt straitjacketed by the Motown assembly-line production formula, and by the time they returned stateside in 1969, they had exited Tamla to resuscitate the T-Bone label. Their next release, the muscular and funky "It's Your Thing," hit number two on the U.S. charts in 1969, and became their most successful record. That year, the Isleys also welcomed a number of new members as younger brothers Ernie and Marvin, brother-in-law Chris Jasper, and family friend Everett Collins became the trio's new backing unit. Spearheaded by Ernie's hard-edged guitar leads, the group began incorporating more and more rock material into its repertoire as the 1970s dawned, and scored hits with covers of Stephen Stills' "Love the One You're With," Eric Burdon & War's "Spill the Wine," and Bob Dylan's "Lay Lady Lay."

In 1973, the Isleys scored a massive hit with their rock-funk fusion cover of their own earlier single "Who's That Lady," retitled "That Lady, Pt. 1"; the album *3 + 3* also proved highly successful, as did 1975's *The Heat Is On*, which spawned the smash "Fight the Power, Pt. 1." As the decade wore on, the group again altered its sound to fit into the booming disco market; while their success on pop radio ran dry, they frequently topped the R&B charts with singles like 1977's "The Pride," 1978's "Take Me to the Next Phase, Pt. 1," 1979's "I Wanna Be With You, Pt. 1," and 1980's "Don't Say Goodnight." While the Isleys' popularity continued into the 1980s, Ernie and Marvin, along with Chris Jasper, defected in 1984 to form their own group, Isley/Jasper/Isley; a year later, they topped the R&B charts with "Caravan of Love." On March 31, 1986, O'Kelly died of a heart attack; Rudolph soon left to join the ministry, but the group reunited in 1990. Although the individual members continued with solo work and side projects, the Isley Brothers forged on in one form or another throughout the decade; in 1996, now consisting of Ronald, Marvin, and Ernie, they released the album *Mission to Please*. Ronald and Ernie hooked up several years later for *Eternal* (2001), a brand-new selection of R&B cuts featuring collaborative efforts with Jill Scott, Jimmy Jam and Terry Lewis, and Raphael Saadiq. On that particular release, Ronald also introduced the alter ego Mr. Biggs.

Sam & Dave

Formed 1961 in Miami, FL

Perhaps no act epitomized soul music as the secularization of gospel more than Sam & Dave. The original pairing of Sam Moore and Dave Prater met in Florida in 1961, and they recorded unsuccessfully for several years before being signed to Atlantic Records in 1965. Atlantic persuaded their Memphis affiliate Stax Records to produce them, and in December that year the writing and production team of Isaac Hayes and David Porter delivered the crisply soulful "You Don't Know Like I Know." Hayes and Porter became the *éminence grises* behind Sam & Dave, much as Holland-Dozier-Holland pulled the strings behind the Supremes. They wrote, they produced—and the result was a string of hits, including "Soul Man," "Hold On! I'm Comin'," and "I Thank You," songs that survive as the very epitome of Southern soul. Certainly, Sam & Dave's hits are among the most soulful ever to crack the Hot 100. Their albums often bore the hallmarks of hasty execution, though. The dissolution of the partnership between Stax and Atlantic virtually sealed the fate of Sam & Dave; there were a few more hits (and, later, a revival of interest thanks to the Blues Brothers), but the glory days were over.

Samuel Moore and David Prater were both raised in the South, where they sang in church as children. During the '50s, they performed in soul and R&B clubs before meeting each other at the King of Hearts club in Miami in 1961. Moore was hosting an amateur-night contest where Prater was singing. Once Dave forgot the lyrics to Jackie Wilson's "Doggin' Around," Sam coached him through the song. Following that night, the singers became a duo and soon became a popular local Miami act and signed with Roulette Records, releasing a handful of singles. In 1965, they signed with Atlantic Records, but producer Jerry Wexler moved the band to the label's Stax subsidiary.

Working with Stax's house band and songwriters/producers Isaac Hayes and David Porter, Sam & Dave created a body of sweaty, gritty soul that ranks among the finest and most popular produced in the late '60s. The duo's 1966 debut, "You Don't' Know Like I Know," kicked off a series of Top Ten R&B hits that included "Hold On! I'm Comin'" (1966), "You Got Me Hummin'" (1966), "When Something Is Wrong With My Baby" (1967), "Soul Man" (1967), and "I Thank You" (1968). However, the duo's career began to unravel in 1968, when Stax's distribution deal with Atlantic ended. Since Sam & Dave were signed with Atlantic, not Stax, they no longer had access to the production team of Hayes and Porter or the house band of Booker T. & the MG's, and their recorded work took a slight dip in quality. Though the switch of labels was unfortunate, what really caused the duo's demise was their volatile relationship. While the duo had enormous creative energy, they frequently fought off-stage. Nicknamed "Double Dynamite," Sam & Dave became famous for their energetic, infectious live performances during the late '60s, which complemented the overall high quality of their studio work. They may have communicated on-stage, but behind the scenes, it was reported that the duo could hardly stand each other's presence. The tension caused Sam & Dave to part ways in 1970, just a few years after their heyday.

During the '70s, Sam & Dave reunited several times to little attention. At the end of the decade, John Belushi and Dan Aykroyd's Blues Brothers routine—which borrowed heavily from Sam & Dave—sparked a resurgence of interest in the duo, and the pair performed a number of concerts during 1980. However, their personal animosity had not faded, and they separated after a performance on New Year's Eve 1981. For the next few years, Prater toured as Sam & Dave with vocalist Sam Daniels. During the mid-'80s, Moore revealed the sources of the duo's tensions in a series of interviews. He disclosed that he had been addicted to drugs during the '70s. Prater was arrested in 1987 for selling crack to an undercover policeman. A year later, he died in a car accident. Moore continued to perform sporadically, most notably on Bruce Springsteen's 1992 album *Human Touch*. Sam & Dave were inducted into the Rock & Roll Hall of Fame that same year.

Percy Sledge

Born Nov 25, 1941 in Leighton, AL

Percy Sledge will forever be associated with "When a Man Loves a Woman," a pleading, soulful ballad he sang with wrenching, convincing anguish and passion. Sledge sang all of his songs that way, delivering them in a powerful rush where he quickly changed from soulful belting to quavering, tearful pleas. It was a voice that made him one of the key figures of deep Southern soul during the late '60s. Sledge recorded at Muscle Shoals studios in Alabama, where he frequently sang songs written by Spooner Oldham and Dan Penn. Not only did he sing deep soul, but Sledge was among the pioneers of country-soul, singing songs by Charlie Rich and Kris Kristofferson in a gritty, passionate style. During the '70s, his commercial success quickly faded away, but Sledge continued to tour and record into the '90s.

While he worked as a hospital nurse in the early '60s, Sledge began his professional music career as a member of the Southern soul vocal group the Esquires Combo. On the advice of local disc jockey Quin Ivy, he went solo in 1966. Ivy fancied himself a record producer and he agreed to help shape Sledge's song "When a Man Loves a Woman" into a full-fledged single, hiring Spooner Oldham to play a distinctive, legato organ phrase. Ivy released the single independently and quickly licensed it to Atlantic Records, who quickly bought out Sledge's contract. "When a Man Loves a Woman" became a huge hit in the summer of 1966, topping both the pop and R&B charts. It was quickly followed that year by two Top Ten R&B hits, "Warm and Tender Love" and "It Tears Me Up," which were both in the vein of his first hit. Although few of his subsequent singles were hits—only "Take Time to Know Her" reached the R&B Top Ten in 1968—many of the songs, which were often written by Dan Penn and/or Oldham, were acknowledged as classics among soul aficionados.

Despite his strong reputation among deep soul fans, Sledge's sales had declined considerably by the early '70s, and he headed out on the club circuit in America and England. In 1974, he left Atlantic for Capricorn Records, where he surprisingly returned to the R&B Top 20 with "I'll Be Your Everything." Instead of re-igniting his career, the single was a last gasp, as far as chart success was concerned. Over the next two decades he continued to tour, and in the late '80s, "When a Man Loves a Woman" experienced a resurgence in popularity, due to its inclusion in movie soundtracks and in television commercials. Following its appearance in a 1987 Levi commercial in the U.K., the single was re-released and climbed to number two. Two years later, he won the Rhythm and Blues Foundation's Career Achievement Award. Sledge was able to turn this revived popularity into a successful career by touring constantly, playing over 100 shows a year into the '90s. In 1994, he released *Blue Night*, his first collection of new material in over a decade, to uniformly positive reviews.

Kim Weston

Born: Agatha Natalie Weston

Born Dec 30, 1939 in Detroit, MI

Best known as a duet partner of Marvin Gaye, Kim Weston also charted with some of her own solo sides during the '60s, although she never had the breakout success of a Martha Reeves or Diana Ross. Born Agatha Natalie Weston in Detroit in 1939, she started singing in her church choir at age three, and by her teenage years had joined a touring gospel group called the Wright Specials. She signed with Motown during the company's early days, scoring a minor R&B hit in 1963 with "Love Me All the Way." The following year, she recorded her first duet with Gaye, "What Good Am I Without You," but made the tactical error of turning down a chance to record "Dancing in the Street," which subsequently became a smash hit for Martha & the Vandellas. She enjoyed her biggest solo hit in 1965 with "Take Me in Your Arms (Rock Me a Little While)" and followed it up in 1966 with the equally soulful "Helpless," both of which helped make her reputation among soul collectors. Also in 1966, she cut an entire album of duets with Gaye, *Take Two*, which produced the Top Five R&B classic "It Takes Two." By the time it was peaking on the charts in early 1967, however, Weston had already left Motown; she and her husband, producer William "Mickey" Stevenson, moved to MGM, but a pair of albums there (*For the First Time* and *This Is America*) proved to be commercial failures. Weston subsequently recorded for Volt (*Kim Kim Kim*), People (*Big Brass Four Poster*, an album of jazz standards with the Hastings Street Jazz Experience), and Johnny Nash's Banyan Tree, all without much success. She did, however, chart with her version of the anthem "Lift Ev'ry Voice and Sing" in 1970. Weston largely disappeared from the music industry during the '70s; in 1987, Weston became the first of many Motown artists to work with British producer Ian Levine on the Motorcity label, re-recording many of her old hits for the Northern soul market; her two albums for Motorcity, 1990's *Investigate* and 1992's *Talking Loud*, also featured some new material.

Disco

Disco marked the dawn of the modern era of dance-based popular music. Growing out of the increasingly groove-oriented sound of early '70s and funk, disco emphasized the beat above anything else, even the singer and the song. Disco was named after discotheques, clubs that played nothing but music for dancing. Most of the discotheques were gay clubs in New York, and the DJs in these clubs specifically picked soul and funk records that had a strong, heavy groove. After being played in the disco, the records began receiving radio play and respectable sales. Soon, record companies and producers were cutting records created specifically for discos. Naturally, these records also had strong pop hooks, so they could have crossover success. Disco albums frequently didn't have many tracks—they had a handful of long songs that kept the beat going. Similarly, the singles were issued on 12-inch records, which allowed for extended remixes. DJs could mix these tracks together, matching the beats on each song since they were marked with how fast they were in terms of beats per minute. In no time, the insistent, pounding disco beat dominated the pop chart, and everyone cut a disco record, from rockers like the Rolling Stones and Rod Stewart to pop acts like the Bee Gees and new wave artists like Blondie. There were disco artists that became stars—Donna Summer, Chic, the Village People, and KC & the Sunshine Band were brand names—but the music was primarily a producer's medium, since they created the tracks and wrote the songs. Disco lost momentum as the '70s became the '80s, but it didn't die—it mutated into a variety of different dance-based genres, ranging from dance-pop and hip-hop to house and techno.

Hues Corporation

Formed 1969 in Los Angeles, CA
Disbanded in 1977

A Los Angeles vocal trio, the Hues Corporation enjoyed two big hits in the mid-'70s, notably "Rock the Boat" in 1974 for RCA. While it was lightweight, mainly pop work, it did take The Hues Corporation to number two on the R&B charts and get them their lone pop chart topper. The next single, "Rockin' Soul," peaked at number six on the R&B charts and number 18 on the pop charts. They had their final R&B hit the next year with "Love Corporation," which reached number 15, but it was evident that the audience was losing interest in their material. "I Caught Your Act" was the last release in 1977. H. Ann Kelley, Flemming Williams, and Bernard "St. Clair Lee" Henderson were the original lineup. Tom Brown replaced Williams in the wake of "Rock the Boat's" success. He was then replaced by Karl Russell in 1975. —Ron Wynn

Van McCoy

Born: Jan 6, 1944 in Washington, D.C.
Died: Jul 6, 1979 in Englewood, NJ

Although best known to the listening public at large for his lone headlining hit, the disco blockbuster "The Hustle," Van McCoy in fact enjoyed a long and remarkably prolific career behind the scenes as a songwriter and producer, piling up a series of soul hits prior to his premature death at the age of just 39. Born Van Allen Clinton McCoy on January 6, 1940, in Washington, D.C., as a child he sang with the Metropolitan Baptist Church choir, and by the age of 12 he was writing his own songs in addition to performing in local amateur shows alongside older brother, Norman Jr.

The McCoy siblings eventually partnered with high-school friends Freddy Smith and Paul Comedy in the doo wop combo the Starlighters. Serving as their lead vocalist, writer, and music director, Van masterminded the Starlighters' 1956 debut single, "The Birdland," a novelty dance record that generated enough local interest to earn them an invitation to tour the East Coast in support of drummer Vi Burnsides. As military and marital obligations forced the group to dissolve during the months to follow, McCoy entered Howard University to study psychology, but dropped out after a year to pursue a full-time career in music, relocating to Philadelphia and forming his own label, Rockin' Records. In 1959 Rockin' issued McCoy's debut solo single, "Hey Mr. DJ." While not a major hit, the record did earn the attention of Scepter Records owner Florence Greenberg, who hired him as a staff writer and A&R rep—there he penned the 1962 hit "Stop the Music" for the Shirelles before signing on with producers Jerry Lieber and Mike Stoller as a writer with their Tiger and Daisy labels. Over the next several years McCoy penned a series of hits, among them Jackie Wilson's "I Get the Sweetest Feeling," Gladys Knight & the Pips' "Giving Up," Betty Everett's "Getting Mighty Crowded," Ruby & the Romantics' "When You're Young and in Love," and—best of all—Barbara Lewis' celestial "Baby, I'm Yours." With then-girlfriend Kendra Spotswood, he also wrote, produced, and performed a series of pseudonymous singles, including the Pacettes' "You Don't Know Baby," Jack & Jill's "Two of a Kind," and the Fantastic Vantastics' "Gee What a Boy." (Under the name Sandi Sheldon, Spotswood also recorded the McCoy-penned stomper "You're Gonna Make Me Love You," one of the crown jewels of Britain's Northern soul club scene.)

In 1966 McCoy signed to Columbia to record a solo LP, the Mitch Miller-produced *Nighttime Is a Lonely Time*; the following year he formed his own short-lived label, Vando, as well as his own production company, VMP (Van McCoy Productions, natch). Beginning in 1971, McCoy began a long and fruitful collaboration with fellow songwriter and producer Charles Kipps—together they helmed a series of sessions, including David Ruffin's acclaimed 1975 Motown comeback, *Who I Am*, which yielded the smash "Walk Away from Love." McCoy also arranged several hits for Philly soul legends the Stylistics, but despite his success as a writer and producer, he still sought approval as a performer. In 1972 he issued a solo LP, *Soul Improvisations* (later retitled *From Disco to Love*), but it went nowhere.

Expectations were similarly low for 1975's Avco label effort *Disco Baby*—McCoy authored "The Hustle" after hearing about the dance from New York City disc jockey David Todd, and the song, written in under an hour, was the last track recorded for the album. "The Hustle" went on to top the Billboard pop charts in July 1975, also earning a Grammy, although McCoy acknowledged he felt extreme discomfort in his new and narrow role as a disco hitmaker—a series of follow-up albums (among them *The Disco Kid*, 1976's *The Real McCoy* and *Rhythms of the World*, and 1979's *Lonely Dancer*) failed to recapture the massive popularity of "The Hustle," however, and he gradually receded back into the shadows, producing new talent including Faith, Hope & Charity. He died of a massive heart attack in Englewood, NJ, on July 6, 1979, exactly six months shy of his 40th birthday. —Jason Ankeny

Silver Convention

Formed 1974 in Munich, Germany

Best remembered for their disco smash "Fly Robin Fly," the Munich, Germany-based ensemble Silver Convention was formed by producers Silvester Levay and Michael Kunze, debuting in 1975 with the LP *Save Me* and scoring a U.K. hit with the title track. After topping the American charts with "Fly Robin Fly," Levay and Kunze recruited a trio of vocalists—Linda Thompson (not to be confused with the same-named singer and wife of guitarist Richard Thompson), Ramona Wulf, and Penny McLean—who began appearing publicly under the Silver Convention banner; they were featured on the follow-up, "Get Up and Boogie (That's Right)," which was also a smash in 1976. While another single, "Telegram," proved a success that same year in the annual Eurovision Song Contest, Silver Convention's popularity quickly faded, and by the end of the decade the group was no more. —Jason Ankeny

Rose Royce

Formed 1973 in Los Angeles, CA

Rose Royce—the Los Angeles-based group comprised of Henry Garner (drums), Terral "Terry" Santiel (congas), Lequeint "Duke" Jobe (bass), Michael Moore (saxophone), Rose Norwalt (lead vocals), Kenny Copeland (trumpet, lead vocals), Kenji Brown (guitar, lead vocals), Freddie Dunn (trumpet), and Michael Nash (keyboards)—was actually formed by Copeland and Garner. Both were preparing for graduation from high school, and contemplating their careers. Joined by Dunn and Moore, the two decided to go the route of the music business under the name Total Concept Unlimited (and later as Magic Wand). They auditioned for Edwin Starr, and he hired them as his backup band.

The group's association with Starr enabled them to interact with numerous music industry personalities. One in particular was Motown producer Norman Whitfield. Whitfield gradually became associated with the group by hiring them for recording sessions; the group also worked with Yvonne Fair, the Undisputed Truth, and the Temptations through Whitfield's influence. After a couple of years of seasoning, the group began production on their debut album under Whitfield's supervision. Also during this time, MCA Records was seeking an artist for the soundtrack to the movie *Car Wash*. Whitfield convinced executives that the band was more than competent for the job. So the material that Whitfield had assembled for the group's debut album became the soundtrack's material.

The movie *Car Wash* and the soundtrack were big hits, and they also propelled the group, now known as Rose Royce, into national notoriety. Released in late 1976, the soundtrack featured three Billboard R&B Top Ten singles: "Car Wash," "I Wanna Get Next to You," and "I'm Going Down." The former was also a number one single on the Billboard pop charts.

To offset any negative rhetoric regarding their legitimacy, the group released its follow-up album, *Rose Royce II: In Full Bloom*, and bloom it did. The group returned to the Top Ten with "Do Your Dance" and "Ooh Boy," silencing all critics. In 1978, they released their third album, entitled *Rose Royce III: Strikes Again!*, and it featured "I'm in Love (And I Love the Feeling)" and "Love Don't Live Here Anymore." Both singles cracked the Billboard R&B Top Five.

The group followed with a string of hits that roamed the charts, but never gained the chart status that their previous songs did. They became very popular in England and remain a marquee attraction there. —Craig Lytle

Thelma Houston

Born May 7, 1943 in Leland, MS

Singer Thelma Houston is best known for her number one pop classic disco cover of "Don't Leave This Way." Originally a hit for Harold Melvin and the Blue Notes featuring Teddy Pendergrass, the Gamble & Huff/Cary Gilbert song soars through the gospel music-honed vocals of the Leland, MS, native. Houston's energetic performance takes the song in the same way that Aretha Franklin takes "Repect"—with no disrespect to either artist.

The singer came from humble beginnings. Her mother picked cotton to support Houston and her three sisters. During her youth, the family relocated to Long Beach, CA. As an adult, Houston graduated from high school, got married, had two children, and was later divorced. She got a job in the health care field. Staying active in music, she became a member of the Art Reynolds Singers, singing lead on their popular single cover of "Glory Glory Hallelujah," on Capitol. Fifth Dimension manager Marc Gordon was impressed by her vocal skills and helped to get her a recording deal with Dunhill Records. In 1969, renowned songwriter Jimmy Webb produced her debut LP *Wildflower*. One single, a cover of Laura Nyro's "Save the Country," charted in early 1970.

During 1971, Houston signed with Motown, with her label debut *Thelma Houston* being issued on the MoWest imprint. Over the next few years, the singer issued numerous singles that failed to be hits, though one Motown single, the catchy "You've Been Doing Wrong for So Long," lingered in the lower half of the R&B charts. She can be seen in the classic Billy Dee Williams/James Earl Jones Negro League baseball movie, *The Bingo Long Traveling All Stars and Motor Kings*, produced by Motown and released through Universal Pictures. Houston's background vocals are woven throughout

Jermaine Jackson's 1976 gold LP, *My Name Is Jermaine*.

Finally, synchronicity in Houston's favor came in a big way in the form of the release of the 1976 LP *Any Way You Like It*, produced by Hal Davis (Diana Ross' "Love Hangover") and issued on Motown's Tamla imprint. Davis had heard the Blue Notes' version at a party while he was in the process of recording tracks for the album. First taking off in disco and on both disco-oriented and soul music radio stations, "Don't Leave This Way," went to number one R&B in February 1977 and number one pop in April 1977 (Billboard). It can be found on Rhino's *Disco Box, Billboard Top Hits: 1975–1979, Disco Nights, Vol. 9: Motown Dance, 70s Disco Ball Party Pack*, and *The Disco Years, Vol. 1: Turn the Beat Around*. A 12" version is on *Pure Disco* [Polygram] and *Essential 12": The 70s*.

Her other hits include "If It's the Last Thing I Do," "I'm Here Again," "Saturday Night, Sunday Morning," and the RCA single "If You Feel It." A pre-mega stardom Jimmy Jam and Terry Lewis produced the smooth, percolating Top 20 R&B dance track, "You Used to Hold Me So Tight," from her 1984 MCA album, *Qualifying Heat*. She duets with the Winans on a cover of Bill Withers' "Lean on Me," the title track of the same named 1989 Morgan Freeman movie. She does backing vocals on guitarist Scott Henderson's 1997 Atlantic CD, *Tore Down House*.

Thelma Houston appeared on cable channel VH1's *100 Greatest Dance Songs* during October 2000. —Ed Hogan

Donna Summer

Born Dec 31, 1948 in Boston, MA

Donna Summer's title as the "Queen of Disco" wasn't mere hype—she was one of the very few disco performers to enjoy a measure of career longevity, and her consistent chart success was rivaled in the disco world only by the Bee Gees. Summer was certainly a talented vocalist, trained as a powerful gospel belter, but then again, so were many of her contemporaries. Of major importance in setting Summer apart were her songwriting abilities and her choice of talented collaborators in producers/songwriters Giorgio Moroder and Pete Bellotte, which resulted in a steady supply of high-quality (and, often, high-concept) material. But what was more, few vocalists could match the sultry, unfettered eroticism Summer brought to many of her best recordings, which seemed to embody the spirit of the disco era perfectly. The total package made Summer the ultimate disco diva, one of the few whose star power was even bigger than the music.

Summer was born LaDonna Andre Gaines on December 31, 1948, and grew up in Boston's Mission Hill section. Part of a religious family, she first sang in her church's gospel choir, and as a teenager performed with a rock group called the Crow. After high school, she moved to New York to sing and act in stage productions, and soon landed a role in a German production of Hair. She moved to Europe around 1968–1969, and spent a year in the German cast, after which she became part of the Hair company in Vienna. She joined the Viennese Folk Opera, and later returned to Germany, where she settled in Munich and met and married Helmut Sommer, adopting an Anglicized version of his last name. Summer performed in various stage musicals and worked as a studio vocalist in Munich, recording demos and background vocals. Her first solo recording was 1971's "Sally Go 'Round the Roses," but success would not come until 1974, when she met producers/songwriters Giorgio Moroder and Pete Bellotte while working on a Three Dog Night record. The three teamed up for the single "The Hostage," which became a hit around Western Europe, and Summer released her first album, *Lady of the Night*, in Europe only. In 1975, the trio recorded "Love to Love You Baby," a disco-fied reimagining of Serge Gainsbourg and Jane Birkin's lush, heavy-breathing opus "Je T'aime . . . Moi Non Plus." Powered by Summer's graphic moans, "Love to Love You Baby" became a massive hit in Europe, and drew the attention of Casablanca Records, which put the track out in America. It climbed to number two on the singles charts, and became a dance-club sensation when Moroder remixed the track into a 17-minute, side-long epic on the LP of the same name.

In the wake of "Love to Love You Baby," albums (as opposed to just singles) became an important forum for Summer and her producers. The 1976 follow-up *Love Trilogy* contained another side-long suite in "Try Me (I Know We Can Make It Work)," and demonstrated Moroder and Bellotte's growing sophistication as arrangers with its lush, sweeping strings. *Four Seasons of Love*, released later in the year, was a concept album with one track dedicated to each season, and 1977's *I Remember Yesterday* featured a variety of genre exercises. Despite the album's title, it produced the most forward-looking single in Summer and Moroder's catalog, the monumental "I Feel Love." Eschewing the strings and typical disco excess, "I Feel Love" was the first major pop hit recorded with an entirely synthesized backing track; its lean, sleek arrangement and driving, hypnotic pulse laid the groundwork not only for countless Euro-dance imitators, but also for the techno revolution of the '80s and '90s. It became Summer's second Top Ten hit in the U.S., and she followed it with *Once Upon a Time*, another concept album, this one retelling the story of Cinderella for the disco era.

Summer's albums were selling well, bolstered by her popularity in the dance clubs, and she was poised to become a major pop hitmaker as well. Her acting turn in the 1978 disco-themed comedy *Thank God It's Friday* produced another hit in "Last Dance," which won her a Grammy for Best Female R&B Vocal (as well as an Oscar for songwriter Paul Jabara). Doubtlessly benefiting from the added exposure, the double-LP set *Live and More* became Summer's first number one album later that year. It featured one side of new studio material, including a disco cover of the psychedelic pop epic "MacArthur Park" that became her first number one pop single early the next year. Her 1979 double-LP *Bad Girls* featured more of her songwriting contributions than ever, and went straight to number one, as did the lusty singles "Bad Girls" and the rock-oriented "Hot Stuff," which made Summer the first female artist ever to score three number one singles in the same calendar year. Her greatest-hits package *On the Radio* also topped the charts, the first time any artist had ever hit number one with three consecutive double LPs; the newly recorded title track became another hit, and Summer's duet with Barbra Streisand, "No More Tears (Enough Is Enough)," became her fourth number one single.

At the peak of her success, Summer decided to leave Casablanca, and became the first artist signed to the new Geffen label. Sensing that the disco era was coming to a close, Summer attempted to modify her style to include more R&B and pop/rock on her first Geffen album, 1980's *The Wanderer*; the album and its title track were both hits. Not wanting to alienate her core audience, Summer returned to pure dance music on an attempted follow-up; however, Geffen deemed *I'm a Rainbow* not worthy of release (it was finally issued in 1996). Instead, Summer ended her collaboration with Moroder and Bellotte and teamed up with Quincy Jones for 1982's *Donna Summer*. "Love Is in Control (Finger on the Trigger)" was a significant hit, but none of its follow-ups did very well. With producer Michael Omartian, Summer moved back into post-disco dance music and urban R&B with 1983's *She Works Hard for the Money*; its title track was a smash and became a feminist anthem of sorts. However, with her career momentum slowing, it also marked the end of Summer's prime. Despite winning a gospel Grammy for "Forgive Me," Summer's 1984 follow-up *Cats Without Claws* flopped, as did the 1987 comeback effort *All Systems Go*. Hiring the British production team of Stock, Aitken & Waterman, Summer scored her last major success with the 1989 Top Ten single "This Time I Know It's for Real," from the album *Another Place & Time*; around the same time, she began denouncing her earlier, "sinful" disco material. 1991's lackluster, urban-styled *Mistaken Identity* effectively killed her career momentum, and none of her new '90s albums produced that elusive hit. However, she did make some noise on the dance charts with "Melody of Love," from the excellent 1994 retrospective *Endless Summer*, and reunited with Moroder for the 1997 non-LP single "Carry On," which won the inaugural Grammy for Best Dance Recording. Summer subsequently signed a deal with Sony, which primed her for re-establishment with the 1999 greatest-hits live album *VH1 Presents: Live and More Encore!*; it featured the new song "I Will Go With You (Con Te Partiro)," which had some success on the dance charts. —Steve Huey

The Trammps

Formed 1973 in Philadelphia, PA
Disbanded in 1980

Disco's most soulful vocal group began in the '60s as the Volcanos, and were also called the Moods. Gene Faith was the original lead vocalist, with Earl Young, Jimmy Ellis, guitarist Dennis Harris, keyboardist Ron Kersey, organist John Hart, bassist Stanley Wade, and drummer Michael Thomas. But by the time they'd gone through various identities and emerged as the Trammps in the mid-'70s, the lineup featured lead vocalist Ellis, Harold and Stanley Wade, Robert

Upchurch, and Young. A snappy revival of Judy Garland's '40s tune "Zing Went the Strings of My Heart" was their first chart single, reaching number 17 on the R&B list in 1972. Despite their well-deserved reputation and boisterous, jubilant harmonies and sound, the Trammps were never huge commercial successes even during disco's heyday. Indeed, they had only three R&B Top Ten hits from 1972 through 1978, and such wonderful records as "Soul Bones," "Ninety-Nine and a Half," and "I Feel Like I've Been Livin' (On the Dark Side of the Moon)" stiffed on the charts though they were beloved by club audiences and R&B fans alike. Their only huge hit was "Disco Inferno" in 1977, which was a number nine R&B single in 1977 and was also featured in *Saturday Night Fever*. Yet it missed the pop Top Ten, peaking at number 11. But the Trammps' prowess can't be measured by chart popularity; Ellis' booming, joyous vocals brilliantly championed the celebratory fervor and atmosphere that made disco both beloved and hated among music fans. —Ron Wynn

Evelyn Champagne King

Born Jun 29, 1960 in New York, NY [The Bronx]

Singer Evelyn "Champagne" King first came to fame with the million-selling '70s disco smashes "Shame" and "I Don't Know If It's Right." Born July 1, 1960, in the Bronx, NY, she had a showbiz lineage. Her uncle was actor/singer/dancer Avon Long, who first played Sportin' Life in the play *Porgy and Bess* and later starred in the '70s play *Bubblin' Brown Sugar*. Her father, Erik King, was a singer and often augmented groups that appeared at New York's Apollo Theater. By her teens, King had relocated to Philadelphia with her mother, and began singing in several groups. To make ends meet, King and her mother became cleaning women. For a teenager, King's voice was quite mature; many at first thought she was a grown woman.

While working one night at Philadelphia International Records' recording base, producer T. Life overheard some tantalizing vocals coming from a washroom. There he discovered 16-year-old Evelyn King and her mother. Signing the singer to a production deal and a contract with RCA, Life's first single with Evelyn "Champagne" King was "Dancin' Dancin' Dancin'." Her debut LP *Smooth Talk* was released August 1977. But it was a song written by John Fitch and Reuben Cross called "Shame," that gave her career-launching success. The extended mix began gaining radio play and eventually the Top Ten on the R&B and pop charts by spring 1978. The follow-up, "I Don't Know If It's Right" also went gold, peaking at number seven R&B, number 23 pop in fall 1978. *Smooth Talk* went gold, and she made two more LPs with T. Life: *Music Box* and *Call on Me*.

After teaming with a new producer, Kashif, King recorded two number one R&B hits during the early '80s, "I'm in Love" and "Love Come Down." Several of her LPs also placed high on the charts, including 1980's *Call on Me*, the following year's *I'm in Love*, and 1982's *Get Loose*. She signed to EMI-Manhattan in 1988, and was teamed with Leon F. Sylvers III for *Flirt*, which included the tender ballad

"Kisses Don't Lie." On *The Girl Next Door*, the singer worked with house producer Marshall Jefferson.

In 1990, King recorded the album *I'll Keep a Light On* for the British label Expansion, whose featured musicians were Larry Graham, Jeff Lorber, and Paul Jackson, Jr. Many of the singer's classic sides are on *Love Come Down: The Best of Evelyn "Champagne" King*. —Ed Hogan

A Taste of Honey

Formed 1971 in Los Angeles, CA

A Taste of Honey had two huge hits that were very dissimilar from each other— "Boogie Oogie Oogie" and a cover of Kyu Sakamoto's 1963 gold hit "Sukiyaki." The former was foot-stomping disco and the latter was languid and lush. Around 1971, singer/bassist/guitarist Janice Marie Johnson and keyboardist Perry Kimble decided to start a band after meeting at an audition for vacation cruise gigs for Princess Cruises. Taking their group name from one of their favorite songs, the band added several friends to the lineup and began playing Southern California bars and military bases in the U.S. and abroad. Their lead singer, Greg Walker, quit to join Santana and guitarist Hazel Payne was added. After meeting with producer Fonce Mizell and his brother Larry, the group were signed to Capitol Records.

The group's first single, "Boogie Oogie Oogie," was inspired by an unresponsive audience during a date at a military base; Johnson believed the crowd was chauvinistic toward the group's two female guitar players. The notorious bass solo intro came about when Johnson was warming up before the recording session, unaware that she was being recorded. The single sold more than two million copies and topped Billboard's charts for three weeks in fall 1978. The follow-up single, the slinky and funky "Do It Good," went to number 13 R&B and number 79 pop, and *A Taste of Honey* went platinum.

After hearing Linda Ronstadt's version of Smokey Robinson's "Ooh Baby Baby," Johnson decided that the group (now Johnson and Payne) should remake a classic song. In their pre-Capitol days, Johnson used to sing the lyrics to Sakamoto's "Sukiyaki" when the group toured Japan and performed at the Yamaha Song Festival. She contacted her Japanese sub-publisher, who in turn contacted the original writers, Ei Rokusuke and Hashida Nakamura Rokusuke, to get permission to redo the song with English lyrics. Two translators were employed, and one of them came up with lyrics that were close to the maudlin theme of the original song, translated into English as "I Look up When I Walk." Johnson decided to add her own original lyrics to the song. At first she thought her lyrics were too simple, but producer George Duke encouraged her to write from her heart. A publishing-rights dispute almost stopped the song from being released. After it was recorded, Johnson found out that one of the original writers had signed his rights away years before. His publisher had Johnson give up all songwriting and publishing rights to her new version before Capitol was able to release it. The bassist relented, knowing that this song would be the one to take A Taste of Honey out of the disco category. But Capitol wasn't too keen on "Sukiyaki," promising to release it as a single but then releasing "Rescue Me" (number 16 R&B, summer 1980) and "I'm Talkin 'Bout You" (number 64 R&B, late 1980). Others discouraged Johnson for donning Japanese attire and doing a fan dance while performing the song. Forced by album track radio play, the label finally released "Sukiyaki" as a single, which went to number one R&B and number three pop in spring 1981. The *Twice as Sweet* LP went to number 36 pop in spring 1981. After "Sukiyaki" was a hit, the duo went to Japan and toured with Kyu Sakamoto. A Taste of Honey also covered Smokey Robinson & the Miracles' "I'll Try Something New." Johnson released a solo Capitol LP, *One Taste of Honey*, which yielded a charting single, the softly "Sukiyaki"-ish "Love Me Tonite," (number 67 R&B), in summer 1984. The Burger King national fast food chain began using "Boogie Oogie Oogie" in a national TV ad campaign in summer 1999, introducing another generation to the late-'70s smash. The track has also been sampled by hip-hop and rap artists MC Lyte, Mack 10, and others. Around the same time, Johnson announced plans for an EP, *Hiatus of the Heart*, for her own Tastebuds label to be released in 2000. She also said she had projects with Ice Cube and Con Funk Shun founder Felton C. Pilate II. Payne tours Japan with her own Top 40 band. Perry Kimble died in 1999. A Taste of Honey's greatest hits can be found on *Anthology* (One Way, 1995) and "Sukiyaki" is listed on *Smooth Grooves: A Sensual Collection, Vol. 7* (Rhino, 1996). —Ed Hogan

Village People

Formed 1977 in New York, NY

Part clever concept, part exaggerated camp act, the Village People were worldwide sensations during disco's heyday and keep reviving like the phoenix. Producer Jacques Morali in 1977 assembled a group designed to attract gay audiences while parodying (some claimed exploiting) that same constituency's stereotypes. Songwriters Phil Hurtt and Peter Whitehead were tabbed to compose songs with gay underpinnings, and roles and costumes were carefully selected; among them were a cowboy, biker, soldier, policeman, and construction worker complete with hard hat. The group clicked first in England with the single "San Francisco (You Got Me)" in 1977, then reaped stateside honors with "Macho Man" in 1978. "Y.M.C.A." and "In the Navy" were worldwide smashes, both peaking at number two on the pop charts. After two more successful singles, "Go West" and "Can't Stop the Music," the group's fortunes plummeted, in large part due to their participation in the ill-fated film also titled *Can't Stop the Music*. —Ron Wynn

Chic

Formed 1977 in New York, NY

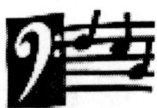
There can be little argument that Chic was disco's greatest band; and, working in a heavily producer-dominated field, they were most definitely a *band*. By the time Chic appeared in the late '70s, disco

was already slipping into the excess that eventually caused its downfall. Chic bucked the trend by stripping disco's sound down to its basic elements; their funky, stylish grooves had an organic sense of interplay that was missing from many of their overproduced competitors. Chic's sound was anchored by the scratchy, James Brown-style rhythm guitar of Nile Rodgers and the indelible, widely imitated (sometimes outright stolen) bass lines of Bernard Edwards; as producers, they used keyboard and string embellishments economically, which kept the emphasis on rhythm. Chic's distinctive approach not only resulted in some of the finest dance singles of their time, but also helped create a template for urban funk, dance-pop, and even hip-hop in the post-disco era. Not coincidentally, Rodgers and Edwards wound up as two of the most successful producers of the '80s.

Rodgers and Edwards first met in 1970, when both were jazz-trained musicians fresh out of high school. Edwards had attended New York's High School for the Performing Arts and was working in a Bronx post office at the time, while Rodgers' early career also included stints in the folk group New World Rising and the Apollo Theater house orchestra. Around 1972, Rodgers and Edwards formed a jazz-rock fusion group called the Big Apple Band. This outfit moonlighted as a backup band, touring behind smooth soul vocal group New York City in the wake of their 1973 hit "I'm Doin' Fine Now." After New York City broke up, the Big Apple Band hit the road with Carol Douglas for a few months, and Rodgers and Edwards decided to make a go of it on their own toward the end of 1976. At first they switched their aspirations from fusion to new wave, briefly performing as Allah & the Knife Wielding Punks, but quickly settled into dance music. They enlisted onetime LaBelle drummer Tony Thompson and female vocalists Norma Jean Wright and Alfa Anderson, and changed their name to Chic in summer 1977 so as to avoid confusion with Walter Murphy & the Big Apple Band (who'd just hit big with "A Fifth of Beethoven").

Augmented in the studio by keyboardists Raymond Jones and Rob Sabino, Chic recorded the demo single "Dance, Dance, Dance (Yowsah, Yowsah, Yowsah)" and shopped it around to several major record companies, all of which declined it. The small Buddah label finally released it as a 12" in late 1977, and as its club popularity exploded, Atlantic stepped in, signed the group, and re-released the single on a wider basis. "Dance, Dance, Dance" hit the Top Ten, peaking at number six, and made Chic one of the hottest new groups in disco. Chic scrambled to put together their self-titled first album, which spawned a minor follow-up hit, "Everybody Dance," in early 1978. At this point, Wright left to try her hand at a solo career (with assistance from Rodgers and Edwards), and was replaced by Luci Martin. It was a good time to come onboard; "Le Freak," the first single from sophomore album *C'est Chic*, was an out-of-the-box smash, spending five weeks on top of the charts toward the end of 1978 and selling over four-million copies (which made it the biggest-selling single in Atlantic's history). Follow-up "I Want Your Love" reached number seven, cementing the group's new star status, and *C'est Chic* became one of the rare disco albums to go platinum.

1979's *Risqué* was another solidly constructed LP that also went platinum, partly on the strength of Chic's second number one pop hit, "Good Times." "Good Times" may not have equaled the blockbuster sales figures of "Le Freak," but it was the band's most imitated track: Queen's number one hit "Another One Bites the Dust" was a clear rewrite, and the Sugarhill Gang lifted the instrumental backing track wholesale for the first commercial rap single, "Rapper's Delight," marking the first of many times that Chic grooves would be recycled into hip-hop records. Also in 1979, Rodgers and Edwards took on their first major outside production assignment, producing and writing the Sister Sledge smashes "We Are Family" and the oft-sampled "He's the Greatest Dancer." This success, in turn, landed them the chance to work with Diana Ross on 1980's *Diana* album, and they wrote and produced "Upside Down," her first number one hit in years, as well as "I'm Coming Out."

The disco fad was fading rapidly by that point, however, and 1980's *Real People* failed to go gold despite another solid performance by the band. Changing tastes put an end to Chic's heyday, as Rodgers and Edwards' outside production work soon grew far more lucrative, even despite aborted projects with Aretha Franklin and Johnny Mathis. Several more Chic LPs followed in the early '80s, with diminishing creative and commercial returns, and Rodgers and Edwards disbanded the group after completing the lackluster *Believer* in 1983. Later that year, both recorded solo LPs that sank without a trace. Hungry for acceptance and respect in the rock mainstream (especially after accusations that *they* had ripped off Queen instead of the other way around), both Rodgers and Edwards sought out high-profile production and session work over the rest of the decade. Rodgers produced blockbuster albums like David Bowie's *Let's Dance*, Madonna's *Like a Virgin*, and Mick Jagger's *She's the Boss*. Edwards wasn't as prolific as a producer, but did join the one-off supergroup the Power Station along with Tony Thompson as well as Robert Palmer and members of avowed Chic fans Duran Duran; he later produced Palmer's commercial breakthrough, *Riptide*. Edwards also worked with Rod Stewart (*Out of Order*), Jody Watley, and Tina Turner, while Rodgers' other credits include the Thompson Twins, the Vaughan Brothers, INXS, and the B-52's' comeback *Cosmic Thing*.

Rodgers and Edwards re-formed Chic in 1992 with new vocalists Sylver Logan Sharp and Jenn Thomas, and an assortment of session drummers in Thompson's place; they toured and released a new album, *Chic-ism*. In 1996, the reconstituted Chic embarked on a tour of Japan; sadly, on April 18, Edwards passed away in his Tokyo hotel room due to a severe bout of pneumonia. Rodgers continued to tour occasionally with a version of Chic, and, in 1999, his Sumthing Else label issued a recording of Edwards' final performance with the band, *Live at the Budokan*.
—Steven Thomas Erlewine

Sylvester

Born: Sep 1944 in Los Angeles, CA
Died: Dec 16, 1988 in San Francisco, CA

Along with the Village People, '70s disco artist Sylvester was one of the few artists of the era not afraid to openly acknowledge his homosexuality. Born Sylvester James during September 1944 in Los Angeles, CA, Sylvester was introduced to music at an early age by his grandmother, Julia Morgan, who was a jazz singer. While still a youngster, Sylvester began singing in gospel groups, while finding further inspiration from the likes of Bessie Smith and Billie Holiday, among others. After relocating to San Francisco in the late '60s, Sylvester began to perform in a musical production called Women of the Blues, before becoming the star attraction of a transvestite vocal group called the Cockettes in the early '70s. After leaving the band in 1973, Sylvester signed on with the Hot Band and issued such releases as *Scratch My Flower* and *Bazaar* the same year. Sylvester's dance-happy funk style eventually transformed into disco, as his flamboyant and over-the-top stage act created quite a following for the singer in the San Francisco area. He also issued some of his best-known recordings around the end of the decade—1977's *Sylvester* and 1979's in-concert *Living Proof*—while racking up such popular disco hits as "You Make Me Feel (Mighty Real)" and "Dance (Disco Heat)."

1979 saw Sylvester receive three Billboard awards and another for Best Male Disco Act from *Disco International Magazine*, as well as landing a bit part in Bette Midler's 1979 movie, *The Rose*. But by the dawn of the '80s, disco was being considered increasingly passé and the singer's career began to slow down (funny enough, Sylvester's backup singers, Martha Wash and Izora Rhodes, would go on to form the Weather Girls, and score one of 1982's big dance hits with "It's Raining Men"). Although he continued to issue albums throughout the '80s, Sylvester's career came to an abrupt and tragic end on December 16, 1988, when he died from AIDS-related complications. Despite his passing, Sylvester's music remains popular on dance floors worldwide, while "You Make Me Feel (Mighty Real)" has been covered over the years by three separate artists: former lead singer of Bronski Beat and the Communards Jimmy Somerville (on his 1989 solo debut *Read My Lips*), comedian/actor/singer Sandra Bernhard (on her 1994 release *Excuses for Bad Behavior, Pt. 1*), and by former Ten City lead singer Byron Stingily (on his 1998 solo debut, *The Purist*), whose version hit number one on the U.S. dance chart the same year. —Greg Prato

Kool & the Gang

Formed 1964 in Jersey City, NJ

Formed as a jazz ensemble in the mid-'60s, Kool & the Gang became one of the most inspired and influential funk units during the '70s, and one of the most popular R&B groups of the '80s after their breakout hit "Celebration" in 1979. Just as funky as James Brown or Parliament (and sampled almost as frequently), Kool & the Gang relied on their jazz backgrounds and long friendship to form a tightly knit group with the interplay and improvisation of a jazz outfit, plus the energy and spark of a band with equal ties to soul, R&B, and funk.

Robert "Kool" Bell and his brother Ronald (or Khalis Bayyan) grew up in Jersey City, NJ, and picked up the music bug from their father. A professional boxer, he was also a serious jazz lover and a close friend of Thelonious Monk. With Robert on bass and Ronald picking up an array of horns, the duo formed the Jazziacs in 1964 with several neighborhood friends: trombone player Clifford Adams, guitarists Charles Smith and Woody Sparrow, trumpeter Robert "Spike" Michens, alto saxophonist Dennis Thomas, keyboard player Ricky West, and drummer Funky George Brown (all of whom, except Michens and West, still remained in the group more than 30 years later).

The growing earthiness of soul inspired the Jazziacs to temper their jazz sensibilities with rhythms more akin to R&B, and the newly renamed Soul Town Band began playing clubs in Greenwich Village. After a mix-up with a club owner resulted in the group being billed Kool & the Flames, they moderated the title to Kool & the Gang and found a leg up with the tiny De-Lite Records. Three singles from their self-titled debut album hit the pop charts, and although the position wasn't incredibly high, Kool & the Gang became a quick success on the R&B charts. Always a staple of their appeal, the group's live act was documented on two 1971 LPs, *Live at the Sex Machine* and *Live at P.J.'s*, including left-field covers of "Walk On By" and "Wichita Lineman" (as well as the not so unusual "I Want to Take You Higher").

Studio albums followed in 1972 and 1973, but it was with Kool & the Gang's sixth LP, *Wild and Peaceful*, that they hit the big time. "Funky Stuff" became their first Top 40 hit at the end of 1973. Then both "Jungle Boogie" and "Hollywood Swinging" reached the pop Top Ten. During the next four years, however, Kool & the Gang could only manage an occasional Top 40 hit ("Higher Plane," "Spirit of the Boogie"), and though they did win a Grammy award for "Open Sesame" (from the *Saturday Night Fever* soundtrack), the rise of disco—a movement centered around producers and vocalists, in direct contrast to the group's focus on instrumentalists—had appeared to end their popularity.

Then, in 1979, the group added two new vocalists, Earl Toon, Jr. and, more importantly, James "J.T." Taylor, a former Jersey nightclub singer. Kool & the Gang also began working with jazz fusion arranger Eumir Deodato, who produced their records from 1979 to 1982. The first such album, *Ladies Night*, was their biggest hit yet, the first of three consecutive platinum albums, with the Top Ten singles "Too Hot" and the title track. *Celebrate!*, released in 1980, spawned Kool & the Gang's only number one hit, "Celebration," an anthem favored by innumerable wedding receptions since. With Deodato, the group produced several more hits, including the singles "Take My Heart (You Can Have It if You Want It)," "Get Down on It," and "Big Fun," and the albums *Something Special* in 1981 and *As One* a year later. After Deodato left the fold in late 1982, Kool & the Gang proved their success wasn't solely due to him; they had two immense hits during 1984–1985 ("Joanna" and "Cherish"), as well as two more Top Tens, "Misled" and "Fresh." The group's string of seven gold or platinum records continued until 1986's *Forever*, after which James "J.T." Taylor amicably left the group for a solo career.

Although Taylor did reasonably well with his solo recordings (many of which were produced by Ronald Bell), Kool & the Gang quickly sank without him. They replaced Taylor with three vocalists, Skip Martin (formerly of the Dazz Band), Odeen Mays, and Gary Brown, but failed to chart their albums *Sweat* (1989) and *Unite* (1993). Taylor finally returned to the group in 1995 for the release of a new album, *State of Affairs*. —John Bush

Gloria Gaynor

Born Sep 7, 1949 in Newark, NJ

Perhaps second only to Donna Summer, Gloria Gaynor has become one of the best-known female disco artists from the '70s due to the ongoing success of her monster 1979 hit (and subsequent "woman's anthem"), "I Will Survive." Born Gloria Fowles on September 7, 1949, in Newark, NJ, the singer (who began going by Gloria Gaynor by the early '70s), first sang as part of the obscure R&B outfit the Soul Satisfiers before being discovered by MGM Records head honcho Mike Curb (eventual leader of the Curb label and Lieutenant Governor of California), who decided to sign the singer to his label after several auditions. Gaynor began issuing albums on a regular basis beginning in 1975 and with her 1976 release *Never Can Say Goodbye*, the singer became one of the first-ever dance artists to issue an album aimed primarily for club use (there were no breaks between the songs, as one track would automatically segue into the next), a method used to this day by DJs and certain dance artists.

Although Gaynor enjoyed a few moderate hits, it wasn't until the release of 1979's aforementioned disco gem "I Will Survive" that Gaynor racked up her first true smash hit. The song was awarded the first and only Grammy Award for Best Disco Recording in 1980 (the category was discontinued upon disco's fall from favor shortly afterward) and although Gaynor was unable to follow up "I Will Survive" with another sizeable hit, the track subsequently took on a life of its own. It remains popular in dance clubs and has appeared on countless movie soundtracks and dance/disco compilations. Gaynor continues to issue albums and play shows (especially in Europe) and during the late '90s issued an autobiography (also titled *I Will Survive*), as well as appearing for a two-week run on Broadway's hit musical *Smokey Joe's Café*. —Greg Prato

Anita Ward

Born 1957 in Memphis, TN

Perhaps more so than any other genre in the history of popular music, the '70s disco scene was littered with countless one-hit wonders, including Anita Ward. Born during 1957 in Memphis, TN, Ward developed an interest in music at an early age, although it was gospel and not the

up-tempo dance style she'd become synonymous with years later. Ward went on to sing with the Rust College A Cappella Choir (which included recording alongside renowned Metropolitan Opera vocalist Leontyne Price), as well as issuing an obscure album recorded by her own gospel quartet. But after graduation, Ward didn't automatically set out to pursue a career in music and instead became a substitute teacher in the Memphis elementary school system. It wasn't long before Ward realized music was too much a part of her life to ignore and her manager put her in contact with singer/songwriter Frederick Knight (who had scored a substantial hit on his own in the summer of 1972 with "I've Been Lonely for So Long"). Knight signed on to help produce a three-song demo session with Ward, but once the tape was rolling, Knight became so taken by Ward's singing ability that the sessions soon produced an album's worth of material.

Upon listening back to their work, both agreed that they were still one song short, which resulted in Knight digging up an old track titled "Ring My Bell" that he had originally penned for a young teenybopper singer, Stacy Lattisaw (who would later score several hits in the early '80s). The song's original lyrics dealt with teens chatting away on the phone and even though Knight gave the track a quick lyrical overhaul, Ward was less than enthusiastic about the song. Still, she agreed to record it (with Knight providing most of the musical accompaniment himself, including one of the first uses of synth drums on a record), which only took a total of two days to record. "Ring My Bell" turned out to be the best track of the bunch, resulting in a recording contract with the TK label, and the release of Ward's debut album, *Songs of Love*, in 1979. It didn't take long for "Ring My Bell" to scale the charts and it peaked at number one during the summer (out-gunning such other future disco-classics as Donna Summer's "Hot Stuff" and "Bad Girls," plus Sister Sledge's "We Are Family," all of which were in the Top Five) and remained on the charts for five months solid.

Since the song was a fluke to begin with, there weren't any other tracks on the album that really resembled "Ring My Bell" (most were ballads and mid-tempo songs), resulting in the album disappearing from the charts soon after. A follow-up single, "Don't Drop My Love," could only make it as far as number 87 on the charts in December of the same year, signaling that Ward's 15 minutes had come and gone, delegating her to one-hit wonder status. Although Ward only scored a lone hit during her brief recording career, a 12-track best-of set was released in 1998, unsurprisingly titled *Ring My Bell*; a remix of the track, "Ring My Bell 2000," was issued shortly thereafter. —Greg Prato

The Sugarhill Gang

Formed in 1979

Though the Sugarhill Gang inaugurated the history of recorded hip-hop with their single "Rapper's Delight," a multi-platinum seller and radio hit in 1979, the group was cooked up to cash in on a supposed novelty item. Music-industry producer and label-owner Sylvia Robinson had become aware of the massive hip-hop block parties occurring around the New York area during the late '70s, so she gathered three local rappers (Master Gee, Wonder Mike, and Big Bank Hank) to record a single. Infectious and catchy, "Rapper's Delight" borrowed the break from Chic's "Good Times" and became a worldwide hit, eventually selling more than eight million copies. Most industry people figured rap for a short-lived trend, and though they were dead wrong, the Sugarhill Gang certainly didn't carry the torch; despite several modest hits ("8th Wonder," "Apache") the trio faded quickly and was gone by the mid-'80s, only returning in 1999 with *Jump on It*, a rap album for children. —John Bush

Take the Reggae Test

1. Jamaica has the greatest output per capita of music.
2. Jamaican music largely borrowed from American music, especially jazz.
3. After WWII Jamaicans played music played by British soldiers stationed there during the war.
4. The first records made in Jamaica were made by Syrian owned Federal Records.
5. Former Prime Minister Edward Seaga started WIRL records in 1958 and was one of the first to record local Jamaican artists.
6. Chris Blackwell started Island Records in 1968 and his first hit was "I Shot the Sheriff."
7. Clement "Coxsone" Dodd and Duke Reid had competing sound systems in the late 1940s.
8. Many Jamaicans had no radio and looked to the Sound Systems for entertainment.
9. Coxsone & Reid opened recording studios and began making records in 1959.
10. "Oh Carolina" by Shaggy was first a hit for Bob Marley in 1960.
11. Jamaica gained independence from Great Britain in 1972.
12. Mento is a kind of Jamaican herbal tea.
13. Ska represented the optimism of the post-independence period in Jamaica.
14. Ska was a Jamaicanized blend of American jazz and R&B.
15. The Skatellites were made up of seasoned, veteran jazz musicians, many of whom graduated from the Catholic Alpha Boys School in Kingston.
16. Many ska hits like the Skatellites' "Guns of Navarone" were instrumentals.
17. Coxsone's Studio 1 label dominated ska.
18. Ska was very popular in many parts of the UK.
19. British Skinheads followed Jamaican music and played it widely at their parties.
20. The ghetto youth identified with the ska bands.
21. In 1963 Bob Marley cut his first record "Simmer Down" for Chinese Jamaican businessman Byron Lee and immediately rose to international fame.
22. Bob Marley was heavily impacted by the music prevalent in the post-independence period.
23. The post-independence period was marked in a significant improvement in the standard of living of the average Jamaican.
24. In 1966 Bob Marley moved to the US where he worked on a line at a Chrysler plant in Wilmington, Delaware.
25. Prince Buster ska records were a big hit in the UK through Blue Beat Records.
26. "My Boy Lollipop" by Millie Small peaked at number two on the pop chart in the US in 1964 at the height of Beatlemania and sold 7 million copies worldwide.
27. By 1967 Duke Reid & Coxsone lost their dominance after reggae gained popularity.
28. Rock steady is ska sped up and lasted only about one year.
29. Rock steady's success proved that the public was accepting of new beats.

30. Duke Ried's recording of Alton Ellis' "Girl I've Got a Date" was one of the first rock steady hits.
31. The Rude Boys was a gang of truant students at Alpha Boys School who influenced rock steady.
32. Ska had a walking bass; rock steady had a tenser melodic bass.
33. Rock steady was orchestrated initially by Trinidadian guitarist Lynn Taitt.
34. In 1969 Desmond Dekker's "Israelites" was a Top-10 hit in the US.
35. Prince Buster, who used to work for Coxsone, started to accentuate the offbeat with his guitarist Jah Jerry. He is credited with being the first to crystallize the reggae beat.
36. Bob Marley was the first to use the word reggae in a song "Roots Rock Reggae."
37. Toots and the Maytals—"54-46"—are credited as the first to use the word reggae in music with their record "Do The Reggay."
38. Unlike in the US, the Jamaican church had minimal impact on reggae music.
39. Jamaican society was divided between one group that looked to the USA and the west for musical and social inspiration and another that looked to Africa.
40. Duke Reid and Byron Lee would have nothing to do with Rasta lyrics.
41. Reggae music, especially bands like the Wailers and Steel Pulse [Rally Round], was the first black music genre that gave real recognition and honor to Africa.
42. Through reggae Rastafari became pervasive and accepted throughout the Caribbean and Africa.
43. In reggae music, Babylon refers to an area in the Euphrates delta in Iraq.
44. The tempo of reggae is slower than rock steady was.
45. The early reggae pioneers got the best musicians in Jamaica to work with them.
46. Since the mid 50s, socially conscious lyrics dominated Jamaican music.
47. Reggae and dub were pioneered by Bunny Lee, Lee "Scratch" Perry and King Tubby.
48. Bunny Lee made three albums in one night.
49. Lee Perry was house producer from Coxsone and Tubby cut masters for Reid.
50. Lee Perry was the first to record DJ toasting over dubs.
51. Lee Perry began to slow down the beat in 1970s as illustrated in "Police and Theives."
52. Bunny Lee and Lee Perry were able to deal the Jamaican musical establishment a severe blow from which they have never recovered—as Rasta music gained acceptance worldwide.
53. The first rap, remix and dub records were made in Jamaica.
54. King Tubby was the first to create a dub plate—the song minus the lead vocal.
55. In the mid 70s King Tubby was the first to begin the practice of recycling beats.
56. The Wailers started Tuff Gong in 1968 and had a deal with Johnny Nash that paid them $50 JA each per week.
57. In 1970 Big Youth's "Wake the Town" was the first DJ to record toasting on records—Jamaican form of early rap.
58. Record business people welcomed DJs being recorded.

59. Lee Perry hooked up with and recorded the Wailers in 1969.
60. Lee Perry added Aston and Carlton Barrett to the Wailers, completing their sound.
61. In 1972 reggae went international with the release of "Harder they Come" starring Bob Marley.
62. In 1972 The Wailers signed to Island Records and their album *Catch a Fire* was released to an international audience.
63. In 1972 Bob Marley didn't have dreadlocks.
64. Bob Marley refused to sign recording contracts, a nightmare for record companies.
65. Peter Tosh once pulled a machete on Chris Blackwell and is well known for advocating the legalization of marijuana in the song "Bush Doctor."
66. Since the mid 70s most Jamaican elections have been peaceful and orderly.
67. In 1974 Peter Tosh and Bunny Wailer left the Wailers causing the band to break up.
68. In 1975 Channel One studio launched the careers of Sly Dunbar and Robbie Shakespeare who produced Black Uhuru's "Guess Who's Coming to Dinner."
69. In the mid 70s Jamaican ghetto youth gravitated to the blend of Garveyism, American Black Power and Rastafarianism expressed in reggae.
70. Bob Marley died in 1990 after writing the classic reggae anthem "War" produced by Roots Radics.
71. In the early 1980s Greggory Isaacs released the classic ska hit "Night Nurse."
72. In 1980 Sugar Minott begins recording ghetto youth with his 'Youth Promotion' sound system and dancehall is born when "Ring the Alarm" was recorded by Tenor Saw.
73. In 1980 Sly & Robbie and Roots Radics were the dominant beat producers.
74. In 1985 King Jammy and Black Scorpio were the dominant sound systems in Jamaica.
75. The influx of cocaine, guns, gangterism in the mid-80s reflected in dancehall lyrics.
76. Dancehall DJs continued the reggae tradition of dealing mainly with conscious lyrics as illustrated in Admiral Bailey's 1987 "Punanny."
77. Jamaican producers favored organic production techniques and tended to not jump on new technologies.
78. Shabba Ranks signed a major record deal with a US multi-national record company. He also has three top-40 hits on the US pop chart including "Wicked in a Bed."
79. England has traditionally been a better market for Jamaican music than the US.

African-American Music Map

Style	1880	1890	1900	1910	1920	1930	1940	1950	1960	1970	1980	1990	Main Artists
WORK SONGS	■	■											Black workers sang these songs in the fields.
SPIRITUALS	■	■	■										Harlem Spiritual Ensemble, Golden Gate Quartet, Mahalia Jackson
COUNTRY BLUES			■	■	■	■	■						Blind Blake, Alberta Hunter, Professor Longhair, Leadbelly, Big Bill Broonzy
PREWAR COUNTRY BLUES					■	■	■						Tommy Johnson, Blind Blake, Sleepy John Estes, Blind Willie McTell
CLASSIC FEMALE BLUES					■	■							Ma Rainey, Bessie Smith, Mamie Smith, Ida Cox, Ella Fitzgerald, Billie Holiday
DELTA BLUES					■	■	■						Charley Patton, Son House, Mississippi John Hurt, Robert Johnson
ACOUSTIC BLUES						■	■	■					Son House, Lonnie Johnson, Mississippi John Hurt, Kokomo Arnold
JUMP BLUES							■	■					Big Joe Turner, Dizzy Gillespie, Nat King Cole, Lavern Baker
RHYTHM & BLUES							■	■	■				Ray Charles, Ruth Brown, Drifters, Coasters
ELECTRIC CHICAGO BLUES								■	■				Howlin' Wolf, Sonny Boy Williamson II, Muddy Waters
ELECTRIC BLUES								■	■	■			Muddy Waters, Howlin' Wolf, Buddy Guy, Cub Koda
DOO WOP								■	■				Frankie Lymon, Platters, Drifters, Jackie Wilson, Coasters
"SOUL" BLUES									■	■			Bobby Blue Bland, Albert King, Johnnie Taylor, Etta James, B.B. King
ROCKABILLY								■					Chuck Berry, Little Richard, Fats Domino
MODERN ELECTRIC BLUES										■	■	■	B.B. King, Albert King, Bobby Blue Bland, Robert Cray, Buddy Guy
SOUL									■	■			Ray Charles, Ruth Brown, Aretha Franklin, James Brown, Marvin Gaye
DETROIT SOUL "MOTOWN"									■	■			Smokey Robinson, Supremes, Temptations, Four Tops, Jackson 5
FUNK										■	■		James Brown, Sly Stone, George Clinton, Funkadelic, Rick James, Prince
DISCO										■			Donna Summer, Chic, Gloria Gaynor, Village People, Trammps
HOUSE											■		Bomb the Bass, M People, Farley Jackmaster Funk, Larry Heard, Deep Dish
RAP											■	■	Curtis Blow, Run-DMC, LL Cool J, Dr Dre, Public Enemy
RAGTIME		■	■	■	■								Tom Turpin, Scott Joplin, Eubie Blake, James P. Johnson
NEW ORLEANS JAZZ				■	■	■							Buddy Bolden, Freddie Keppard, King Olliver, Sidney Bechet, Louis Armstrong
DIXIELAND				■	■								Louis Armstrong, Sidney Bechet, Bud Freeman
CLASSIC JAZZ					■	■							Louis Armstrong, James P. Johnson, Coleman Hawkins, Earl Hines, Fats Waller
SWING						■	■						Fletcher Henderson, Louis Armstrong, Lester Young, Art Tatum, Earl Hines, Count Basie
BOOGIE WOOGIE						■	■						Jimmy Yancey, Albert C. Ammons, Pete Johnson, Meade Lux Lewis
STRIDE						■							Fats Waller, James P. Johnson, Luckey Roberts, Willie "the Lion" Smith
BLUES JAZZ							■	■					Pete Johnson, Joe Turner, Chuck Painey
BIG BAND						■	■	■					Duke Ellington, Earl Hines, Fletcher Henderson, Count Basie
BOP (BEBOP)							■	■	■				Charlie Parker, Dizzy Gillespie, Bud Powell, Max Roach
COOL								■	■				Lester Young, Miles Davis, Gerry Mulligan, Stan Getz
HARD BOP								■	■				Thelonius Monk, Miles Davis, J.J. Johnson, Freddie Hubbard, Art Blakey
SOUL JAZZ									■				George Benson, King Curtis, Houston Person, Jimmy McGriff
GROOVE									■				Charles Mingus, Wes Montgomery, Archie Shepp
AVANT GARDE									■	■			John Coltrane, Archie Shepp, Betty Carter, Wayne Shorter
MODAL									■				John Coltrane, Miles Davis, Thelonious Monk, Bill Evans
FREE JAZZ									■	■			Cecil Taylor, Omette Coleman, Archie Shepp, John Coltrane
FUSION										■	■		Bill Evans, McCoy Tyner, Ahmad Jamal, Thelonius Monk, Gil Evans
POST BOP											■	■	Herbie Hancock, Terence Blanchard, Keith Jarrett, Wynton Marsalis, Max Roach
ACID JAZZ												■	Brand New Heavies, Incognito, Galliano, James Taylor, Jamiroquai

African-American Music Map

#	GENRE	ARTIST	BIRTHPLACE	BORN	DIED	80	90	00	10	20	30	40	50	60	70	80	90	INSTRUMENT	STYLES
1	RAGTIME	Tom Turpin	Bowie City, TX	1867	4/1/17	■	■	■	■									Piano	Ragtime
2	RAGTIME	Scott Joplin	Bowie City, TX	24-Nov-1865	4/1/17	■	■	■	■									Piano	Ragtime
3	RAGTIME	Eubie Blake	Baltimore, MD	7-Feb-1883	2/12/83			■	■	■	■	■	■	■	■	■		Piano	Ragtime
4	BLUES	W.C. Handy	Muscle Shoals, AL	16-Nov-1873	3/28/58		■	■	■	■	■	■	■					Piano	Father of the Blues, Early American Blues
5	BLUES	Ma Rainey	Columbus, GA	26-Apr-1886	12/22/39			■	■	■	■							Vocals	Blues, Classic Female Blues
6	BLUES	Frank Stokes	Whitehaven, TN	1-Jan-1888	9/12/55			■	■	■	■	■	■					Vocals, Guitar	Prewar Country Blues, Acoustic Memphis Blues
7	BLUES	Mamie Smith	Cincinnati, OH	26-May-1883	10/30/46			■	■	■	■	■						Vocals	First vocalist to record a blues song
8	BLUES	Papa Charlie Jackson	New Orleans, LA	1885	1938			■	■	■	■							Vocals, Guitar, Banjo	Country Blues
9	BLUES	Leadbelly	Shiloh, LA	21-Jan-1888	12/6/49			■	■	■	■	■						Vocals, Guitar	Folk-Blues, Country Blues, Acoustic Blues
10	BLUES	Charlie Patton	Edwards, MS	3-Apr-1891	4/28/34				■	■	■							Vocals, Guitar	Slide Guitar Blues, Delta Blues, Acoustic Blues, Blues Revival, Country Blues
11	BLUES	Big Bill Broonzy	Scott, MS	26-Jun-1893	8/15/58				■	■	■	■	■					Vocals, Guitar, Mandolin	Acoustic Chicago Blues
12	BLUES	Mississippi John Hurt	Teoc, MS	3-Jul-1893	11/2/66				■	■	■	■	■	■				Vocals, Harmonica, Guitar	Delta Blues, Blues Revival, Country Blues, Acoustic Blues
13	BLUES	Bessie Smith	Chattanooga, TN	15-Apr-1894	9/26/37				■	■	■							Vocals	Classic Jazz, Blues
14	BLUES	Blind Blake	Jackson, FL	1895	1933				■	■	■							Vocals	Blues, Country Blues, Acoustic Blues
15	BLUES	Tommy Johnson	Terry, MS	1896	11/1/56				■	■	■	■	■					Vocals, Guitar	Delta Blues, Country Blues, Acoustic Blues
16	BLUES	Ida Cox	Toccoa, GA	25-Feb-1896	11/10/67				■	■	■	■	■	■				Vocals	Classic Female Blues, Blues
17	BLUES	Lonnie Johnson	New Orleans, LA	8-Feb-1899	6/16/70				■	■	■	■	■	■	■			Vocals, Guitar	Country Blues, Jazz Blues
18	BLUES	Sleepy John Estes	Ripley, TN	25-Jan-1899	6/5/77				■	■	■	■	■	■	■			Vocals, Guitar	Classic Jazz, Acoustic Blues Memphis Blues, Piedmont Blues, Country Blues
19	BLUES	Leroy Carr	Nashville, TN	27-Mar-05	4/29/35					■	■							Vocals, Piano	Blues, Piano Blues
21	BLUES	Lightnin' Hopkins	Centerville, TX	15-Mar-12	1/30/82					■	■	■	■	■	■	■		Vocals, Guitar, Piano	Country Blues, Acoustic Texas Blues, Blues Revival
22	BLUES	Kokomo Arnold	Lovejoys Stn., GA	15-Feb-1901	11/8/68					■	■	■	■	■				Vocals, Guitar	Acoustic Chicago Blues, Acoustic Blues
23	BLUES	Son House	Riverton, MS	21-Mar-1902	10/19/88					■	■	■	■	■	■	■		Vocals, Guitar	Slide Guitar Blues, Delta Blues, Acoustic Blues, Work Songs
25	BLUES	Robert Johnson	Hazelhurst, MS	8-May-11	8/16/38					■	■							Vocals, Guitar	Blues, Slide Guitar Blues, Delta Blues
26	BLUES	Big Joe Turner	Kansas City, MO	18-May-11	11/24/85					■	■	■	■	■	■	■		Vocals	Jump Blues, Swing Jazz, Blues, Rock & Roll, R&B
27	BLUES	Lightnin' Slim	St. Louis, MO	13-Mar-13	7/24/74						■	■	■	■	■			Vocals, Guitar	Swamp Blues, Louisiana Blues
28	BLUES	Sonny Boy Williamson I	Jackson, TN	30-Mar-14	6/1/48						■	■						Vocals, Harmonica	Harmonica Blues, Acoustic Chicago Blues, Chicago Blues
29	BLUES	Big Walter Horton	Horn Lake, MS	16-Apr-17	12/8/81						■	■	■	■	■	■		Vocals, Harmonica	Harmonica Blues, Juke Joint Blues, Memphis Blues
30	BLUES	Blind Lemon Jefferson	Coachman, TX	11-Jul-1897	12/11/29				■	■								Vocals, Guitar	Blues, Country Blues
31	BLUES	T-Bone Walker	Linden, TX	28-May-10	3/16/75					■	■	■	■	■	■			Vocals, Guitar	Texas Blues, Electric Texas Blues (first to electrify guitar)
32	BLUES	Howlin' Wolf	West Point, MS	10-Jun-10	1/10/76						■	■	■	■	■			Vocals, Guitar	Electric Blues, Electric Chicago Blues

African-American Music Map

#	GENRE	ARTIST	BIRTHPLACE	BORN	DIED	80	90	00	10	20	30	40	50	60	70	80	90	INSTRUMENT	STYLES
33	BLUES	Muddy Waters	Rolling Fork, MS	4-Apr-15	4/30/83							■	■	■	■	■		Vocals, Guitar	Slide Guitar Blues, Blues Revival, Delta Blues, Electric Chicago Blues
34	BLUES	John Lee Hooker	Clarksdale, MS	17-Aug-20								■	■	■	■	■	■	Vocals, Guitar	Detroit Blues, Blues Revival, Delta Blues, Country Blues
36	BLUES	B.B. King	Indianola, MS	16-Sep-25									■	■	■	■	■	Vocals, Guitar	Blues, Modern Electric Blues, Soul Blues
37	BLUES	Guitar Slim	Greenwood, MS	10-Dec-26	2/7/59							■	■					Vocals, Guitar	New Orleans Blues
38	BLUES	Bobby Blue Bland	Rosemark, TN	27-Jan-30									■	■	■	■	■	Vocals, Guitar	Modern Electric Texas Blues, Soul Blues
39	BLUES	Little Walter	Marksville, LA	1-May-30	2/15/68								■	■				Vocals, Harmonica	Electric Harmonica Blues (King of Genre)
40	BLUES	Lavern Baker	Chicago, IL	11-Nov-29	3/10/97								■	■	■	■	■	Vocals	Jump Blues, R&B
41	BLUES	Etta James	Los Angeles, CA	25-Jan-38									■	■	■	■	■	Vocals	Classic Female Blues, Blues, Soul Blues, R&B
42	BLUES	Albert King	Indianola, MS	25-Apr-23	12/21/92								■	■	■	■	■	Vocals, Guitar	Modern Electric Blues, Soul Blues
43	BLUES	Buddy Guy	Chicago, IL	30-Jul-36									■	■	■	■	■	Vocals, Guitar	Modern Chicago Electric Blues
44	JAZZ	Bill Johnson	New Orleans, LA	10-Aug-1872	12/3/72		■	■	■									Bass	New Orleans Jazz (First to pluck instead of bow the bass)
45	JAZZ	Tony Jackson	New Orleans, LA	5-Jun-1876	4/20/21		■	■	■	■								Piano	Ragtime, Blues
46	JAZZ	Buddy Bolden	New Orleans, LA	6-Sep-1877	11/4/31		■	■										Cornet	New Orleans Jazz (One of the first jazz musicians)
47	JAZZ	Freddie Keppard	New Orleans, LA	27-Feb-1890	7/15/33			■	■	■	■							Cornet	New Orleans Jazz (Introduced jazz to LA)
48	JAZZ	King Olliver	New Orleans, LA	11-May-1885	4/8/38			■	■	■	■							Cornet	New Orleans Jazz
49	JAZZ	Lucky Roberts	Philadelphia, PA	7-Aug-1887	2/5/68				■	■	■	■	■	■				Piano	Jazz, Stride, Blues
50	JAZZ	James P. Johnson	New Brunswick, NJ	1-Feb-1894	11/17/55				■	■	■	■	■					Piano	Ragtime, Jazz, Stride
51	JAZZ	Jelly Roll Morton	New Orleans, LA	20-Oct-1890	7/10/41				■	■	■	■						Piano	New Orleans Jazz (Claims to have invented jazz in 1902)
53	JAZZ	Sidney Becket	New Orleans, LA	14-May-1897	5/14/59				■	■	■	■	■					Soprano Sax, Clarinet	New Orleans Jazz, Dixieland
54	JAZZ	Willie "the Lion" Smith	Goshen, NY	25-Nov-1897	4/18/73					■	■	■	■	■	■			Piano	Classic Jazz, Stride
56	JAZZ	Duke Ellington	Washington, DC	29-Apr-1899	5/24/74					■	■	■	■	■	■			Piano	Orchestral Jazz, Swing, Prog. Big Band, Big Band
57	JAZZ	Louis Armstrong	New Orleans, LA	4-Aug-1901	7/6/71					■	■	■	■	■	■			Vocals, Trumpet	Dixieland Revival, Vocal Jazz, New Orleans Jazz, Pop
58	JAZZ	Earl Hines	Dusquesne, PA	28-Dec-1903	4/22/83					■	■	■	■	■	■	■		Piano	Jazz, Classic Jazz, Swing, Big Band
59	JAZZ	Coleman Hawkins	St. Joseph, MO	21-Nov-04	5/19/69					■	■	■	■	■				Tenor Sax	Mainstream Jazz, Classic Jazz, Swing, Bop
60	JAZZ	Fats Waller	New York, NY	21-May-04	12/15/43					■	■	■						Vocals, Piano, Organ	Jive, Classic Jazz, Stride, Swing
62	JAZZ	Cab Calloway	Rochester, NY	25-Dec-07	11/18/94						■	■	■	■	■	■	■	Vocals	Vocal Jazz, Jive, Swing, Vocal
63	JAZZ	Art Tatum	Toledo, OH	13-Oct-09	11/5/56						■	■	■					Piano	Jazz, Swing
65	JAZZ	Jimmy Yancey	Chicago, IL	1894	9/17/51					■	■	■	■					Piano	Boogie Woogie, Piano Blues
67	JAZZ	Count Basie	Red Bank, NJ	21-Aug-04	4/26/84						■	■	■	■	■	■		Piano	Swing, Piano Blues, Big Band
68	JAZZ	Meade Max Lewis	Chicago, IL	4-Sep-05	6/7/64						■	■	■	■				Piano	Boogie Woogie, Piano Blues
70	JAZZ	Lester Young	Woodville, MS	27-Aug-09	3/15/59						■	■	■					Tenor Sax, Clarinet	Mainstream Jazz, Swing, Cool Jazz, Swing
71	JAZZ	Teddy Wilson	Austin, TX	24-Nov-12	7/31/86						■	■	■	■	■	■		Piano	
73	JAZZ	Billie Holiday	Baltimore, MD	7-Apr-15	7/17/59						■	■	■					Vocals	Vocal Jazz, Trad Pop, Swing, Ballads, Classic Blues

African-American Music Map

#	GENRE	ARTIST	BIRTHPLACE	BORN	DIED	1880	1890	1900	1910	1920	1930	1940	1950	1960	1970	1980	1990	INSTRUMENT	STYLES
74	JAZZ	Nat King Cole	Montgomery, AL	31-Mar-17	2/15/65						■	■	■	■				Vocals, Piano	Vocal Jazz, Trad Pop, Standards, Ballads, Bop
75	JAZZ	Ella Fitzgerald	Newport News, VA	25-Apr-17	6/15/96						■	■	■	■	■	■	■	Vocals	Vocal Jazz, Trad Pop, Swing, Bop, Classic Female Blues
77	JAZZ	Louis Jordan	Brinkley, AR	8-Jul-08	2/4/75						■	■	■	■	■			Vocals, Alto Sax	East Coast Blues, Jump Blues, Swing, Urban Blues
78	JAZZ	Thelonious Monk	Rocky Mount, NC	10-Oct-17	2/17/82							■	■	■	■	■		Piano	Jazz, Modal Music, Hard Bop, Post Bop, Bop
79	JAZZ	Dizzy Gillespie	Cheraw, SC	21-Oct-17	1/6/93						■	■	■	■	■	■	■	Trumpet	Vocal Jazz, Afro-Cubase Jazz, Jump Blues, Pop
80	JAZZ	Charlie Parker	Kansas City, KS	29-Aug-20	3/12/55							■	■					Alto Sax	Bop, Big Band
81	JAZZ	Sarah Vaughn	Newark, NJ	27-Mar-24	4/3/90							■	■	■	■	■		Vocals	Vocal Jazz, Trad Pop, Standards, Ballads, Bop
82	JAZZ	Dinah Washington	Tuscaloosa, AL	29-Aug-24	12/14/63							■	■	■				Vocals	Vocal Jazz, Trad Pop, Standards, Classic Female Blues
83	JAZZ	Bud Powell	New York, NY	27-Sep-24	7/31/66							■	■	■				Piano	Bop
84	JAZZ	Miles Davis	Alton, IL	25-May-26	9/28/91							■	■	■	■	■	■	Trumpet	Jazz Rock, Modal Music, Bop
85	JAZZ	Oscar Peterson	Montreal, QC	15-Aug-25								■	■	■	■	■	■	Piano	Swing, Bop
86	JAZZ	John Coltrane	Hamlet, NC	23-Sep-26	7/17/67							■	■	■				Soprano & Tenor Sax	Avante Garde Jazz, Modal Music, Free Jazz, Hard Bop
87	JAZZ	Ruth Brown	Portsmouth, VA	12-Jan-28								■	■	■	■	■	■	Vocals	Jump Blues, Jazz, Blues, R&B
88	JAZZ	Betty Carter	Flint, MI	16-May-30	9/26/98								■	■	■	■	■	Vocals	Vocal Jazz, Bop, Avante Garde
89	JAZZ	Sonny Rollins	New York, NY	7-Sep-30									■	■	■	■	■	Tenor Sax	Hard Bop, Post-Bop, Bop
90	JAZZ	Nina Simone	Tryon, NC	21-Feb-33									■	■	■	■	■	Vocals	Vocal Jazz, Standards, Brazil
91	JAZZ	Nancy Wilson	Chillicothe, OH	20-Feb-37									■	■	■	■	■	Vocals	Vocal Jazz, Trad Pop Standards, Pop, Bop, R&B
92	JAZZ	McCoy Tyner	Philadelphia, PA	12-Nov-38									■	■	■	■	■	Piano	Hard Bop, Post-Bop
93	ROCK	Chuck Berry	St. Louis, MO	18-Oct-26									■	■	■	■	■	Vocals, Guitar	Rock & Roll
94	ROCK	Fats Domino	New Orleans, LA	26-Feb-28									■	■	■	■	■	Vocals, Piano	New Orleans R&B, Piano Blues, Rock & Roll, R&B
95	ROCK	Bo Diddley	McComb, MS	30-Dec-28									■	■	■	■	■	Vocals, Guitar	Rock & Roll, Rock & Roll, R&B
96	ROCK	Ray Charles	Albany, GA	23-Sep-30									■	■	■	■	■	Vocals, Piano	Country Soul, Jazz Blues, Pop, Bop, Urban Blues, Piano Blues, R&B
97	ROCK	Sam Cooke	Clarkedale, MS	22-Jan-31	12/11/64								■	■				Vocals	Pop/Rock, Ballads, Big Band, R&B
98	VOCAL	Lena Horne	Brooklyn, NY	30-Jun-17							■	■	■	■	■	■	■	Vocals	Vocal Jazz, Swing, Show Tunes, Trad Pop
99	VOCAL	Harry Belafonte	New York, NY	1-Mar-27									■	■	■	■	■	Vocals	Trad Pop, Caribbean Folk, Trad Folk, Vocal
100	VOCAL	Etta Jones	Aiken, SC	25-Nov-28								■	■	■	■	■	■	Vocals	Vocal Jazz, Standards

York University—Department of Fine Arts — FA1520—Song Listing — 2004-2005

#	Pop	R&B	Year	Label	Artist	Song	Writer
1		10	Dec-26	Okeh	Louis Armstrong	Muskrat Ramble	Ray Gilbert, Kid Ory
2			Mar-27	Paramount	Blind Lemon Jefferson	Match Box Blues	Blind Lemon Jefferson
3			Oct-27	Paramount	Blind Lemon Jefferson	One Dime Blues	Blind Lemon Jefferson
4			Oct-27	Paramount	Ida Cox	Give me a Break Blues	Ida Cox
5			Jun-28	Paramount	Ma Rainey	Prove it on me Blues	Ma Rainey
6			Dec-28	Okeh	Mississippi John Hurt	Ain't No Tellin'	Mississippi John Hurt
7			May-29	Columbia	Bessie Smith	Nobody Know You When You're Down & Out	James Cox
8			Aug-29	Paramount	Blind Blake	Police Dog Blues	Blind Blake
9		10	Sep-29	Okeh	Louis Armstrong	Ain't Misbehavin'	Brooks, Razaf, Fats Waller
10			Sep-29	Okeh	Louis Armstrong	I Ain't Got Nobody	Roger Graham, Spencer Williams
11			Dec-29	Okeh	Louis Armstrong	St Louis Blues	W.C. Handy
12			May-30	Okeh	Louis Armstrong	Tiger Rag	DaCosta, Edwards, LaRocca, Ragas
13		10	Oct-30	Okeh	Louis Armstrong	Body & Soul	Eyton, Green, Heyman, Sour
14			Oct-30	Columbia	Memphis Minnie	What's The Matter With The Mill	Joe McCoy, Memphis Minnie
15			Feb-31	Okeh	Lonnie Johnson	Low Down St Louis Blues	Lonnie Johnson
16			Feb-31	Okeh	Mamie Smith	Jenny's Ball	Jimmy Reed
17			Oct-31	Victor	Blind Willie McTell	Southern Can is Mine	Blind Willie McTell
18		5	Feb-32	Columbia	Louis Armstrong	Chinatown my Chinatown	William Jerome, Jean Schwarz
19		1	Mar-32	Columbia	Louis Armstrong	All of Me	Gerald Marks, Seymour Simons
20			Aug-33	Columbia	Billie Holiday	Your Mother's Son-In-Law	Mann Holiner, Alberta Nichols
21			Nov-33	Columbia	Billie Holiday	What A Little Moonlight Can Do	Harry Woods
22			Jan-34	Paramount	Charley Patton	Revenue man Blues	Charley Patton
23			Jul-35	Victor	Sleepy Joe Estes	Someday Baby	Sleepy Joe Estes
24			Nov-35	Columbia	Billie Holiday	Swing, Brother, Swing	Bishop, Raymond, Williams
25			Mar-36	Columbia	Billie Holiday	Easy To Love	Cole Porter
26			Sep-36	Columbia	Billie Holiday	God Bless The Child	Arthur Herzog Jr, Billie Holiday
27			Nov-36	Columbia	Billie Holiday	Billie's Blues	Billie Holiday
28			Jan-37	Columbia	Billie Holiday	Speak Low	Ogden Nash, Kurt Weill
29			Jun-37	History	Robert Johnson	Stones in my Passway	Robert Johnson
30			Jun-37	History	Robert Johnson	Stop Breakin Down	Robert Johnson
31			Jun-37	History	Robert Johnson	Sweet Home Chicago	Robert Johnson
32			Apr-38	Decca	Louis Armstrong	Jeepers Creepers	Johnny Mercer, Harry Warren
33			Nov-38	Columbia	Billie Holiday	Miss Brown To You	Rainger, Robin, Whiting
34			Feb-39	Okeh	Big Bill Broonzy	Spreadin' Snakes Blues	Big Bill Broonzy
35			Apr-39	Commodore	Billie Holiday	Fine & Mellow	Herzog Holiday
36			Apr-39	Commodore	Billie Holiday	Strange Fruit	Lewis Allan
37		10	Apr-39	Decca	Louis Armstrong	When the Saints Go Marching In	Standard
38			May-40	RCA	Sonny Boy Williamson	I've Been Dealing With The Devil	Sonny Boy Williamson
39			May-40	RCA	Sonny Boy Williamson	Train Fare Blues	Sonny Boy Williamson
40			Jun-40	Okeh	Memphis Minnie	Nothing In Ramblin	Memphis Minnie
41			Mar-41	Jazz Unlimited	Billie Holiday	Georgia On My Mind	Hoagy Carmichael, Stuart Gorrell
42		1	Nov-42	Decca	Nat King Cole	That Ain't Right	Nat King Cole

123

	Pop	R&B	Year	Label	Artist	Song	Writer
43	19	1	Nov-43	Capitol	Nat King Cole	All For You	Nat King Cole
44			Mar-44	Decca	Billie Holiday	Don't Explain	Arthur Herzog Jr., Billie Holiday
45	9	1	Apr-44	Capitol	Nat King Cole	Straighten Up & Fly Right	Nat King Cole
46			Apr-44	Verve	Billie Holiday	My Man	Charles, Pollack, Willemetz, Yvain
47	20	1	Sep-44	Capitol	Nat King Cole	Gee, Baby, Ain't I Good To You	Andy Razaf, Don Redman
48			Sep-44	Decca	Billie Holiday	There is no Greater Love	Isham Jones, Marty Symes
49			Mar-45	Verve	Billie Holiday	Stars Fell On Alabama	Mitchell Parish, Frank Perkins
50			Mar-45	Verve	Billie Holiday	April In Paris	Vernon Duke, E.Y. Harburg
51	11		Aug-46	Capitol	Nat King Cole	Route 66	Bobby Troup
52			Sep-46	Columbia	Muddy Waters	Hard Day Blues	McKinley Morganfield, Muddy Waters
53	3	3	Nov-46	Capitol	Nat King Cole	The Christmas Song	Mel Torme, Robert Wells
54	1	3	Nov-46	Capitol	Nat King Cole	For Sentimental Reasons (I Love You)	William Best, Dee Watson
55			Jul-47	Omega	Louis Armstrong	Mack The Knife	Blitzstein, Brecht, Kurt Weill
56			Sep-47	Decca	Billie Holiday	My Sweet Hunk O'Trash	James P. Johnson, F.E. Miller
57			Oct-47	MCA	Louis Armstrong	Cabaret	Henri Betti, Jerry Seelen
58			Apr-48	Verve	Billie Holiday	I Cover The Waterfront	Johnny Green, Edward Heyman
59		1	Sep-48	Mercury	Dinah Washington	Am I Asking Too Much	Glenn Miller, Whitman
60			Jul-49	Legacy	Ray Charles	Sentimental Blues	William York
61		1	Jul-49	Mercury	Dinah Washington	Baby Get Lost	Leonard Feather
62	1	2	Jul-50	Capitol	Nat King Cole	Nature Boy	Eden Ahbez
63	1	3	May-51	Capitol	Nat King Cole	Too Young	Sylvia Dee, Sidney Lippman
64			Jul-51	Legacy	Ray Charles	Rockin' Chair Blues	Ray Charles
65			Jul-51	Legacy	Ray Charles	She's On the Ball	Ray Charles
66	40		Oct-51	Decca	Louis Armstrong	A Kiss to Build a Dream On	Hammerstein II, Kalmar, Ruby
67	12		Nov-51	Capitol	Nat King Cole	Unforgettable	Irving Gordon
68	8		Jul-52	Capitol	Nat King Cole	Walking My Baby Back Home	Fred E. Ahlert, Roy Turk
69	2	10	Feb-53	Capitol	Nat King Cole	Pretend	Belloc, Douglas, LaVere, Parman
70	6		Feb-54	Capitol	Nat King Cole	Answer Me	Raunch, Sigman, Winkler
71	1		Nov-54	Atlantic	Ray Charles	I Gotta Woman	Ray Charles, Renald Richard
72	8	1	Dec-54	DooTone	The Penguins	Earth Angel	Belvin, Hodge, Williams
73	20	11	Mar-55	Chess	The Moonglows	Sincerely	Alan Freed, Harvey Fuqua
74	7		Mar-55	Capitol	Nat King Cole	Darling Je Vous Aime Beaucoup	Anna Sosenko
75	2		May-55	Capitol	Nat King Cole	A Blossom Fell	Barnes, Cornelius, J.G. Johnson
76	8		May-55	Capitol	Nat King Cole	If I May (with the Four Knights)	Rosemary McCoy, Charlie Singleton
77	79	10	Oct-55	Atco	The Coasters	Smokey Joe's Cafe	Leiber-Stoller
78	5	1	Oct-55	Mercury	The Platters	Only You	Ram-Rand
79	1	1	Dec-55	Mercury	The Platters	The Great Pretender	Buck Ram
80	17	1	Jan-56	Specialty	Little Richard	Tutti-Frutti	Richard Penneman
81		8	Feb-56	Atlantic	The Coasters	Down in Mexico	Leiber-Stoller
82	6	1	Feb-56	Gee	Frankie Lymon & The Teenagers	Why do Fools Fall in Love	Frankie Lymon
83	6	1	Apr-56	Specialty	Little Richard	Long Tall Sally	Richard Penneman
84			Apr-56	Verve	Louis Armstrong	Sweet Lorraine	Carter Burwell, Mitchell Parish
85	95	6	Jun-56	Federal	James Brown & the Famous Flame	Please Please Please	James Brown-Johnny Terry

	Pop	R&B	Year	Label	Artist	Song	Writer
86	1	1	Jul-56	Mercury	The Platters	My Prayer	Kennedy-Boulanger
87	25	15	Oct-56	Chess	The Moonglows	See Saw	Roquel Davis, Charles Sutton
88	3	1	Mar-57	Atlantic	The Coasters	Searchin'	Leiber-Stoller
89	8	2	Mar-57	Atlantic	The Coasters	Young Blood	Leiber-Stoller
90	21	4	Apr-57	Specialty	Little Richard	Lucille	Richard Penneman
91	39	24	Jun-57	Decca	Mills Brothers	Queen of the Senior Prom	Stella Lee, Jack Richards
92	10	1	Jun-57	Specialty	Little Richard	Jenny Jenny	Richard Penneman
93	6	1	Jul-57	Capitol	Nat King Cole	Send For Me	Ollie Jones
94	1	1	Jul-57	Capitol	Nat King Cole	Mona Lisa	Ray Evans, Jay Livingston
95	46	1	Aug-57	Duke	Bobby Bland	Farther Up The Road	Joe Medwick, Don Robey
96			Sep-57	Decca	Billie Holiday	Good Morning Heartache	Drake, Fisher, Higginbotham
97	1	1	Oct-57	Keen	Sam Cooke	You Send Me	Sam Cooke
98	8	1	Oct-57	Specialty	Little Richard	Keep A Knockin	Richard Penneman
99	34	14	Nov-57	Atlantic	Ray Charles	Swanee River Rock (Talkin''Bout That River)	Ray Charles
100	22	7	Feb-58	Brunswick	Jackie Wilson	To Be Loved	Gordy-Carlo-Gordy
101			Feb-58	Columbia	Billie Holiday	You've Changed	Bill Carey, Carl Fischer
102			Feb-58	Columbia	Billie Holiday	The End of a Love Affair	Edward Redding
103			Feb-58	Specialty	Little Richard	You Don't Know What Love Is	Gene DePaul, Don Raye
104	10	1	Mar-58	Specialty	Little Richard	Good Golly Miss Molly	Blackwell-Marascallo
105	21	7	Mar-58	Dot	Mills Brothers	Get a Job	Beal, Edwards, Horton, Lewis
106	1	1	Apr-58	Mercury	The Platters	Twilight Time	Ram-A&M Nevins-Dunn
107	5	2	Apr-58	Capitol	Nat King Cole	Looking Back	Brook Benton, Hendricks, Otis
108	8	1	May-58	Chess	Chuck Berry	Johnny B. Goode	Chuck Berry
109	1	1	Jun-58	Atlantic	The Coasters	Yakety Yak	Leiber-Stoller
110	48	1	Jun-58	Federal	James Brown & the Famous Flame	Try Me	James Brown
111	4	1	Aug-58	End	Little Anthony & the Imperials	Tears on my Pillow	Sylvester Bradford, Al Lewis
112	6	1	Oct-58	Atlantic	Clyde McPhatter	A Lover's Question	Brook Benton, Jimmy Williams
113	7	1	Oct-58	Brunswick	Jackie Wilson	Lonely Teardrops	Gordy-Carlo-Gordy
114	1	1	Dec-58	Mercury	The Platters	Smoke Gets in your Eyes	Harbach-Kern
115	2	2	Jan-59	Atlantic	The Coasters	Charlie Brown	Leiber-Stoller
116	13	2	Mar-59	Brunswick	Jackie Wilson	That's Why (I Love You So)	Gordy-Carlo-Gordy
117	9	14	May-59	Capitol	Nat King Cole	Along Came Jones	Gordy-Carlo-Gordy
118	20	6	Jun-59	Brunswick	Jackie Wilson	I'll Be Satisfied	Gordy-Carlo-Gordy
119	6	1	Jul-59	Atlantic	Ray Charles	What'd I Say	Ray Charles
120	7	1	Aug-59	Atlantic	The Coasters	Poison Ivy	Leiber-Stoller
121	36	29	Nov-59	Atlantic	The Coasters	Run Red Run	Leiber-Stoller
122	17	47	Nov-59	Atlantic	The Coasters	What About Us	Leiber-Stoller
123	5	1	Jan-60	Mercury	Dinah Washington	Baby (You've Got What It Takes)	Brook Benton, Clyde Otis, Stein
124	8	1	Feb-60	Mercury	The Platters	Harbour Lights	Kennedy-Williams
125	4	3	Mar-60	Brunswick	Jackie Wilson	Night	Lehman-Miller
126	15	1	Mar-60	Brunswick	Jackie Wilson	Doggin' Around	Tarnopol
127	23	2	Mar-60	Motown/Anna	Barrett Strong	Money (That's What I Want)	Gordy-Bradfield
128	38	1	Apr-60	Fire	Buster Brown	Fannie Mae	Buster Brown
129	33	7	May-60	Federal	James Brown & the Famous Flame	Think	Lowman Pauling

	Pop	R&B	Year	Label	Artist	Song	Writer
130	7	1	May-60	Mercury	Dinah Washington	A Rocking Good Time	Brook Benton, Clyde Otis, DeJesus
131	15	1	May-60	Brunswick	Jackie Wilson	Doggin' Around	Lena Agree
132	15	1	Jun-60	Brunswick	Jackie Wilson	A Woman, A Lover, A Friend	Wyche
133	24	1	Jun-60	Mercury	Dinah Washington	This Bitter Earth	Clyde Otis
134	7	1	Jun-60	Mercury	Brook Benton & Dinah Washington	A Rockin' Good Way (To Mess Around and Fall in	Benton, DeJesus, Clyde Otis
135	31	1	Jul-60	Fire	Bobby Marchan	There's Something On Your Mind-Part 2	Big Jay McNeely
136	1	2	Aug-60	Parkway	Chubby Checker	The Twist	Hank Ballard
137	2	1	Aug-60	RCA	Sam Cooke	Chain Gang	Sam Cooke
138	7	1	Aug-60	Mercury	Brook Benton	Kiddio	Brook Benton, Clyde Otis
139	32	10	Sep-60	Brunswick	Jackie Wilson	Am I The Man	Hamilton-King
140	8	20	Sep-60	Brunswick	Jackie Wilson	Alone At last	Lehman
141	1	3	Oct-60	Herald	Maurice Williams	Stay	Maurice Williams
142	2	1	Oct-60	Motown/Tamla	The Miracles	Shop Around	Gordy-Robinson
143	1		Oct-60	ABC-Paramount	Ray Charles	Georgia On My Mind	Hoagy Carmichael, Stuart Gorrell
144	1	1	Oct-60	Atlantic	The Drifters	Save The Last Dance For Me	Doc Pomus, Mort Shuman
145	6	1	Nov-60	King	Hank Ballard & The Midnighters	Let's Go, Let's Go, Let's Go	Hank Ballard
146	7	1	Nov-60	Vee-Jay	Jerry Butler	He Will Break Your Heart	Butler, Carter, Curtis Mayfield
147	9	25	Dec-60	Brunswick	Jackie Wilson	My Empty Arms	Kasha-Hunter
148	1	2	Dec-60	Sceptre	The Shirelles	Will You Still Love Me Tomorrow	King-Goffin
149	28		Dec-60	ABC-Paramount	Ray Charles	Ruby	Mitchell Parish, Heinz Roemheld
150	43	1	Feb-61	Duke	Bobby Bland	I Pity The Fool	Deadric Malone
151	1	1	Feb-61	Parkway	Chubby Checker	Pony Time	John Berry, Don Covay
152	3	2	Feb-61	Sceptre	The Shirelles	Dedicated to the One I Love	Panting-Bass
153	1	1	Mar-61	Colpix	The Marcels	Blue Moon	Lorenz Hart, Richard Rodgers
154	23	16	Apr-61	Atlantic	The Coasters	Little Egypt (Ying-Yang)	Leiber-Stoller
155	40	8	Apr-61	King	James Brown & the Famous Flame	Bewildered	Whitcup-Powell
156	8	1	Apr-61	Impulse	Ray Charles	One Mint Julep	Rudy Toombs
157	1	1	Apr-61	Minit	Ernie K-Doe	Mother-In-Law	Allen Toussaint
158	4	1	May-61	Atlantic	Ben E. King	Stand By Me	King-Glick
159	4	2	May-61	Sceptre	The Shirelles	Mama Said	Dixon-Denson
160	47	4	Jun-61	King	James Brown & the Famous Flame	I Don't Mind	James Brown
161	6	1	Jun-61	Vee-Jay	The Pips	Every Beat Of My Heart	Johnny Otis
162	3	2	Jul-61	Satellite	Mar-Keys	Last Night	Axton-Caple-Newman-Smith-Moman
163	1	1	Jul-61	Beltone	Bobby Lewis	Tossin' And Turnin'	Ritchie Adams, Malou Rene
164	49	2	Aug-61	King	James Brown & the Famous Flame	Baby You're Right	James Brown-Joe Tex
165	1	1	Aug-61	Motown/Tamla	The Marvelettes	Please Mr. Postman	Dobbins-Garrett-Holland-Bateman-G
166	3	1	Sep-61	Beltone	The Jive Five	My True Story	Eugene Pitt, Oscar Waltzer
167	30	6	Oct-61	Motown	Eddie Holland	Jamie	William Stevenson
168	1	1	Oct-61	ABC-Paramount	Ray Charles	Hit The Road Jack	Ray Charles
169	7	1	Nov-61	Fury	Lee Dorsey	YA YA	Dorsey, Levy, Lewis, Robinson
170	1	4	Dec-61	Parkway	Chubby Checker	The Twist	Hank Ballard
171	8	3	Jan-62	Sceptre	The Shirelles	Baby It's You	David-Williams-Bacharach
172	9	1	Jan-62	ABC-Paramount	Ray Charles	Unchain My Heart	Teddy Powell, Bobby Sharp
173	3	1	Jan-62	A.F.O.	Barbara George	I Know (You Don't Love Me' No More)	Barbara George

	Pop	R&B	Year	Label	Artist	Song	Writer
174	8	2	Feb-62	Motown	Mary Wells	The One Who Really Loves You	William Robinson Jr.
175	1	1	Feb-62	Vee-Jay	Gene Chandler	Duke of Earl	Dixon, Edwards, Bernie Williams
176	7	4	Mar-62	Mercury	Clyde McPhatter	Lover Please	Billy Swan
177	1	3	Mar-62	Sceptre	The Shirelles	Soldier Boy	Dixon-Green
178	9	1	Mar-62	Keen	Sam Cooke	Twistin' The Night Away	Sam Cooke
179	17	1	Apr-62	Enjoy	King Curtis	Soul Twist	King Curtis
180	2	1	Apr-62	Cameo	Dee Dee Sharp	Mashed Potato Time	Brianhert, Jon Sheldon
181	35	5	May-62	King	James Brown & the Famous Flame	Night Train	Washington-Simpkins-Forrest
182	1	1	May-62	ABC-Paramount	Ray Charles	I Can't Stop Loving You	Don Gibson
183	3	1	Jun-62	Motown/Gordy	The Contours	Do You Love Me	Berry Gordy
184	17	7	Jul-62	Motown/Tamla	The Marvelettes	Beechwood 4-5789	Gordy-Gaye-Stevenson
185	46	8	Jul-62	Motown/Tamla	Marvin Gaye	Stubborn Kind Of Fellow	Gordy-Gaye-Stevenson
186	9	1	Jul-62	Motown/Tamla	Mary Wells	You Beat Me To The Punch	Robinson-White
187	2	5	Aug-62	ABC-Paramount	Ray Charles	You Don't Know Me	Eddy Arnold, Cindy Walker
188	8	1	Aug-62	Jamie	Barbara Lynn	You'll Lose A Good Thing	Huey P. Meaux, Barabra Lynn
189	2	7	Aug-62	Capitol	Nat King Cole	Ramblin' Rose	Noel Sherman, Joe Sherman
190	1	1	Aug-62	Dimension	Little Eva	The Loco-Motion	Gerry Goffin, Carole King
191	3	1	Sep-62	Stax	Booker T. & The MG's	Green Onions	Jones-Cropper-Steinberg-Jackson
192	7	1	Oct-62	Motown	Mary Wells	Two Lovers	William Robinson Jr.
193	8	1	Nov-62	Motown/Tamla	The Miracles	You've Really Got A Hold On Me	William Robinson Jr.
194	5	4	Dec-62	Atlantic	The Drifters	Up On The Roof	Gerry Goffin, Carole King
195	29	23	Dec-62	ABC-Paramount	Ray Charles	Your Cheating Heart	Hank Williams
196	8	1	Dec-62	Lenox	Esther Phillips	Release Me	McCall, Miller, Pebworth, Yount
197	7	1	Dec-62	ABC-Paramount	Ray Charles	You are my Sunshine	Jimmie Davis, Charles Mitchell
198	5	1	Feb-63	Brunswick	Jackie Wilson	Baby Workout	Wilson-Tucker
199	29	6	Feb-63	Motown/Gordy	Martha & The Vandellas	Come And Get These Memories	Holland-Dozier-Holland
200	33	1	Mar-63	Duke	Bobby Bland	That's The Way Love Is	Deadric Malone
201	20	9	Mar-63	ABC-Paramount	Ray Charles	Don't Set Me Free	Teddy Powell
202	1	1	Mar-63	Kapp	Ruby & The Romantics	Our Day Will Come	Mort Garson, Bob Hilliard
203	9	7	Apr-63	Atlantic	The Drifters	On Broadway	Weil-Mann-Leiber-Stoller
204	10	2	Apr-63	Motown/Tamla	Marvin Gaye	Pride & Joy	Whitfield-Gaye-Stevenson
205	1	1	Apr-63	Laurie	The Chiffons	He's So Fine	Ronnie Mack
206	8	7	Apr-63	ABC-Paramount	Ray Charles	Take These Chains From My Heart	Hy Heath, Fred Rose
207	37	30	May-63	Atlantic	Wilson Pickett	If You Need Me	Pickett-Bateman-Sanders
208	18	6	May-63	King	James Brown & the Famous Flame	Prisoner of Love	Robin-Columbo-Gaskin
209	1	1	May-63	Motown/Tamla	Little Stevie Wonder	Fingertips - Pt.2	Paul-Cosby
210	6	11	May-63	Capitol	Nat King Cole	Those Lazy-Hazy-Crazy Days Of Summer	Hans Carste, Charles Tobias
211	1	1	Jun-63	SPQR	Jimmy Soul	If You Wanna Be Happy	Frank Guida, Joseph Royster
212	10	1	Jun-63	RCA	Sam Cooke	Another Saturday Night	Sam Cooke
213	10	3	Jul-63	Atlantic	Doris Troy	Just One Look	Payne-Carroll
214	4	1	Jul-63	Motown/Gordy	Martha & The Vandellas	(Love is Like A) Heatwave	Holland- Dozier-Holland
215	8	3	Jul-63	Motown/Tamla	The Miracles	Mickey's Monkey	Holland-Dozier-Holland
216	3	1	Jul-63	Atlantic	Barbara Lewis	Hello Stranger	Barbara Lewis
217	10	10	Aug-63	Colpix	Freddie Scott	Hey Girl	Gerry Goffin, Carole King

	Pop	R&B	Year	Label	Artist	Song	Writer
218	4	3	Sep-63	ABC-Paramount	Ray Charles	Busted	Harlan Howard
219	12	19	Sep-63	Capitol	Nat King Cole	That Sunday, That Summer	Joe Sherman, George David Weiss
220	4	1	Oct-63	United Artists	Garnet Mimms & The Enchanters	Cry Baby	Meade, Russell
221	19	1	Oct-63	Galaxy	Little Johnny Taylor	Part-Time Love	Clay Hammond
222	10	5	Nov-63	Stax	Rufus Thomas	Walking the Dog	Rufus Thomas
223	4	1	Nov-63	ABC-Paramount	The Impressions	It's All Right	Curtis Mayfield
224	20	20	Dec-63	ABC-Paramount	Ray Charles	That Lucky Old Sun	Haven Gillespie, Harry Beasley Smith
225	11	1	Jan-64	Motown/Gordy	The Temptations	The Way You Do The Things You Do	Robinson-Rodgers
226	8	8	Jan-64	Scepter	Dionne Warwick	Anyone Who Had a Heart	Burt Bacharach, H. David
227	23	1	Feb-64	King	James Brown & the Famous Flame	Oh Baby Don't You Weep	James Brown
228	1	1	Mar-64	Motown	Mary Wells	My Guy	William Robinson Jr.
229	13	13	Mar-64	Motown/Tamla	Brenda Holloway	Every Little Bit Hurts	Ed Cobb
230		39	Mar-64	ABC-Paramount	Ray Charles	Baby, Don't You Cry	Buddy Johnson, Ned Washington
231	1		Apr-64	MCA	Louis Armstrong	Hello Dolly	Jerry Herman
232	1	1	May-64	Red Bird	Dixie Cups	Chapel Of Love	Barry, Greenwich, Phil Spector
233	6	6	May-64	Scepter	Dionne Warwick	Walk On By	Burt Bacharach, Hal David
234	4	4	Jul-64	Atlantic	The Drifters	Under the Boardwalk	Resnick-Young
235	11	1	Jul-64	Motown	Four Tops	Baby I Need Your Loving	Holland-Dozier-Holland
236	1	1	Jul-64	Motown	The Supremes	Where Did Our Love Go	Holland-Dozier-Holland
237	1	1	Jul-64	Motown	Martha & The Vandellas	Dancing In The Streets	Stevenson-Gaye-Hunter
238	24	24	Sep-64	King	James Brown & the Famous Flame	Out of Sight	Ted Wright
239	1	1	Sep-64	Motown	The Supremes	Baby Love	Holland-Dozier-Holland
240	1	3	Oct-64	Motown	The Supremes	Come See About Me	Holland-Dozier-Holland
241	1	1	Oct-64	Red Bird	The Shangri-Las	Leader of the Pack	Barry, Greenwich, Morton
242	6	2	Nov-64	DCP	Little Anthony & the Imperials	Goin' out of my Head	Teddy Randazzo, Bob Weinstein
243	5	2	Nov-64	Dial	Joe Tex	Hold What You've Got	Guy Draper, Joe Tex
244	6	4	Nov-64	Motown/Tamla	Marvin Gaye	How Sweet It Is (To Be Loved By You)	Holland-Dozier-Holland
245	1	1	Dec-64	Motown/Gordy	The Temptations	My Girl	Robinson-White
246	24	9	Jan-65	Motown	Four Tops	Ask The Lonely	Stevenson-Hunter
247	4	1	Jan-65	Motown/Soul	Jr. Walker & The All Stars	Shotgun	Autry DeWalt
246	7	3	Jan-65	RCA	Sam Cooke	Shake	Sam Cooke
249	8	5	Feb-65	Motown/Gordy	Martha & The Vandellas	Nowhere To Run	Holland-Dozier-Holland
250	25	12	Feb-65	Motown/Tamla	Brenda Holloway	When I'm Gone	William Robinson Jr.
251	16	4	Mar-65	Motown/Tamla	The Miracles	Ooo Baby Baby	Robinson-Moore
252	1	1	Apr-65	Motown	Four Tops	I Can't Help Myself (Sugar Pie Honey Bunch)	Holland-Dozier-Holland
253	22	1	Apr-65	Atlantic	Solomon Burke	Got to Get You Off My Mind	Burke, Burke, Moore
254			Apr-65	Paramount	Son House	Death Letter	Son House
255	25	1	May-65	Checker	Little Milton	We're Gonna Make It	Barge, Davis, Miner, Smith
256	8	1	May-65	Motown	Marvin Gaye	I'll be Doggone	Moore, Robinson, Tarplin
257	1	1	May-65	Motown	The Supremes	Back in My Arms Again	Holland-Dozier-Holland
258	21	2	Jun-65	Atlantic	Otis Redding	I've Been Loving You Too Long (To Stop Now)	Redding-Butler
259	16	2	Jun-65	Motown/Tamla	The Miracles	The Tracks of My Tears	Robinson-Moore
260	11	5	Jul-65	Atlantic	Barbara Lewis	Baby, I'm Yours	Van McCoy
261	10	5	Jul-65	DCP	Little Anthony & the Imperials	Hurt So Bad	Hart, Randazzo, Wilding

	Pop	R&B	Year	Label	Artist	Song	Writer
262	5	2	Jul-65	Motown	Four Tops	It's The Same Old Song	Holland-Dozier-Holland
263	3	1	Jul-65	Motown/Tamla	Stevie Wonder	Uptight (Everything's Alright)	Cosby-Moy-Wonder
264	21	1	Aug-65	Atlantic	Wilson Pickett	In the Midnight Hour	Pickett-Cropper
265	8	1	Aug-65	King	James Brown	Papa's Got A Brand New Bag	James Brown
266	88	4	Sep-65	JoDa	Johnny Nash	Let's Move & Groove Together	Unknown
267	50	4	Sep-65	Motown/Gordy	Kim Weston	Take Me In Your Arms	Holland-Dozier-Holland
268	11	5	Oct-65	Atlantic	Barbara Lewis	Make Me Your Baby	Atkins-Miller
269	23	1	Oct-65	Dial	Joe Tex	I Want to (Do everything for you)	Joe Tex
270	33	1	Oct-65	Checker	Fontella Bass	Rescue Me	Raynard Miner, C. Smith
271	3	1	Nov-65	King	James Brown	I Got You (I Feel Good)	James Brown
272	7	3	Nov-65	Motown/Tamla	The Marvellettes	Don't Mess With Bill	William Robinson Jr.
273	90	7	Nov-65	Stan	Sam & Dave	You Don't Know Like I Know	Hayes-Porter
274	8	1	Nov-65	Motown	Marvin Gaye	Ain't That Peculiar	Moore, Robinson, Rogers, Tarplin
275	72	3	Dec-65	Motown/VIP	The Elgins	Darling Baby	Holland-Dozier-Holland
276	12	6	Jan-66	Motown/Tamla	Isley Brothers	This Old Heart Of Mine (Is Weak For You)	Holland-Dozier-Holland-Moy
277	29	1	Jan-66	Dial	Joe Tex	A Sweet Woman Like You	Joe Tex Arrington
278	6	5	Jan-66	ABC-Paramount	Ray Charles	Crying Time	Buck Owens
279	16	1	Feb-66	Excello	Slim Harpo	Baby Scratch my Back	Slim Harpo
280	42	6	Mar-66	King	James Brown	Ain't That A Groove	James Brown-Nat Jones
281	20	4	Mar-66	Motown	Jr. Walker & The All Stars	(I'm A) Road Runner	Holland-Dozier-Holland
282	21	1	Mar-66	Stax	Sam & Dave	Hold On! I'm Comin'	Hayes-Porter
283	13	1	Mar-66	Atlantic	Wilson Pickett	634-5789 (Soulsville, USA)	Steve Cropper, Eddie Floyd
284	1	1	Apr-66	Atlantic	Percy Sledge	When A Man Loves A Woman	Lewis, Wright
285	8	5	Apr-66	Scepter	Dionne Warwick	Message To Michael	Burt Bacharach, Hal David
286	19	10	Apr-66	ABC-Paramount	Ray Charles	Together Again	Buck Owens
287	29	1	Apr-66	Motown	The Temptations	Get Ready	Smokey Robinson
288	7	2	May-66	Karen	The Capitols	Cool Jerk	Don Storball
289	8	1	May-66	King	James Brown	It's a Man's World	James Brown-Betty Newsome
290	13	1	May-66	Motown/Gordy	The Temptations	Ain't Too Proud To Beg	Eddie Holland
291	7	6	Jun-66	Motown	Jimmy Ruffin	What Becomes Of A Broken Heart	Weatherspoon, Riser, Dean
292	9	1	Jul-66	Motown	Stevie Wonder	Blowin In the Wind	Bob Dylan
293	18	3	Jul-66	Motown	Jr. Walker & The All Stars	How Sweet It Is (To Be Loved By You)	Holland-Dozier-Holland
294	1	1	Jul-66	Motown	The Supremes	You Can't Hurry Love	Holland-Dozier-Holland
295	78	14	Jul-66	Philly Int'l	The Intruders	(We'll Be) United	Gamble-Huff
296	31	1	Jul-66	ABC-Paramount	Ray Charles	Let's Go Get Stoned	Armstead, Ashford, Simpson
297	6	1	Aug-66	Atlantic	Wilson Pickett	Land of 1000 Dances	Chris Kenner
298	17	5	Aug-66	Atlantic	Percy Sledge	Warm And Tender Love	Ida Irral Berger, Bobby Robinson
299	3	1	Aug-66	Motown/Gordy	The Temptations	Beauty Is Only Skin Deep	Whitfield-Holland
300	50	9	Aug-66	MotownNtP	The Elgins	Heaven Must Have Sent You	Holland-Dozier-Holland
301	64	8	Aug-66	Stax	Sam & Dave	Said I Wasn't Gonna Tell Nobody	Hayes-Porter
302	11	5	Sep-66	Brunswick	Jackie Wilson	Whispers (Getting Louder)	Acklin-Scott
303	1	1	Sep-66	Motown	Four Tops	Reach Out (I'll Be There)	Holland-Dozier-Holland
304	14	3	Sep-66	Stan	Carla Thomas	B-A-B-Y	Hayes-Porter
305	32	22	Oct-66	ABC	Ray Charles	I Chose To Sing The Blues	Ray Charles. Jimmy Holiday

	Pop	R&B	Year	Label	Artist	Song	Writer
306	50	4	Oct-66	King	James Brown	Don't Be A Dropout	James Brown-Nat Jones
307	20	7	Nov-66	Atlantic	Percy Sledge	It Tears Me Up	Spooner Oldham, Dan Penn
308	6	2	Nov-66	Motown	Four Tops	Standing In The Shadow Of Love	Holland-Dozier-Holland
309	8	1	Nov-66	Motown/Gordy	The Temptations	I Know I'm Losing You	Holland-Whitfield-Grant
310	28	1	Nov-66	Stax	Eddie Floyd	Knock on Wood	Floyd-Cropper
311	77	7	Nov-66	Stax	Sam & Dave	You've Got Me Humming	Hayes-Porter
312	13	1	Nov-66	Capitol	Lou Rawls	Love is a Hurtin' Thing	Dave Linden, Ben Raleigh
313	1	1	Nov-66	Motown	The Supremes	You Keep Me Hangin' On	Holland-Dozier-Holland
314	14	4	Dec-66	Motown/Tamla	Marvin Gaye & Kim Weston	It Takes Two	Stevenson-Moy
315	13	2	Dec-66	Motown/Tamla	The Marvelettes	The Hunter Gets Captured By The Game	William Robinson Jr.
316	2	1	Dec-66	Par-Lo	Aaron Neville	Tell It Like It Is	Davis-Diamond
317	25	4	Dec-66	Volt	Otis Redding	Try A Little Tenderness	Connelly-Woods-Campbell
318	29	7	Jan-67	King	James Brown	Bring It Up	James Brown-Nat Jones
319	42	2	Jan-67	Stax	Sam & Dave	When Something is Wrong with My Baby	Hayes-Porter
320	46	5	Feb-67	King	James Brown	Let Yourself Go	James Brown-Bud Hobgood
321	4	1	Feb-67	Motown	Four Tops	Bernadette	Holland-Dozier-Holland
322	10	1	Feb-67	Motown/Gordy	Martha & The Vandellas	Jimmy Mack	Holland-Dozier-Holland
323	16	1	Feb-67	Soul City	The Fifth Dimension	Go Where You Wanna Go	J. Phillips
324	2	1	Feb-67	Stax	Sam & Dave	Soul Man	Hayes-Porter
325	39	1	Feb-67	Shout	Freddie Scott	Are You Lonely For Me Baby?	Bert Berns
326	1	1	Mar-67	Motown	The Supremes	Love is Here and Now You're Gone	Holland-Dozier-Holland
327	9	1	Mar-67	Atlantic	Aretha Franklin	I Never Loved a Man (The Way I Love You)	Ronnie Shannon
328	2	2	Apr-67	Atlantic	Arthur Conley	Sweet Soul Music	Redding-Conley-Cooke
329	19	3	Apr-67	Motown/Tamla	Marvin Gaye & Tammi Terrell	Ain't No Mountain High Enough	Ashford-Simpson
330	1	1	May-67	Atlantic	Aretha Franklin	Respect	Otis Redding
331	23	5	May-67	Motown/Tamla	Smokey Robinson & The Miracles	More Love	William Robinson Jr.
332	56	16	May-67	Stax	Sam & Dave	Soothe Me	Cooke
333	7	2	Jun-67	Soul City	The Fifth Dimension	Up Up And Away	Jimmy Webb
334	15	5	Jun-67	ABC-TRC	Ray Charles	Here We Go Again	Don Lanier, Red Steagall
335	31	1	Jul-67	Atlantic	Joe Turner	Shake Rattle & Roll	Charles E. Calhoun
336	6	1	Jul-67	Brunswick	Jackie Wilson	Your Love Keeps Lifting Me Higher & Higher	Jackson-Smith-Miner
337	2	1	Jul-67	Motown	Stevie Wonder	I Was Made To Love Her	Cosby, Hardaway, May, Wonder
338	21	1	Jul-67	Money	Bettye Swann	Make Me Yours	Bettye Swann
339	7	1	Aug-67	Atlantic	James Brown	Cold Sweat	James Brown-Alfred Ellis
340	4	1	Aug-67	Atlantic	Aretha Franklin	Baby I Love You	Ronnie Shannon
341	33	6	Sep-67	Atco	King Curtis	Memphis Soul Stew	Curtis Ousley
342	2	1	Sep-67	Motown	Gladys Knight & The Pips	I Heard It Through The Grapevine	Whitfield-Strong
343	4	3	Sep-67	Philly Int'l	Soul Survivors	Expressway to your Heart	Gamble-Huff
344	33	21	Sep-67	ABC-TRC	Ray Charles	In The Heat Of The Night	Bergman, Bergman, Quincy Jones
345	8	1	Sep-67	Atlantic	Wilson Pickett	Funky Broadway	Arlester "Dyke" Christian
346	4	1	Oct-67	Motown/Tamla	Smokey Robinson & The Miracles	Second That Emotion	Robinson-Cleveland
347	8	2	Oct-67	Atlantic	Aretha Franklin	A Natural Woman (You Make Me Feel)	Goffin-King-Wexler
348	10	2	Nov-67	Dial	Joe Tex	Skinny Legs And All	Joe Tex
349	40	11	Nov-67	King	James Brown	Get it Together	Brown-Ellis-Hobgood

#	Pop	R&B	Year	Label	Artist	Song	Writer
350	4	8	Nov-67	Scepter	Dionne Warwick	I Say A Little Prayer	Burt Bacharach, Hal David
351	28	4	Dec-67	King	James Brown	I Can't Stand Myself	James Brown
352	4	1	Dec-67	Motown/Gordy	The Temptations	I Wish It Would Rain	Whitfield-Strong-Penzabene
353	25	9	Dec-67	ABC-TRC	Ray Charles	Yesterday	John Lennon, Paul McCartney
354	2	1	Jan-68	Atlantic	Aretha Franklin	Chain of Fools	Don Covay
355	36	3	Feb-68	King	James Brown	There Was A Time	James Brown-Bud Hobgood
356	29	5	Feb-68	Motown/Gordy	Bobby Taylor & The Vancouvers	Does Your Mama Know About Me	Baird-Chong
357	2	13	Feb-68	Scepter	Dionne Warwick	Theme from Valley of the Dolls	Andre Previn, Dory Previn
358	9	4	Feb-68	Stax	Sam & Dave	I Thank You	Hayes-Porter
359	8	1	Mar-68	Epic	Sly & The Family Stone	Dance To the Music	S. Stewart
360	6	1	Mar-68	King	James Brown	I Got The Feelin	James Brown
361	8	1	Mar-68	Motown/Tamla	Marvin Gaye & Tammi Terrell	Ain't Nothing Like The Real Thing	Ashford-Simpson
362	6	1	Mar-68	Philly Int'l	The Intruders	Cowboys To Girls	Gamble-Huff
363	14	1	Mar-68	ABC-Paramount	The Impressions	We're A Winner	Curtis Mayfield
364	1	1	Mar-68	Volt	Otis Redding	(Sittin' On) The Dock of The Bay	Steve Cropper, Otis Redding
365	1	1	Apr-68	Atlantic	Archie Bell & The Drells	Tighten It Up	Buttier-Bell
366	11	6	Apr-68	Atlantic	Percy Sledge	Take Time To Know Her	Stephen Allen Davis, Al Gallico
367			Apr-68	MCA	Louis Armstrong	Hello Brother	Bob Thiele, George David Weiss
368	[1]		Apr-68	MCA	Louis Armstrong	What a Wonderful World	Bob Thiele, George David Weiss
369	10	23	Apr-68	Scepter	Dionne Warwick	Do You Know The Way To San Jose	Burt Bacharach, Hal David
370	5	1	Apr-68	Atlantic	Aretha Franklin	(Sweet Sweet baby) Since You've Been Gone	Aretha Franklin, Teddy White
371	48	20	May-68	Stan	Sam & Dave	You Don't Know What You Mean To Me	Floyd-Cropper
372	14	2	Jun-68	King	James Brown	Licking Stick	Brown-Ellis-Byrd
373	9	1	Jun-68	Motown	Stevie Wonder	Shoo-Be-Doo-Be-Doo-Da-Day	Cosby, Moy, Wonder
374	3	2	Jun-68	Soul City	The Fifth Dimension	Stoned Soul Picnic	L. Nyro
375	7	1	Jun-68	Atlantic	Aretha Franklin	Think	Aretha Franklin, Teddy White
376	54	19	Jul-68	Stax	Sam & Dave	I Could Never Love Another (After Loving You)	Banks-Jackson
377	13	1	Jul-68	Motown	The Temptations	I Could Never Love Another (After Loving You)	Whitfield-Strong-Penzabene
378	1	1	Jul-68	Uni	Hugh Masekela	Grazing in the Grass	Harry Elston, Philemon Hou
379	35	30	Jul-68	ABC-TRC	Ray Charles	Eleanor Rigby	John Lennon, Paul McCartney
380	6	2	Aug-68	Atlantic	Clarence Carter	Slip Away	Armstrong-Terrell-Daniel
381	15	3	Aug-68	Brunswick	Barbara Acklin	Love Makes a Woman	Davis, Record, Sanders, Simms
382	9	5	Aug-68	Philly Int'l	Archie Bell & The Drells	I Can't Stop Dancing	Gamble-Huff
383	10	1	Aug-68	Cadet	The Dells	Stay in My Corner	Flemons, Miller, Barrett Strong
384	7	1	Aug-68	Motown	Marvin Gaye & Tammi Terrell	You're All I Need To Get By	Ashford, Simpson
385	10	1	Sep-68	King	James Brown	Say it Loud, I'm Black and I'm Proud	James Brown-Alfred Ellis
386	1	1	Sep-68	Motown	Diana Ross & The Supremes	Love Child	Taylor-Wilson-Sawyer-Richards
387	5	21	Oct-68	JAD	Johnny Nash	Hold Me Tight	J Nash
388	6	2	Oct-68	Motown/Gordy	The Temptations	Cloud Nine	Whitfield-Strong
389	2	2	Oct-68	Motown/Tamla	Stevie Wonder	For Once In My Life	Miller-Murden
390	1	1	Oct-68	Motown/Tamla	Marvin Gaye	I Heard It Through The Grapevine	Whitfield-Strong
391	41	18	Nov-68	Stax	Sam & Dave	Soul Sister, Brown Sugar	Hayes-Porter
392	16	1	Nov-68	Vee-Jay	Jerry Butler	Hey, Western Union Man	Butler, Gamble, Huff
393	5	1	Nov-68	Stax	Johnnie Taylor	Who's Making Love	Banks, Crutcher, Davis, Jackson

	Pop	R&B	Year	Label	Artist	Song	Writer
394	3	3	Dec-68	Brunswick	Young-Holt Unlimited	Soulful Strut	Eugene Record, Sonny Sanders
395	31	9	Dec-68	King	James Brown	Goodbye My Love	James Brown
396	8	3	Dec-68	Motown/Tamla	Smokey Robinson & The Miracles	Baby Baby Don't Cry	Robinson-Cleveland-Johnson
397	21	6	Jan-69	Atlantic	Archie Bell & The Drells	Ther's Gonna Be A Showdown	Tyson-Sigler-Felder
398	5	1	Jan-69	Brunswick	Tyrone Davis	Can I Change My Mind	Barry Despenza, Carl Wolfolk
399	1	1	Jan-69	Epic	Sly & The Family Stone	Everyday People	S. Stewart
400	9	2	Jan-69	Motown	David Ruffin	My Whole World Ended (The Moment You Left Me)	Bristol-Fuqua-Sawyer-Roach
401	6	6	Jan-69	Motown/Gordy	Edwin Starr	Twenty-Five Miles	Bristol-Fuqua-Starr
402	15	1	Feb-69	King	James Brown	Give It Up or Turn It Loose	Charles Bobbit
403	7	7	Feb-69	Scepter	Dionne Warwick	This Girl's In Love With You	Burt Bacharach, Hal David
404	4	1	Mar-69	Philly Int'l	Jerry Butler	Only The Strong Survive	Butler, Gamble, Huff
405	1	6	Mar-69	Soul City	The Fifth Dimension	Aquarius/Let The Sunshine In	Rado-Ragni-MacDermot
406	6	1	Mar-69	Motown	The Temptations	Run Away Child Running Wild	Whitfield-Strong
407	22	6	Apr-69	Epic	Sly & The Family Stone	Stand	S. Stewart
408	20	3	Apr-69	King	James Brown	I Don't Want Nobody To Give me Nothing	James Brown
409	4	1	Apr-69	Motown	Jr. Walker & The All Stars	What Does It Take (To Win Your Love)	Bristol-Fuqua-Bullock
410	2	1	Apr-69	T-Neck	The Isley Brothers	It's Your Thing	Isley, Isley, Isley
411	13	1	May-69	Sound Stage	Joe Simon	The Chokin' Kind	Harlan Howard
412	11	1	Jun-69	King	James Brown	Mother Popcorn	James Brown-Alfred Ellis
413	30	11	Jun-69	King	James Brown	The Popcorn	James Brown-Alfred Ellis
414	4	1	Jun-69	Motown	Marvin Gaye	Too Busy Thinking About My Baby	Bradford, Strong, Whitfield
415	14	1	Jul-69	Motown	The Originals	Baby, I'm For Real	Gaye-Gaye
416	1	1	Jul-69	Motown	The Temptations	I Can't Get Next To You	Whitfield-Strong
417	68	15	Jul-69	Philly Int'l	The O'Jays	One Night Affair	Gamble-Huff
418	2	1	Aug-69	Epic	Sly & The Family Stone	Hot Fun In The Summertime	S. Stewart
419	21	1	Aug-69	Curtom Records	The Impressions	Choice of Colors	Curtis Mayfield
420	13	1	Aug-69	Atlantic	Aretha Franklin	Share Your Love With Me	Alfred Braggs, Deadric Malone
421	37	8	Sep-69	King	James Brown	Man's World Part 1	James Brown-Betty Newsome
422	10	1	Sep-69	Cadet	The Dells	Oh, What a Night	Johnny Funches, Marvin Junior
423	1	1	Oct-69	Motown	The Jackson 5	I Want You Back	Perren-Mizell-Gordy-Richards
424	1	23	Oct-69	Soul City	The Fifth Dimension	Wedding Bell Blues	L. Nyro
425	21	2	Nov-69	King	James Brown	Let A Man Come in and Do the Popcorn Pt 1	James Brown
426	24	3	Dec-69	King	James Brown	Ain't it Funky Now	James Brown
427	1	1	Dec-69	Motown	Diana Ross & The Supremes	Someday We'll Be Together	Beavers, Bristol, Fuqua
428	4	1	Jan-70	Cotillion	Brook Benton	Rainy Night in Georgia	Tony Joe White
429	1	1	Jan-70	Epic	Sly & The Family Stone	Thank You	S. Stewart
430	39		Jan-70	JAD	Johnny Nash	Cupid	S. Cooke
431	40	6	Jan-70	King	James Brown	Let A Man Come In and Do the Popcorn Pt 2	James Brown
432	12	4	Jan-70	Motown	The Originals	The Bells	Gaye-Gaye-Gordy-Stover
433	6	17	Jan-70	Scepter	Dionne Warwick	I'll Never Fall In Love Again	Burt Bacharach, Hal David
434	32	3	Feb-70	King	James Brown	It's a New Day	James Brown
435	10	5	Feb-70	Motown	The Supremes	Up The Ladder To The Roof	DiMarco-Wilson
436	1	1	Feb-70	Motown	The Jackson 5	ABC	Perren-Mizell-Gordy-Richards
437	76	30	Feb-70	Philly Int'l	Dusty Springfield	Silly, Silly Fool	Gamble-Huff

	Pop	R&B	Year	Label	Artist	Song	Writer
438	51	20	Mar-70	King	James Brown	Funky Drummer	James Brown
439	13	1	Mar-70	Atlantic	Aretha Franklin	Call Me	Aretha Franklin
440	2	20	May-70	Invictus	Freda Payne	Band of Gold	Holland-Dozier-Holland
441	32	2	May-70	King	James Brown	Brother Rapp	James Brown
442	1	1	May-70	Motown	The Jackson 5	The Love You Save	Perren-Mizell-Gordy-Richards
443	3	2	May-70	Motown/Tamla	The Temptations	Ball Of Confusion	Whitfield-Strong
444	3	1	May-70	Dakar	Tyrone Davis	Turn Back the Hands of Time	Daniels-Thompson
445	3	1	May-70	Stang	The Moments	Love On a Two-Way Street	Keyes/Robinson
446	38	14	Jun-70	Epic	Sly & The Family Stone	I Want To Take You Higher	S. Stewart
447	1	3	Jun-70	Motown/Gordy	Edwin Starr	WAR	Whitfield-Strong
448	3	1	Jun-70	Motown/Tamla	Stevie Wonder	Signed Sealed & Delivered	Wonder-Garrett-Wright-Hardaway
449	14	4	Jun-70	Motown/VIP	The Spinners	It's A Shame	Wonder-Garrett-Wright
450	1	1	Jul-70	Motown	Diana Ross	Ain't No Mountain High Enough	Ashford-Simpson
451	15	4	Aug-70	King	James Brown	Get Up, I Feel Like Being a Sex Machine	Brown-Byrd-Lenhoff
452	11	4	Aug-70	Motown	Four Tops	Still Water	Robinson-Wilson
453	7	20	Aug-70	Rare Earth	Rare Earth	I Know I'm Losing You	Holland-Whitfield-Grant
454	1	1	Sep-70	Motown	The Jackson 5	I'll Be There	Gordy-West-Davis-Hutch
455	1	1	Sep-70	Motown/Tamla	Smokey Robinson & The Miracles	The Tears Of A Clown	Cosby-Robinson-Wonder
456	29	3	Oct-70	Curtom	Curtis Mayfield	(Don't Worry) If There's A Hell Below	Curtis Mayfield
457	13	1	Oct-70	King	James Brown	Super Bad	James Brown
458	9	1	Oct-70	Motown	Gladys Knight & The Pips	If I Were Your Woman	Ware-Sawyer-McMurray
459	7	1	Oct-70	Motown	The Supremes	Stoned Love	Wilson-Samoht
460	2	4	Nov-70	Bell	The Fifth Dimension	One Less Bell To Answer	Bacharach-David
461	34	4	Jan-71	King	James Brown	Get Up, Get into It, Get Involved	Brown-Byrd-Lenhoff
462	2	1	Jan-71	Motown/Tamla	Marvin Gaye	What's Going On	Gaye-Clevelans-Benson
463	1	1	Jan-71	Motown/Tamla	The Temptations	Just My Imagination (Running Away With Me)	Whitfield-Strong
464	17	2	Jan-71	Philly Int'l	Wilson Pickett	Don't Let The Green Grass Fool You	Aikenes-Bellman-Drayton-Turner
465	6	1	Jan-71	Chimneyville	King Floyd	Groove Me	King Floyd
466	4	5	Feb-71	Liberty	Ike & Tina Turner	Proud Mary	J Fogerty
467	25	1	Feb-71	Stax	Rufus Thomas	(Do The) Push and Pull	Rufus Thomas
468	28	1	Feb-71	Stax	Johnnie Taylor	Jody's Got Your Girl and Gone	Baker, Wilson, Davis
469	29	3	Mar-71	King	James Brown	Soul Power	James Brown
470	2	1	Mar-71	Motown	The Jackson 5	Never Can Say Goodbye	Clifton Davis
471	16	8	Apr-71	Motown	The Supremes	Nathan Jones	Wakefield-Caston
472	17	2	May-71	Motown	Gladys Knight & The Pips	I Don't Want To Do Wrong	Bristol-Knight-Guest-Knight-Schaffne
473	3	2	May-71	Motown/Gordy	The Undisputed Truth	Smiling Faces Sometimes	Whitfield-Strong
474	51	10	May-71	Philly Int'l	The Ebonys	You're The Reason Why	Gamble-Huff
475	2	1	May-71	United Art	Cornelius Bros & Sister Rose	Treat Her Like a Lady	E. Cornelius
476	6	1	May-71	Atlantic	Aretha Franklin	Bridge Over Troubled Water	Paul Simon
477	1	1	May-71	Hot Wax	The Honey Cone	Want Ads	Holland-Dozier-Holland
478	12	3	Jun-71	Invictus	Freda Payne	Bring The Boys Home	Holland-Dozier-Holland
479	7	30	Jun-71	Motown/RareEarth	Rare Earth	I Just Want To Celebrate	Rzesses-Fekaris
480	4	1	Jun-71	Motown/Tamla	Marvin Gaye	Mercy Mercy Me	Marvin Gaye
481	25	6	Jun-71	People	James Brown	Escapism	James Brown

	Pop	R&B	Year	Label	Artist	Song	Writer
482	13	1	Jun-71	Atlantic	Wilson Pickett	Don't Knock My Love	Pickett-Shapiro
483	15	1	Jul-71	People	James Brown	Hot Pants	James Brown-Fred Wesley
484	9	3	Jul-71	Volt	The Dramatics	Whatcha See is Whatcha Get	Tony Hester
485	2	1	Jul-71	Stax	Jean Knight	Mr. Big Stuff	Broussard, Washington, Williams
486	2	1	Aug-71	Atlantic	Aretha Franklin	Spanish Harlem	Leiber-Spector
487	22	1	Sep-71	Polydor	James Brown	Make it Funky	James Brown-Charles Bobbit
488	11	1	Sep-71	Hot Wax	The Honey Cone	Stick Up	Holland-Dozier-Holland
489	69	13	Oct-71	Curtom	Curtis Mayfield	Get Down	Curtis Mayfield
490	115	32	Oct-71	Curtom	Curtis Mayfield	We Got To Have Peace	Curtis Mayfield
491	1	1	Oct-71	Enterprise	Isaac Hayes	Theme from Shaft	Isaac Hayes
492	15	1	Oct-71	Atco	The Persuaders	Thin Line Between Love & Hate	Members-Poindexter-Poindexter
493	13	1	Oct-71	Westbound	Denise LaSalle	Trapped By a Thing Called Love	D. LaSalle
494	9	2	Nov-71	Atlantic	Aretha Franklin	Rocksteady	Aretha Franklin
495	1	1	Nov-71	Epic	Sly & The Family Stone	Family Affair	S. Stewart
496	4	4	Nov-71	Motown	Michael Jackson	Got To Be There	Willensky
497	11	3	Nov-71	Philly Int'l	Joe Simon	Drowning In The Sea of Love	Gamble-Huff
498	9	1	Nov-71	Motown	Marvin Gaye	Inner City Blues (Make Me Wanna Holler)	Marvin Gaye
499	3	1	Nov-71	Brunswick	The Chi-Lites	Have You Seen Her	Acklin/Record
500	35	7	Dec-71	Polydor	James Brown	I'm a Greedy Man	James Brown-Charles Bobbit
501	1	1	Jan-72	Stax	Staple Singers	I'll Take You There	Alvertis Isbell
502	1	1	Jan-72	Hi	Al Green	Let's Stay Together	Green-Jackson-Mitchell
503	2	1	Feb-72	Dial	Joe Tex	I Gotcha	Joe Tex
504	23	14	Feb-72	Epic	Sly & The Family Stone	Running Away	S. Stewart
505	27	1	Feb-72	Polydor	James Brown	Talking Loud & Saying Nothing	James Brown-Bobby Byrd
506	1	4	Mar-72	Atlantic	Roberta Flack	The First Time Ever I Saw Your Face	Ewan MacColl
507	5	3	Mar-72	Volt	The Dramatics	In the Rain	Tony Hester
508	8	28	Apr-72	Bell	The Fifth Dimension	Last Night I Didn't Get Any Sleep At All	T. Macaulay
509	1	1	Apr-72	Brunswick	The Chi-Lites	Oh Girl	E Record
510	4	2	Apr-72	Hi	Al Green	Look What You Done For Me	Green-Jackson-Mitchell
511	1	1	Apr-72	MGM	Sammy Davis Jr.	The Candy Man	Bricusse-Newley
512	40	6	Apr-72	Polydor	James Brown	King Heroin	Brown-Bobbit-Matthews-Rosen
513	43	4	Apr-72	Polydor	James Brown	There It Is	James Brown
514	5	1	Apr-72	Atlantic	Aretha Franklin	Day Dreaming	Aretha Franklin
515	44	7	May-72	Polydor	James Brown	Honky Tonk	James Brown
516	2	2	Jun-72	Motown	Michael Jackson	Rockin Robin	Thomas
517	58	7	Jun-72	Philly Int'l	Harold Melvin & The Blue Notes	I Miss You	Gamble-Huff
519	2	1	Jun-72	United Art	Cornelius Bros & Sister Rose	It's Too Late to Turn Back Now	E. Cornelius
520	60	1	Jun-72	United Art	Bobby Womack	Woman's Gotta Have It	Carter-Womack-Womack
521	1	1	Jun-72	Sussex	Bill Withers	Lean On Me	Bill Withers
522	2	1	Jul-72	A&M	Billy Preston	Outa-Space	Greene-Preston
523	64	17	Jul-72	Buddah	The Trammps	Zing Went The Strings Of My Heart	Baker/Felder/Harris/Young
524	4	2	Jul-72	Curtom	Curtis Mayfield	Freddie's Dead (Theme from Superfly)	Curtis Mayfield
525	3	1	Jul-72	Philly Int'l	The O'Jays	Back Stabbers	McFadden-Whitehead-Huff
526	44	3	Jul-72	Polydor	James Brown	I Got A Bag of My Own	James Brown

	Pop	R&B	Year	Label	Artist	Song	Writer
527	3	1	Jul-72	KoKo	Luther Ingram	(If Loving You Is Wrong) I Don't Want To Be Right	Banks-Hampton-Jackson
528	5	1	Aug-72	Atlantic	Roberta Flack & Donny Hathaway	Where is the Love	MacDonald-Slater
529	3	1	Aug-72	Hi	Al Green	I'm Still in Love with You	Green-Jackson-Mitchell
530	11	1	Aug-72	Spring	Joe Simon	Power of Love	Gamble-Huff-Simon
531	1	1	Sep-72	Chess	Chuck Berry	My Ding-A-Ling	Chuck Berry
532	1	5	Sep-72	Motown	Michael Jackson	Ben	Black, Scharf
533	78	12	Sep-72	Philly Int'l	Johnny Williams	Slow Motion (Part 1)	Gamble-Huff
534	18	1	Sep-72	Polydor	James Brown	Get On The Good Foot	Brown-Wesley-Mims
535	3	2	Sep-72	RCA	Main Ingredient	Everybody Plays the Fool	Bailey-Clark-Williams
536	8	5	Oct-72	Curtom	Curtis Mayfield	Superfly	Curtis Mayfield
537	1	38	Oct-72	Epic	Johnny Nash	I Can See Clearly Now	J Nash
538	3	1	Oct-72	Philly Int'l	Harold Melvin & The Blue Notes	If You Don't Know Me By Now	Gamble-Huff
539	1	1	Oct-72	Philly Int'l	Billy Paul	Me & Mrs Jones	Gamble-Huff-Gilbert
540	3	1	Oct-72	Atlantic	The Spinners	I'll Be Around	Bell-Hurtt
541	57	13	Nov-72	Philly Int'l	The O'Jays	992 Arguments	Gamble-Huff
542	3	1	Dec-72	Hi	Al Green	You Ought To Be With Me	Green-Jackson-Mitchell
543	1	1	Jan-73	Philly Int'l	The O'Jays	Love Train	Gamble-Huff
544	1	1	Jan-73	Motown	Stevie Wonder	Superstition	Stevie Wonder
545	3	1	Jan-73	Glades	Timmy Thomas	Why Can't We Live Together	Timmy Thomas
546	27	4	Feb-73	Polydor	James Brown	I Got Ants In My Pants and I want to Dance	James Brown
547	1	2	Feb-73	Atlantic	Roberta Flack	Killing me Softly with His Song	Fox-Gimbel
548	4	1	Feb-73	Atlantic	The Spinners	Could It Be I'm Falling In Love	Steals-Steals
549	5	42	Mar-73	Decca	Dobie Gray	Driftaway	Maurice Williams
550	12	1	Mar-73	Epic	Johnny Nash	Stir It Up	B. Marley
551	10	2	Mar-73	Hi	Al Green	Call Me (Come Back Home)	Green-Jackson-Mitchell
552	63	12	Mar-73	Philly Int'l	Harold Melvin & The Blue Notes	Yesterday I Had The Blues	Gamble-Huff
553	1	3	Mar-73	Tamla	Stevie Wonder	You are the Sunshine of my Life	Stevie Wonder
554	2	1	Mar-73	Soul	Gladys Knight & The Pips	Neither One Of Us (Wants To Be The First To Say	Jim Weatherly
555	79	29	Apr-73	Philly Int'l	Billy Paul	Am I Black Enough For You	Sigler-Hurtt
556	7	1	Apr-73	Motown	The Temptations	Masterpiece	Norm Whitfield
557	36	6	May-73	Philly Int'l	The Intruders	I'll Always Love My Mama	McFadden-Whitehead-Gamble-Huff
558	15	1	May-73	Westbound	Ohio Players	Funky Worm	Ohio Players
559	1	10	May-73	A&M	Billy Preston	Will It Go Round In Circles	Fisher-Preston
560	21	1	May-73	Wand	The Independents	Leaving Me	Jackson-Yancy
561	3	1	May-73	20th Century	Barry White	I'm Gonna Love You Just A Little More Baby	Barry White
562	39	11	Jun-73	Curtom	Curtis Mayfield	Future Shock	Curtis Mayfield
563	10	4	Jun-73	London	Bloodstone	Natural High	McCormick
564	11	1	Jun-73	Atlantic	The Spinners	One of a Kind (Love Affair)	Jefferson
565	28	15	Jul-73	Buddah	Gladys Knight & The Pips	Where Peaceful Waters Flow	Jim Weatherly
566	12	1	Jul-73	Epic	Sly & The Family Stone	If You Want Me To Stay	S. Stewart
567	10	2	Jul-73	Hi	Al Green	Here I Am (Come And Take Me)	Green-Hodges
568	1	1	Jul-73	Motown	Diana Ross	Touch Me In the Morning	Masser-Miller
569	22	1	Jul-73	People	Fred Wesley & The JBs	Doing it to Death	James Brown
570	11	1	Jul-73	Stax	Johnnie Taylor	I Believe in You (You Believe In Me)	Davis

	Pop	R&B	Year	Label	Artist	Song	Writer
571	6	1	Aug-73	T-Neck	Isley Brothers	That Lady (Part 1)	Isley Brothers
572	20	1	Aug-73	Atlantic	Aretha Franklin	Angel	Carolyn Franklin, Sonny Saunders
573	1	1	Aug-73	Motown	Marvin Gaye	Let's Get It On	Marvin Gaye
574	1	1	Sep-73	Buddah	Gladys Knight & The Pips	Midnight Train to Georgia	Jim Weatherly
575	1	1	Sep-73	Philly Int'l	The O'Jays	Now That We Found Love	Gamble-Hull
576	7	1	Sep-73	Philly Int'l	Harold Melvin & The Blue Notes	The Love I Lost	Gamble-Huff
577	50	6	Sep-73	Polydor	James Brown	Sexy, Sexy, Sexy	James Brown
578	4	1	Sep-73	Motown	Stevie Wonder	Higher Ground	Stevie Wonder
579		1	Oct-73	Philly Int'l	The O'Jays	Don't Call Me Brother	Gamble-Hutf
580	1	1	Oct-73	Motown	Eddie Kendricks	Keep On Truckin'	Caston-Wilson
581	7	2	Nov-73	20th Century	Barry White	Never, Never Gonna Give You Up	Barry White
582	88	16	Nov-73	Curtom	Curtis Mayfield	Can't Say Nothin'	Curtis Mayfield
583	4	1	Nov-73	A&M	Billy Preston	Space Race	Billy Preston
584	1	1	Dec-73	20th Century	Love Unlimited Orchestra	Love's Theme	Barry White
585	4	1	Dec-73	Buddah	Gladys Knight & The Pips	I've Got To Use My Imagination	Goffin-Goldberg
586		75	Dec-73	Philly Int'l	The Trammps	Love Epidemic	Harris-Green
587	9	1	Dec-73	Stan	Staple Singers	If You're Ready (Come Go With Me)	Staple Singers
588	8	1	Dec-73	Motown	Stevie Wonder	Living for the City	Stevie Wonder
589	4	2	Jan-74	De-Lite	Kool & The Gang	Jungle Boogie	Bayyan-Kool & the Gang
590	3	1	Jan-74	Atlantic	Aretha Franklin	Until You Come Back To Me (That's What I'm Gonn	Broadnax, Paul, Stevie Wonder
591	19	1	Jan-74	Hi	Al Green	Livin' For You	Green-Mitchell
592	27	1	Feb-74	Motown	The Temptations	Let Your Hair Down	Norm Whitfield
593	2	1	Feb-74	Motown	Eddie Kendricks	Boogie Down	Caston-Poree-Wilson
594	3	1	Mar-74	Buddah	Gladys Knight & The Pips	Best Thing That Ever Happened To Me	Jim Weatherly
595	1	1	Mar-74	Philly Int'l	MFSB (Feat. The Three Degrees)	TSOP (The Sound of Philadelphia)	Gamble-Huff
596	10	8	Mar-74	RCA	Main Ingredient	Just Don't Want To be Lonely	Barrett-Eli-Freeman
597	20	1	Mar-74	Atlantic	The Spinners	Mighty Love	Hawes-Jefferson-Simmons
598	10	1	Mar-74	United Art.	Bobby Womack	Lookin' For A Love	Bacharach-David
599	2	5	Apr-74	Avco	Stylistics	You Make Me Feel Brand New	Bell-Creed
600	9	3	Apr-74	Philly Int'l	The O'Jays	For The Love of Money	Gamble-Huff-Jackson
601	26	1	Apr-74	Polydor	James Brown	The Payback	Brown-Wesley-Starks
602	40	3	May-74	Curtom	Curtis Mayfield	Kung Fu	Curtis Mayfield
603	2	1	May-74	Motown	The Jackson 5	Dancing Machine	Davis-Fletcher-Parks
604	19	1	May-74	Atlantic	Aretha Franklin	I'm In Love	Bobby Womack
605	5	1	Jun-74	Buddah	Gladys Knight & The Pips	On & On	Curtis Mayfield
606		28	Jun-74	Philly Int'l	Bunny Sigler	Love Train	Gamble-Huff
607	1	1	Jun-74	RCA	Hues Corporation	Rock the Boat	W. Holmes
608	4	1	Jun-74	Roxbury	William DeVaughn	Be Thankful For What You Got	Williams DeVaughn
609	1	1	Jun-74	T.K.	George McCrae	Rock Your Baby	Casey-Finch
610	6	1	Jun-74	De-Lite	Kool & The Gang	Hollywood Swinging	Kool & the Gang-West
611	8	1	Jun-74	Atco	Blue Magic	Sideshow	Barrett/Eli
612	17	1	Jul-74	Curtom	The Impressions	Finally Got Myself Together (I'm a Changed Man)	Curtis Mayfield
613	1	2	Jul-74	Atlantic	Dionne Warwick	Then Came You	Sherman Marshall, Philip T. Pugh
614	85	42	Jul-74	Philly Int'l	MFSB	Love is The Message	Gamble-Huff

	Pop	R&B	Year	Label	Artist	Song	Writer
615	3	3	Jul-74	ABC	Rufus & Chaka Khan	Tell me Something Good	Stevie Wonder
616	29	1	Aug-74	Polydor	James Brown	My Thang	James Brown
617	1	1	Aug-74	Atlantic	Roberta Flack	Feel Like Making Love	McDaniels
618	13	2	Sep-74	Mercury	Ohio Players	Skin Tight	Beck-Bonner-Jones-Middlebrook-Ohi
619	2	4	Sep-74	Philly Int'l	The Three Degrees	When Will I See You Again	Gamble-Huff
620	31	1	Sep-74	Polydor	James Brown	Papa Don't Take No Mess	Brown-Wesley-Starks-Bobbit
621	1	1	Sep-74	20th Century	Barry White	Can't Get Enough Of Your Love, Babe	Barry White
622	1	11	Sep-74	Motown	Stevie Wonder	You Haven't Done Nothin'	Stevie Wonder
623	6	1	Oct-74	Back beat	Carl Carlton	Everlasting Love	Buzz Cason, Mac Gayden
624	44	4	Oct-74	Polydor	James Brown	Funky President	James Brown
625	2	1	Oct-74	Roadshow	B.T. Express	Do It ('Til You're Satisfied)	Nichols
626	37	1	Oct-74	De-Lite	Kool & The Gang	Higher Plane	Bayyan-Kool & the Gang
627	1	1	Nov-74	20th Century	Carl Douglas	Kung Fu Fighting	Carl Douglas
628	2	2	Nov-74	20th Century	Barry White	You're The First, The Last My Everything	Radcliffe-Sepe-While
629	7	2	Nov-74	Hi	Al Green	She La La (Make Me Happy)	Al Green
670	31	1	Nov-74	Glades	Latimore	Let's Straighten It Out	Latimore
631	22	1	Nov-74	Truth	Shirley Brown	Woman to Woman	Banks, Marion, Thigpen
632	21	1	Nov-74	Buddah	Gladys Knight & The Pips	I Feel a Song (In My Heart)	Camillo-Sawyer
633	1	1	Dec-74	Mercury	Ohio Players	Fire	Beck-Bonner-Jones-Middlebrook-S
634	9	34	Dec-74	MGM	Gloria Gaynor	Never Can Say Goodbye	Clifton Davis
635	48	17	Dec-74	Philly Int'l	The O'Jays	Sunshine	Sigler-Hurtt
636	11	1	Dec-74	ABC	Rufus & Chaka Khan	You Got the Love	Khan-Parker
637	50	1	Dec-74	Capitol	Tavares	She's Gone	Hall-Oates
638	3	1	Dec-74	Motown	Stevie Wonder	Boogie On Reggae Woman	Stevie Wonder
639	1	1	Feb-75	Epic	Labelle	Lady Marmalade	Crewe-Nolan
640	12	1	Feb-75	Vibration	Shirley and Company	Shame, Shame, Shame	Sylvia Robinson
641	4	1	Feb-75	Roadshow	B.T. Express	Express	Lomas-Risbrook-Rowe-Thompson-W
642	8	1	Mar-75	20th Century	Barry White	What Am I Gonna Do With You	Barry White
643	5	1	Mar-75	Atlantic	Ben E. King	Supernatural Thing—Part 1	Patrick Grant, Gwen Guthrie
644	8	1	Mar-75	Big Three	Hot Chocolate	Emma	Brown-Brown
645	1	1	Mar-75	Columbia	Earth Wind & Fire	Shining Star	White-Bailey-Dunn
646	13	1	Mar-75	Hi	Al Green	L-O-V-E	Al Green
647	15	4	Mar-75	Philly Int'l	Harold Melvin & The Blue Notes	Bad Luck	McFadden-Whitehead-Carstarphen
648	8	1	Mar-75	Spring	Joe Simon	Get Down, Get Down (Get on the Floor)	Raeford Gerald, Joe Simon
649	26	1	Mar-75	Tamla	Smokey Robinson	Baby That's Backatcha	Robinson
650	10	4	Mar-75	ABC	Rufus & Chaka Khan	Once You Get Started	Wright
651	5	1	Apr-75	Atlantic	Ben E. King	Love Won't Let Me Wait	Barrett-Eli
652	1	1	May-75	Avco	Van McCoy	The Hustle	Van McCoy
653	11	5	May-75	Buddah	Gladys Knight & The Pips	Try To Remember/The Way We Were	Schmidt-Hamlish-Bergman-Bergman
654	9	1	Jun-75	Cat	Gwen McCrae	Rockin' Chair	Willie Clarke, Clarence Reid
655	42	1	Jun-75	Philly Int'l	Harold Melvin & The Blue Notes	Hope That We Can Be Together Soon	Gamble-Huff
656	25	Jun-75	Philly Int'l	Archie Bell & The Drells	I Could Dance All Night	Tyson-Sigler-Felder
657	67	9	Jul-75	Curtom	Curtis Mayfield	So In Love	Curtis Mayfield
658	11	1	Jul-75	Philly Int'l	People's Choice	Do It Any Way You Wanna	Leon Huff

	Pop	R&B	Year	Label	Artist	Song	Writer
659		7	Jul-75	Philly Int'l	Archie Bell & The Drells	Let's Groove (Part 1)	Tyson-Sigler-Felder
660	4	1	Jul-75	T-Neck	Isley Brothers	Fight The Power (Part 1)	Isley-Isley-Isley-Isley-Jasper
661	5	1	Aug-75	Atlantic	The Spinners	They Just Can't Stop It the (Games	Hawes-Jefferson-Simmons
662	10	1	Aug-75	Capitol	Tavares	It Only Takes A Minute	Lambert-Potter
663	38	1	Sep-75	Warner	Graham Central Station	Your Love	Larry Graham
664	6	1	Oct-75	Capitol	Natalie Cole	This Will Be	Jackson-Yancey
665	1	1	Oct-75	Mid. Int'l	Silver Convention	Fly Robin Fly	Levay-Prager
666	22	8	Nov-75	Buddah	Gladys Knight & The Pips	Part-Time Love	D. Gates
667	1	1	Nov-75	Curtom	Staple Singers	Let's Do It Again	Staple Singers
668	28	1	Nov-75	Hi	Al Green	Full of Fire	Al Green
669	1	1	Nov-75	Mercury	Ohio Players	Love Roller Coaster	Beck-Bonner-Jones-Middlebrook-Sat
670	1	1	Nov-75	Motown	Diana Ross	Theme from Mahogany (Do You Know	Goffin-Masser
671	5	1	Nov-75	Philly Int'l	The O'Jays	I Love Music	Gamble-Huff
672	12	1	Nov-75	Philly Int'l	Harold Melvin & The Blue Notes	Wake Up Everybody	McFadden-Whitehead-Carstarphen
673	3	1	Dec-75	Big Three	Hot Chocolate	You Sexy Thing	Brown
674	32	1	Dec-75	Capitol	Natalie Cole	Inseprable	Jackson-Yancey
675	2	3	Dec-75	Casablanca	Donna Summer	Love to Love you baby	Bellotte-Moroder-Summer
676	5	1	Dec-75	Columbia	Earth Wind & Fire	Sing A Song	White-MacKay
677	35	10	Feb-76	Buddah	The Trammps	Hold Back The Night	Baker/Felder/Harris/Young
678	5	1	Feb-76	Motown	Commodores	Sweet Love	Commodores
679	5	1	Feb-76	ABC	Rufus & Chaka Khan	Sweet Thing	Khan-Maiden
680	1	1	Mar-76	Capitol	Sylvers	Boogie Fever	Perren-Saint Lewis
681	1	1	Mar-76	Columbia	Johnnie Taylor	Disco Lady	Davis, Scales, Vance
682	79	18	Mar-76	Philly Int'l	The O'Jays	Stairway To Heaven	Gamble-Huff
683	20	1	Mar-76	Philly Int'l	The O'Jays	Livin' For The Weekend	Gamble-Huff-Gilbert
684	2	1	Mar-76	United Art	Maxine Nightingale	Right Back Where We Started	Edwards-Stubbs
685	3	2	Apr-76	Malaco	Dorothy Moore	Misty Blue	Montgomery
686	2	1	Apr-76	Mid. Int'l	Silver Convention	Get Up And Boogie	Levay-Prager
687	3	1	May-76	A&M	Brothers Johnson	I'll Be Good To You	Johnson
688	6	1	May-76	ARC	Earth Wind & Fire	Boogie Wonderland	Lind-Willis
689	25	1	May-76	Capitol	Natalie Cole	Sophisticated Lady	Jackson-Yancey
690	1	1	May-76	Columbia	Manhattans	Kiss & Say Goodbye	Lovett
691	14	1	May-76	United Art	Brass Construction	Movin'	Muter-Williamston-Wong
692	15	5	Jun-76	Casablanca	Parliament	Give Up the Funk (Tear the Roof off the Sucker)	Brailey, Clinton, Collins
693	15	3	Jul-76	Capitol	Tavares	Heaven Must Be Missing An Angel	Freddie Perren, K. Saint Louis
694		8	Jul-76	Curtom	Curtis Mayfield	Only You Babe	Curtis Mayfield
695	2	1	Jul-76	Philly Int'l	Lou Rawls	You'll Never Find Another Love Like Mine	Gamble-Huff
696	45	4	Jul-76	Polydor	James Brown	Get Up Off A That Thing	Brown-Brown-Jenkins
697	1	10	Jul-76	Private Stock	Walter Murphy & Big Apple Band	A Fifth of Beethoven	Walter Murphy
698	12	1	Aug-76	Columbia	Earth Wind & Fire	Getaway	Taylor-Cor
699	1	1	Aug-76	Motown	Diana Ross	Love Hangover	McLeod-Sawyer
700	1	1	Oct-76	ABC	Marilyn McCoo & Billy Davis Jr	You Don't Have to be A Star	Dean-Glover
701	2	1	Oct-76	Atlantic	The Spinners	The Rubberband Man	Bell-Creed
702	7	1	Oct-76	Motown	Commodores	Just to be Close to You	Lionel Ritchie

	Pop	R&B	Year	Label	Artist	Song	Writer
703	6	2	Oct-76	Philly Int'l	The Jacksons	Enjoy Yourself	Gamble-Huff
704	3	1	Nov-76	Bang	Brick	Dazz	Hargis-Irons-Ransom
705	1	1	Dec-76	MCA	Rose Royce	Car Wash	Norm Whitfield
706	1	1	Dec-76	Tamla	Stevie Wonder	I Wish	Stevie Wonder
707	1	1	Jan-77	Tamla	Thelma Houston	Don't Leave Me This Way	Gamble-Huff-Gilbert
708	30	1	Feb-77	ABC	Rufus & Chaka Khan	At Midnight (My Love Will Lift You Up)	Maiden, Washburn
709	5	1	Feb-77	Capitol	Natalie Cole	I've Got Love On my Mind	Jackson-Yancey
710	22	1	Mar-77	Capitol	Tavares	Whodunit	Freddie Perren, K. Saint Louis
711	10	3	Mar-77	MCA	Rose Royce	I Wanna Get Next To You	Norm Whitfield
712	12	7	Apr-77	Dial	Joe Tex	Aint' Gonna Bump No More (With no Big Fat Wo	Buddy Killen, Bennie Lee McGinty
713	28	6	Apr-77	Philly Int'l	The Jacksons	Show You The Way To Go	Gamble-Huff
714	1	1	Apr-77	Tamla	Stevie Wonder	Sir Duke	Stevie Wonder
715	5	3	May-77	Capitol	Sylvers	Hot Line	Perren-Saint Lewis
716	4	1	Jun-77	Motown	Commodores	Easy	Lionel Ritchie
717	5	1	Jul-77	A&M	Brothers Johnson	Strawberry Letter 23	Clyde Otis
718	2	5	Aug-77	Epic	Heatwave	Boogie Nights	Rod Temperton
719	6	9	Sep-77	Casablanca	Donna Summer	I Feel Love	Bellotte-Moroder-Summer
720		29	Sep-77	Curtom	Curtis Mayfield	Do Do Wap Is Strong In Here	Curtis Mayfield
721	5	1	Sep-77	Motown	Commodores	Brick House	Commodores
722	4	1	Oct-77	20th Century	Barry White	It's Estacy When You Lay Down Next To Me	Paris-Pigford
723	18	3	Oct-77	Drive	Peter Brown	Do Ya Wanna Get Funky With Me	Brown-Rans
724	4	1	Nov-77	A&M	L.T.D.	Everytime I Turn Around	Grey-Hanks
725	6	6	Dec-77	Atlantic	CHIC	Dance Dance Dance	Rodgers-Edwards
726	18	2	Dec-77	Epic	Heatwave	Always And Forever	Rod Temperton

York University—Department of Fine Arts — FA1520—Song Listing — 2004–2005

#	Pop	R&B	Year	Label	Artist	Song	Writer	Place
1			Mar-27	Paramount	Blind Lemon Jefferson	Match Box Blues	Blind Lemon Jefferson	Chicago
2			Oct-27	Paramount	Blind Lemon Jefferson	One Dime Blues	Blind Lemon Jefferson	Chicago
3			Oct-27	Paramount	Ida Cox	Give me a Break Blues	Ida Cox	Chicago
4			Jun-28	Paramount	Ma Rainey	Prove it on me Blues	Ma Rainey	New York
5			Dec-28	Okeh	Mississippi John Hurt	Ain't No Tellin'	Mississippi John Hurt	Memphis
6			May-29	Columbia	Bessie Smith	Nobody Know You When You're Down & Out	James Cox	New York
7			Aug-29	Paramount	Blind Blake	Police Dog Blues	Blind Blake	Chicago
8			Oct-30	Columbia	Memphis Minnie	What's The Matter With The Mill	Joe McCoy, Memphis Minnie	Chicago
9			Feb-31	Okeh	Lonnie Johnson	Low Down St Louis Blues	Lonnie Johnson	New York
10			Feb-31	Okeh	Mamie Smith	Jenny's Ball	Jimmy Reed	New York
11			Oct-31	Victor	Blind Willie McTell	Southern Can is Mine	Blind Willie McTell	Atlanta
12			Aug-33	Columbia	Billie Holiday	Your Mother's Son-In-Law	Mann Holiner, Alberta Nichols	
13			Nov-33	Columbia	Billie Holiday	What A Little Moonlight Can Do	Harry Woods	New York
14			Jan-34	Paramount	Charley Patton	Revenue man Blues	Charley Patton	
15			Jul-35	Victor	Sleepy Joe Estes	Someday Baby	Sleepy Joe Estes	Chicago
16			Mar-36	Columbia	Billie Holiday	Don't Explain	Arthur Herzog Jr., Billie Holiday	
17			Mar-36	Columbia	Billie Holiday	Easy To Love	Cole Porter	
18			Sep-36	Columbia	Billie Holiday	God Bless The Child	Arthur Herzog Jr., Billie Holiday	
19			Nov-36	Columbia	Billie Holiday	Billie's Blues	Billie Holiday	New York
20			Nov-36	Columbia	Billie Holiday	Miss Brown To You	Ralph Rainger, Leo Robin, Richard Whiting	
21			Jun-37	History	Robert Johnson	Stones in my Passway	Robert Johnson	Dallas
22			Jun-37	History	Robert Johnson	Stop Breakin Down	Robert Johnson	Dallas
23			Jun-37	History	Robert Johnson	Sweet Home Chicago	Robert Johnson	San Antonio
24			Feb-39	Okeh	Big Bill Broonzy	Spreadin' Snakes Blues	Big Bill Broonzy	Chicago
25			Apr-39	Commodore	Billie Holiday	Fine & Mellow	Herzog Holiday	New York
26			Apr-39	Commodore	Billie Holiday	Strange Fruit	Lewis Allan	
27			May-40	RCA	Sonny Boy Williamson	Train Fare Blues	Sonny Boy Williamson	Chicago
28			May-40	RCA	Sonny Boy Williamson	I've Been Dealing With The Devil	Sonny Boy Williamson	Chicago
29			Jun-40	Okeh	Memphis Minnie	Nothing In Ramblin	Memphis Minnie	Chicago
30			Mar-41	Jazz Unlimited	Billie Holiday	Georgia On My Mind	Hoagy Carmichael, Stuart Gorrell	
31			Nov-42	Decca	Nat King Cole	That Ain't Right	Nat King Cole	Los Angeles
32	19	1	Nov-43	Capitol	Nat King Cole	All For You	Nat King Cole	Los Angeles
33	9	1	Apr-44	Capitol	Nat King Cole	Straighten Up & Fly Right	Nat King Cole	Los Angeles
34			Sep-44	Decca	Billie Holiday	Good Morning Heartache	Drake, Fisher, Higginbotham	
35			Sep-44	Decca	Billie Holiday	My Sweet Hunk O'Trash	James P. Johnson, F.E. Miller	
36			Sep-44	Decca	Billie Holiday	There is no Greater Love	Isham Jones, Marty Symes	
37	20	1	Sep-44	Capitol	Nat King Cole	Gee, Baby, Ain't I Good To You	Andy Razaf, Don Redman	Los Angeles
38			Mar-45	Verve	Billie Holiday	April In Paris	Vernon Duke, E.Y. Harburg	
39			Mar-45	Verve	Billie Holiday	Speak Low	Ogden Nash, Kurt Weill	
40			Mar-45	Verve	Billie Holiday	Stars Fell On Alabama	Mitchell Parish, Frank Perkins	
41			Apr-46	Verve	Billie Holiday	I Cover The Waterfront	Johnny Green, Edward Heyman	
42			Apr-46	Verve	Billie Holiday	My Man	Charles, Pollack, Willemetz, Yvain	
43	11		Aug-46	Capitol	Nat King Cole	Route 66	Bobby Troup	
44			Sep-46	Columbia	Muddy Waters	Hard Day Blues	McKinley Morganfield, Muddy Waters	Chicago
45	1	3	Nov-46	Capitol	Nat King Cole	For Sentimental Reasons (I Love You)	William Best, Dee Watson	Los Angeles
46	3	3	Nov-46	Capitol	Nat King Cole	The Christmas Song	Mel Torme, Robert Wells	Los Angeles
47		1	Sep-48	Mercury	Dinah Washington	Am I Asking Too Much		Tuscaloosa, AL
48		1	Jul-49	Mercury	Dinah Washington	Baby Get Lost		Tuscaloosa, AL

	Pop	R&B	Year	Label	Artist	Song	Writer	Place
49	1	2	Jul-50	Capitol	Nat King Cole	Nature Boy	Eden Ahbez	Los Angeles
50	1	3	May-51	Capitol	Nat King Cole	Too Young	Sylvia Dee, Sidney Lippman	Los Angeles
51			Jul-51	Legacy	Ray Charles	Sentimental Blues	William York	
52			Jul-51	Legacy	Ray Charles	Rockin' Chair Blues	Ray Charles	
53			Jul-51	Legacy	Ray Charles	She's On the Ball		
54	12		Nov-51	Capitol	Nat King Cole	Unforgettable	Irving Gordon	
55	8		Jul-52	Capitol	Nat King Cole	Walking My Baby Back Home	Fred E. Ahlert, Roy Turk	
56	2		Feb-53	Capitol	Nat King Cole	Pretend	Belloc, Douglas, LaVere, Parman	
57	6		Feb-54	Capitol	Nat King Cole	Answer Me	Paunch, Sigman, Winkler	
58	8	1	Dec-54	DooTone	The Penguins	Earth Angel		Los Angeles
59	20	11	Mar-55	Chess	The Moonglows	Sincerely	Anna Sosenko	
60	7		Mar-55	Capitol	Nat King Cole	Darling Je Vous Aime Beaucoup	Barnes, Cornelius, J.C. Johnson	
61	2		May-55	Capitol	Nat King Cole	A Blossom Fell	Rosemary McCoy, Charlie Singleton	
62	8		May-55	Capitol	Nat King Cole	If I May (with the Four Knights)		
63	79	10	Oct-55	Atco	The Coasters	Smokey Joe's Cafe	Stoller-Leiber	New York
64	5	1	Oct-55	Mercury	The Platters	Only You	Ram-Rand	New York
65	1	1	Dec-55	Mercury	The Platters	The Great Pretender	Buck Ram	New York
66	17		Jan-56	Specialty	Little Richard	Tutti-Frutti	Richard Penneman	
67	6	1	Feb-56	Gee	Frankie Lymon & The Teenagers	Why do Fools Fall in Love	Lymon	New York
68	8		Feb-56	Atlantic	The Coasters	Down in Mexico	Stoller-Leiber	New York
69	6	1	Apr-56	Specialty	Little Richard	Long Tall Sally	Richard Penneman	
70	95	6	Jun-56	Federal	James Brown & the Famous Flame	Please Please Please	James Brown - Johnny Terry	Cincinnati
71	1	1	Jul-56	Mercury	The Platters	My Prayer	Kennedy-Boulanger	New York
72	25	15	Oct-56	Chess	The Moonglows	See Saw		
73	3	1	Mar-57	Atlantic	The Coasters	Searchin'	Stoller-Leiber	New York
74	8	2	Mar-57	Atlantic	The Coasters	Young Blood	Stoller-Leiber	New York
75	21	4	Apr-57	Specialty	Little Richard	Lucille	Richard Penneman	
76	10	1	Jun-57	Specialty	Little Richard	Jenny Jenny	Richard Penneman	
77	39	24	Jun-57	Decca	Mills Brothers	Queen of the Senior Prom		Los Angeles
78	1	1	Jul-57	Capitol	Nat King Cole	Mona Lisa	Ray Evans, Jay Livingston	Los Angeles
79	6	1	Jul-57	Capitol	Nat King Cole	Send For Me	Ollie Jones	Los Angeles
80	46	1	Aug-57	Duke	Bobby Bland	Farther Up The Road		Rosemark, TN
81	8	1	Oct-57	Specialty	Little Richard	Keep A Knockin	Richard Penneman	Los Angeles
82	1	1	Oct-57	Keen	Sam Cooke	You Send Me	Sam Cooke	
83	34		Nov-57	Atlantic	Ray Charles	Swanee River Rock (Talkin' 'Bout That River)	Ray Charles	
84			Feb-58	Columbia	Billie Holiday	The End of a Love Affair	Edward Redding	
85			Feb-58	Columbia	Billie Holiday	You Don't Know What Love Is	Gene DePaul, Don Raye	
86			Feb-58	Columbia	Billie Holiday	You've Changed	Bill Carey, Carl Fischer	
87	22	7	Feb-58	Brunswick	Jackie Wilson	To Be Loved	Gordy-Carlo-Gordy	New York
88	10	2	Feb-58	Specialty	Little Richard	Good Golly Miss Molly	Blackwell-Marascallo	
89	21	7	Mar-58	Dot	Mills Brothers	Get a Job		Los Angeles
90	1	1	Apr-58	Mercury	The Platters	Twilight Time	Ram-A&M Nevins-Dunn	New York
91	5		Apr-58	Capitol	Nat King Cole	Looking Back	Brook Benton, Hendricks, Otis	
92	8	1	May-58	Chess	Chuck Berry	Johnny B. Goode	Chuck Berry	Chicago
93	48	1	Jun-58	Federal	James Brown & the Famous Flame	Try Me	James Brown	Cincinnati
94	1	1	Jun-58	Atco	The Coasters	Yakety Yak	Stoller-Leiber	New York
95	4	1	Aug-58	End	Little Anthony & the Imperials	Tears on my Pillow		
96	6	1	Oct-58	Atlantic	Clyde McPhatter	A Lover's Question		
97	7	1	Oct-58	Brunswick	Jackie Wilson	Lonely Teardrops	Gordy-Carlo-Gordy	New York
98	1	1	Dec-58	Mercury	The Platters	Smoke Gets in your Eyes	Harbach-Kern	New York

	Pop	R&B	Year	Label	Artist	Song	Writer	Place
99	2	2	Jan-59	Atlantic	The Coasters	Charlie Brown	Stoller-Leiber	New York
100	13	2	Mar-59	Brunswick	Jackie Wilson	That's Why (I Love You So)	Gordy-Carlo-Gordy	New York
101	9	14	May-59	Atlantic	The Coasters	Along Came Jones	Stoller-Leiber	New York
102	20	6	Jun-59	Brunswick	Jackie Wilson	I'll Be Satisfied	Gordy-Carlo-Gordy	New York
103	6	1	Jul-59	Atlantic	Ray Charles	What'd I Say	Ray Charles	New York
104	6		Jul-59	Atlantic	Ray Charles	What'd I Say (Part 1)	Ray Charles	New York
105	7	1	Aug-59	Atlantic	The Coasters	Poison Ivy	Stoller-Leiber	New York
106	36	29	Nov-59	Atlantic	The Coasters	Run Red Run	Stoller-Leiber	New York
107	17	47	Nov-59	Atlantic	The Coasters	What About Us	Stoller-Leiber	New York
108	5	1	Jan-60	Mercury	Dinah Washington	Baby (You've Got What It Takes)		Tuscaloosa, AL
109	8	1	Feb-60	Mercury	The Platters	Harbour Lights	Kennedy-Williams	New York
110	5	1	Feb-60	Mercury	Brook Benton & Dinah Washington	Baby (You've Got What It Takes)		Tuscaloosa, AL
111	23	2	Mar-60	Motown/Anna	Barrett Strong	Money (That's What I Want)	Gordy-Bradfield	Detroit
112	15	3	Mar-60	Brunswick	Jackie Wilson	Doggin' Around	Tarnopol	New York
113	4	3	Mar-60	Brunswick	Jackie Wilson	Night	Lehman-Miller	New York
114	38		Apr-60	Fire	Buster Brown	Fannie Mae		Cincinnati
115	33	7	May-60	Federal	James Brown & the Famous Flame	Think	Lowman Pauling	Tuscaloosa, AL
116	7	1	May-60	Mercury	Dinah Washington	A Rocking Good Time		
117	15	3	May-60	Brunswick	Jackie Wilson	Doggin' Around		
118	15	1	Jun-60	Brunswick	Jackie Wilson	A Woman, A Lover, A Friend		New York
119	24	1	Jun-60	Mercury	Dinah Washington	This Bitter Earth	Wyche	Tuscaloosa, AL
120	7	1	Jun-60	Mercury	Brook Benton & Dinah Washington	A Rockin' Good Way (To Mess Arounf and Fall In Love)		
121	31	1	Jul-60	Fire	Bobby Marchan	There's Something On Your Mind-Part 2		New York
122	24	1	Jul-60	Mercury	Dinah Washington	This Bitter Earth		
123	2	1	Aug-60	RCA	Sam Cooke	Chain Gang	Sam Cooke	Los Angeles
124	1	2	Aug-60	Parkway	Chubby Checker	The Twist		
125	7	1	Aug-60	Mercury	Brook Benton	Kiddio		
126	8	20	Sep-60	Brunswick	Jackie Wilson	Alone At last	Lehman	New York
127	32	10	Sep-60	Brunswick	Jackie Wilson	Am I The Man	Hamilton-King	New York
128	1	3	Oct-60	Herald	Maurice Williams	Stay	Maurice Williams	New York
129	2	1	Oct-60	Motown/Tamla	The Miracles	Shop Around	Gordy-Robinson	Detroit
130	1 (1)		Oct-60	ABC-Paramount	Ray Charles	Georgia On My Mind	Hoagy Carmichael, Stuart Gorrell	
131	1	1	Oct-60	Atlantic	The Drifters	Save The Last Dance For Me		
132	6	1	Nov-60	King	Hank Ballard & The Midnighters	Let's Go, Let's Go, Let's Go		
133	7	1	Nov-60	Vee-Jay	Jerry Butler	He Will Break Your Heart		
134	9	25	Dec-60	Brunswick	Jackie Wilson	My Empty Arms	Kasha-Hunter	New York
135	1	2	Dec-60	Sceptre	The Shirelles	Will You Still Love Me Tomorrow	King-Goffin	New York
136	28		Dec-60	ABC-Paramount	Ray Charles	Ruby	Mitchell Parish, Heinz Roemheld	
137	43	1	Feb-61	Duke	Bobby Bland	I Pity The Fool	Pauling-Bass	Rosemark, TN
138	3	2	Feb-61	Sceptre	The Shirelles	Dedicated to the One I Love		New York
139	1	1	Feb-61	Parkway	Chubby Checker	Pony Time		
140	1	1	Mar-61	Colpix	The Marcels	Blue Moon	Rudy Toombs	
141	8		Mar-61	Impulse	Ray Charles	One Mint Julep [1]	Whitcup-Powell	Cincinnati
142	40	8	Apr-61	King	James Brown & the Famous Flame	Bewildered	Stoller-Leiber	
143	23	16	Apr-61	Atlantic	The Coasters	Little Egypt (Ying-Yang)		
144	8	1	Apr-61	Impulse	Ray Charles	One Mint Julep		
145	1	1	Apr-61	Minit	Ernie K-Doe	Mother-In-Law		
146	4	1	May-61	Atlantic	Ben E. King	Stand By Me	King-Glick	New York
147	4	2	May-61	Sceptre	The Shirelles	Mama Said	Dixon-Denson	New York
148	47	4	Jun-61	King	James Brown & the Famous Flame	I Don't Mind	James Brown	Cincinnati

Pop	R&B	Year	Label	Artist	Song	Writer	Place
149	6	1	Jun-61	Vee-Jay	The Pips	Every Beat Of My Heart	Axton-Caple-Newman-Smith-Moman	Memphis
150	3	2	Jul-61	Satellite	Mar-Keys	Last Night		
151	1	1	Jul-61	Beltone	Bobby Lewis	Tossin' And Turnin'		Cincinnati
152	49	2	Aug-61	King	James Brown & the Famous Flame	Baby You're Right	James Brown - Joe Tex	
153		1	Aug-61	Motown/Tamla	The Marvellettes	Please Mr. Postman	Dobbins-Garrett-Holland-Bateman-G	Detroit
154	3	1	Sep-61	Beltone	The Jive Five	My True Story		
155	1 (2)		Sep-61	ABC-Paramount	Ray Charles	Hit The Road Jack	Percy Mayfield	
156	30	6	Oct-61	Motown	Eddie Holland	Jamie	William Stevenson	Detroit
157	1		Oct-61	ABC Paramount	Ray Charles	Hit The Road Jack	Ray Charles	
158	7	1	Nov-61	Fury	Lee Dorsey	YA YA		
159	1	4	Dec-61	Parkway	Chubby Checker	The Twist		
160	1		Dec-61	ABC-Paramount	Ray Charles	Unchain My Heart	Teddy Powell, Bobby Sharp	
161	8	3	Jan-62	Sceptre	The Shirelles	Baby It's You	David-Williams-Bacharach	New York
162	9	1	Jan-62	ABC Paramount	Ray Charles	Unchain My Heart		
163	3	1	Jan-62	A.F.O.	Barbara George	I Know (You Don't Love Me No More)		
164	8	2	Feb-62	Motown	Mary Wells	The One Who Really Loves You	William Robinson Jr.	Detroit
165	1	1	Feb-62	Vee-Jay	Gene Chandler	Duke of Earl		
166	7	4	Mar-62	Mercury	Clyde McPhatter	Lover Please		
167	3		Mar-62	Sceptre	The Shirelles	Soldier Boy		
168	9		Mar-62	Keen	Sam Cooke	Twistin' The Night Away	Dixon-Green	New York
169	17		Apr-62	Enjoy	King Curtis	Soul Twist		
170	2		Apr-62	Cameo	Dee Dee Sharp	Mashed Potato Time		
171	35	5	May-62	King	James Brown & the Famous Flame	Night Train	Washington-Simpkins-Forrest	Cincinnati
172	(5)		May-62	ABC Paramount	Ray Charles	I Can't Stop Loving You	Don Gibson	
173	1		May-62	ABC Paramount	Ray Charles	I Can't Stop Loving You		
174	3		Jun-62	Motown/Gordy	The Contours	Do You Love Me	Berry Gordy	Detroit
175	46	8	Jul-62	Motown/Tamla	Marvin Gaye	Stubborn Kind Of Fellow	Gordy-Gaye-Stevenson	Detroit
176	9		Jul-62	Motown/Tamla	Mary Wells	You Beat Me To The Punch	Robinson-White	Detroit
177	17	7	Aug-62	Motown/Tamla	The Marvellettes	Beachwood 4-5789	Gordy-Gaye-Stevenson	Detroit
178	2 (1)		Aug-62	ABC-Paramount	Ray Charles	You Don't Know Me	Eddy Arnold, Cindy Walker	
179	8	1	Aug-62	Jamie	Barbara Lynn	You'll Lose A Good Thing		
180	2		Aug-62	Capitol	Nat King Cole	Ramblin' Rose	Noel Sherman, Joe Sherman	
181	1	1	Aug-62	Dimension	Little Eva	The Loco-Motion		
182	3		Sep-62	Stax	Booker T. & The MG's	Green Onions	Jones-Cropper-Steinberg-Jackson	Memphis
183	7	1	Oct-62	Motown	Mary Wells	Two Lovers	William Robinson Jr.	Detroit
184	8	1	Nov-62	Motown/Tamla	The Miracles	You've Really Got A Hold On Me	William Robinson Jr.	Detroit
185	7		Dec-62	ABC-Paramount	Ray Charles	You Are My Sunshine	Jimmie Davis, Charles Mitchell	
186	5	4	Dec-62	Atlantic	The Drifters	Up On The Roof	King-Goffin	New York
187	29		Dec-62	ABC-Paramount	Ray Charles	Your Cheating Heart	Hank Williams	
188	8	1	Dec-62	Lenox	Esther Phillips	Release Me		
189	7		Dec-62	ABC Paramount	Ray Charles	You are my Sunshine		
190	5	1	Feb-63	Brunswick	Jackie Wilson	Baby Workout	Wilson-Tucker	New York
191	29	6	Feb-63	Motown/Gordy	Martha & The Vandellas	Come And Get These Memories	Holland-Dozier-Holland	Detroit
192	33	1	Mar-63	Duke	Bobby Bland	That's The Way Love Is		Rosemark, TN
193	20		Mar-63	ABC-Paramount	Ray Charles	Don't Set Me Free	Teddy Powell	
194		1	Mar-63	Kapp	Ruby & The Romantics	Our Day Will Come		
195	10	2	Apr-63	Motown/Tamla	Marvin Gaye	Pride & Joy	Whitfield-Gaye-Stevenson	Detroit
196	9	7	Apr-63	Atlantic	The Drifters	On Broadway	Weil-Mann-Leiber-Stotler	New York
197	1	1	Apr-63	Laurie	The Chiffons	He's So Fine		
198	8		Apr-63	ABC-Paramount	Ray Charles	Take These Chains From My Heart	Hy Heath, Fred Rose	

	Pop	R&B	Year	Label	Artist	Song	Writer	Place
199	18	6	May-63	King	James Brown & the Famous Flame	Prisoner of Love	Robin-Columbo-Gaskin	Cincinnati
200	1	1	May-63	Motown/Tamla	Little Stevie Wonder	Fingertips - Pt.2	Paul-Cosby	Detroit
201	37	30	May-63	Atlantic	Wilson Pickett	If You Need Me	Pickett-Bateman-Sanders	Memphis
202		6	May-63	Capitol	Nat King Cole	Those Lazy-Hazy-Crazy Days Of Summer	Hans Carste, Charles Tobias	
203	1	1	Jun-63	SPQR	Jimmy Soul	If You Wanna Be Happy		
204	10	1	Jun-63	RCA	Sam Cooke	Another Saturday Night		
205	10	3	Jul-63	Atlantic	Doris Troy	Just One Look	Payne-Carroll	New York
206	4	1	Jul-63	Motown/Gordy	Martha & The Vandellas	(Love is Like A) Heatwave	Holland-Dozier-Holland	Detroit
207	8	3	Jul-63	Motown/Tamla	The Miracles	Mickey's Monkey	Holland-Dozier-Holland	Detroit
208	3	1	Jul-63	Atlantic	Barbara Lewis	Hello Stranger		
209	10	10	Aug-63	Colpix	Freddie Scott	Hey Girl		
210	4		Sep-63	ABC-Paramount	Ray Charles	Busted	Harlan Howard	
211	1	1	Sep-63	Motown	Martha & The Vandellas	Heat Wave		
212	12		Sep-63	Capitol	Nat King Cole	That Sunday, That Summer	Joe Sherman, George David Weiss	
213	4	1	Oct-63	United Artists	Garnet Mimms & The Enchanters	Cry Baby		
214	19		Oct-63	Galaxy	Little Johnny Taylor	Part-Time Love		
215	10	5	Nov-63	Stax	Rufus Thomas	Walking the Dog	Rufus Thomas	Memphis
216	4	1	Nov-63	ABC Paramount	The Impressions	It's All Right		
217	20		Dec-63	ABC-Paramount	Ray Charles	That Lucky Old Sun	Haven Gillespie, Harry Beasley Smith	
218	8	8	Jan-64	Scepter	Dionne Warwick	Anyone Who Had a Heart		
219	11	1	Jan-64	Motown/Gordy	The Temptations	The Way You Do The Things You Do	Robinson-Rodgers	Detroit
220	23	25	Feb-64	King	James Brown & the Famous Flame	Oh Baby Don't You Weep		Cincinnati
221	13	13	Mar-64	Motown/Tamla	Brenda Holloway	Every Little Bit Hurts	Ed Cobb	Detroit
222	1	1	Mar-64	Motown	Mary Wells	My Guy	William Robinson Jr.	Detroit
223	39		Mar-64	ABC-Paramount	Ray Charles	Baby, Don't You Cry	Buddy Johnson, Ned Washington	
224	1	1	May-64	Red Bird	Dixie Cups	Chapel Of Love		New Orleans
225	6	6	May-64	Scepter	Dionne Warwick	Walk On By		New York
226	11	1	Jul-64	Motown	Four Tops	Baby I Need Your Loving	Holland-Dozier-Holland	Detroit
227	1	1	Jul-64	Motown	Martha & The Vandellas	Dancing In The Streets	Stevenson-Gaye-Hunter	Detroit
228	1	1	Jul-64	Motown	The Supremes	Where Did Our Love Go	Holland-Dozier-Holland	Detroit
229	4	4	Jul-64	Atlantic	The Drifters	Under the Boardwalk	Resnick-Young	New York
230	24	24	Sep-64	King	James Brown & the Famous Flame	Out Of Sight	Ted Wright	Cincinnati
231	1	1	Sep-64	Motown	The Supremes	Baby Love	Holland-Dozier-Holland	Detroit
232	1	3	Oct-64	Motown	The Supremes	Come See About Me	Holland-Dozier-Holland	Detroit
233	1	1	Oct-64	Red Bird	The Shangri-Las	Leader of the Pack		New York
234	5	2	Nov-64	Dial	Joe Tex	Hold What You've Got	Joe Tex	New York
235	6	2	Nov-64	DCP	Little Anthony & the Imperials	Goin' out of my Head		New York
236	6	6	Nov-64	Motown/Tamla	Marvin Gaye	How Sweet It Is (To Be Loved By You)	Holland-Dozier-Holland	Detroit
237	1	1	Dec-64	Motown/Gordy	The Temptations	My Girl	Robinson-White	Detroit
238	24	9	Jan-65	Motown	Four Tops	Ask The Lonely	Stevenson-Hunter	Detroit
239	4	3	Jan-65	Motown/Soul	Jr. Walker & The All Stars	Shotgun	Autry DeWalt	Detroit
240	7	2	Jan-65	RCA	Sam Cooke	Shake	Sam Cooke	Los Angeles
241	25	12	Feb-65	Motown/Tamla	Brenda Holloway	When I'm Gone	William Robinson Jr.	Detroit
242	8	5	Feb-65	Motown/Gordy	Martha & The Vandellas	Nowhere To Run	Holland-Dozier-Holland	Detroit
243	16	4	Mar-65	Motown/Tamla	The Miracles	Ooo Baby Baby	Robinson-Moore	Detroit
244	1	1	Apr-65	Motown	Four Tops	I Can't Help Myself (Sugar Pie Honey Bunch)	Holland-Dozier-Holland	Detroit
245	22		Apr-65	Atlantic	Solomon Burke	Got to Get You Off My Mind		
246			Apr-65	Paramount	Son House	Death Letter		
247	25	1	May-65	Checker	Little Milton	We're Gonna Make It	Son House	New York
248	8	1	May-65	Motown	Marvin Gaye	I'll be Doggone		

	Pop	R&B	Year	Label	Artist	Song	Writer	Place
249	1	1	May-65	Motown	The Supremes	Back in My Arms Again	Holland-Dozier-Holland	Detroit
250	21	2	Jun-65	Atlantic	Otis Redding	I've Been Loving You Too Long (To Stop Now)	Redding-Butler	Memphis
251	16	2	Jun-65	Motown/Tamla	The Miracles	The Tracks of My Tears	Robinson-Moore	Detroit
252	11	5	Jul-65	Atlantic	Barbara Lewis	Baby, I'm Yours	Van McCoy	New York
253	5	2	Jul-65	Motown	Four Tops	It's The Same Old Song	Holland-Dozier-Holland	Detroit
254	10	5	Jul-65	DCP	Little Anthony & the Imperials	Hurt So Bad		New York
255	3	1	Jul-65	Motown/Tamla	Stevie Wonder	Uptight (Everything's Alright)	Cosby-Moy-Wonder	Detroit
256	8	1	Aug-65	King	James Brown & the Famous Flame	Papa's Got A Brand New Bag	James Brown	Cincinnati
257	21	1	Aug-65	Atlantic	Wilson Pickett	In the Midnight Hour	Pickett-Cropper	Memphis
258	88	4	Sep-65	JoDa	Johnny Nash	Let's Move & Groove (Together)		
259	50	4	Sep-65	Motown/Gordy	Kim Weston	Take Me In Your Arms	Holland-Dozier-Holland	Detroit
260	11	3	Oct-65	Atlantic	Barbara Lewis	Make Me Your Baby	Atkins-Miller	New York
261	23	1	Oct-65	Dial	Joe Tex	I Want to (Do everything for you)		
262	33	2	Oct-65	Checker	Fontella Bass	Rescue Me		
263	3	1	Nov-65	King	James Brown & the Famous Flame	I Got You (I Feel Good)	James Brown	Cincinnati
264	90	7	Nov-65	Stax	Sam & Dave	You Don't Know Like I Know	Hayes-Porter	Memphis
265	7	3	Nov-65	Motown/Tamla	The Marvelettes	Don't Mess With Bill	William Robinson Jr.	Detroit
266	8	1	Nov-65	Motown	Marvin Gaye	Ain't That Peculiar		
267	72	3	Dec-65	Motown/VIP	The Elgins	Darling Baby	Holland-Dozier-Holland	Detroit
268	12	6	Jan-66	Motown/Tamla	Isley Brothers	This Old Heart Of Mine (Is Weak For You)	Holland-Dozier-Holland-Moy	Detroit
269	29	1	Jan-66	Dial	Joe Tex	A Sweet Woman Like You		
270	6	1	Jan-66	ABC-Paramount	Ray Charles	Crying Time	Buck Owens	
271	16	1	Feb-66	Excello	Slim Harpo	Baby Scratch my Back		
272	42	6	Mar-66	King	James Brown & the Famous Flame	Ain't That A Groove	James Brown-Nat Jones	Cincinnati
273	20	4	Mar-66	Motown	Jr. Walker & The All Stars	(I'm A) Road Runner	Holland-Dozier-Holland	Detroit
274	21	9	Mar-66	Stax	Sam & Dave	Hold On, I'm Coming	Hayes-Porter	Memphis
275	13	1	Mar-66	Atlantic	Wilson Pickett	634-5789 (Soulsville, USA)		
276	8	5	Apr-66	Scepter	Dionne Warwick	Message To Michael	Lewis-Wright	New York
277	1	1	Apr-66	Atlantic	Percy Sledge	When A Man Loves A Woman		New York
278	19	2	Apr-66	ABC-Paramount	Ray Charles	Together Again	Buck Owens	
279	29	1	Apr-66	Motown	The Temptations	Get Ready	Holland-Dozier-Holland	Detroit
280	8	1	May-66	King	James Brown & the Famous Flame	It's a Man's World	James Brown-Betty Newsome	Cincinnati
281	7	2	May-66	Karen	The Capitols	Cool Jerk	Don Storball	New York
282	13	1	May-66	Motown/Gordy	The Temptations	Ain't Too Proud To Beg	Eddie Holland	Detroit
283	7	6	Jun-66	Motown	Jimmy Ruffin	What Becomes Of A Broken Heart	Weatherspoon-Riser-Dean	Detroit
284	31	4	Jun-66	ABC	Ray Charles	Let's Go Get Stoned	Armstead, Ashford, Simpson	
285	18	3	Jul-66	Motown	Jr. Walker & The All Stars	How Sweet It Is (To Be Loved By You)	Holland-Dozier-Holland	Detroit
286	9	1	Jul-66	Motown	Stevie Wonder	Blowin In the Wind	Bob Dylan	Detroit
287	78	14	Jul-66	Philly Int'l	The Intruders	(We'll Be) United	Gamble-Huff	Philadelphia
288	1	1	Jul-66	Motown	The Supremes	You Can't Hurry Love	Holland-Dozier-Holland	Detroit
289	31	1	Jul-66	ABC Paramount	Ray Charles	Let's Go Get Stoned		
290	17	5	Aug-66	Atlantic	Percy Sledge	Warm And Tender Love		
291	64	1	Aug-66	Stax	Sam & Dave	Said I Wasn't Gonna Tell Nobody	Hayes-Porter	Memphis
292	50	9	Aug-66	Motown/VIP	The Elgins	Heaven Must Have Sent You	Holland-Dozier-Holland	Detroit
293	3	1	Aug-66	Motown/Gordy	The Temptations	Beauty Is Only Skin Deep	Whitfield-Holland	Detroit
294	6	1	Aug-66	Atlantic	Wilson Pickett	Land of 1000 Dances	Chris Kenner	Memphis
295	9	1	Aug-66	Motown	Stevie Wonder	Blowin' in the Wind		
296	14	3	Sep-66	Stax	Carla Thomas	B-A-B-Y	Hayes-Porter	Memphis
297	1	1	Sep-66	Motown	Four Tops	Reach Out (I'll Be There)	Holland-Dozier-Holland	Detroit
298	11	5	Sep-66	Brunswick	Jackie Wilson	Whispers (Getting Louder)	Acklin-Scott	Chicago

	Pop	R&B	Year	Label	Artist	Song	Writer	Place
299	32		Oct-66	ABC	Ray Charles	I Chose To Sing The Blues	Ray Charles, Jimmy Holiday	
300	50	4	Oct-66	King	James Brown & the Famous Flame	Don't Be A Dropout	James Brown-Nat Jones	Cincinnati
301	28	1	Nov-66	Stax	Eddie Floyd	Knock on Wood	Floyd-Cropper	Memphis
302	6	2	Nov-66	Motown	Four Tops	Standing In The Shadow Of Love	Holland-Dozier-Holland	Detroit
303	20	7	Nov-66	Atlantic	Percy Sledge	It Tears Me Up		
304	77		Nov-66	Stax	Sam & Dave	You've Got Me Humming	Hayes-Porter	Memphis
305	8	1	Nov-66	Motown/Gordy	The Temptations	I Know I'm Losing You	Whitfield-Holland-Grant	Detroit
306	13	1	Nov-66	Capitol	Lou Rawls	Love is a Hurtin' Thing		
307	1	1	Nov-66	Motown	The Supremes	You Keep Me Hangin' On	Holland-Dozier-Holland	Detroit
308	2	1	Dec-66	Par-Lo	Aaron Neville	Tell It Like It Is	Davis-Diamond	New Orleans
309	14	4	Dec-66	Motown/Tamla	Marvin Gaye & Kim Weston	It Takes Two	Stevenson-Moy	Detroit
310	25	4	Dec-66	Volt	Otis Redding	Try A Little Tenderness	Connelly-Woods-Campbell	Memphis
311	13		Dec-66	Motown/Tamla	The Marvelettes	The Hunter Gets Captured By The Game	William Robinson Jr.	Detroit
312	29	7	Jan-67	King	James Brown & the Famous Flame	Bring It Up	James Brown-Nat Jones	Cincinnati
313	42	3	Jan-67	Stax	Sam & Dave	When Something is Wrong with My Baby	Hayes-Porter	Memphis
314	4	1	Feb-67	Motown	Four Tops	Bernadette	Holland-Dozier-Holland	Detroit
315	46	5	Feb-67	King	James Brown & the Famous Flame	Let Yourself Go	James Brown-Bud Hobgood	Cincinnati
316	10	1	Feb-67	Motown/Gordy	Martha & The Vandellas	Jimmy Mack	Holland-Dozier-Holland	Detroit
317		1	Feb-67	Stax	Sam & Dave	Soul Man	Hayes-Porter	Memphis
318	16		Feb-67	Soul City	The Fifth Dimension	Go Where You Wanna Go	J. Phillips	
319	39	1	Feb-67	Shout	Freddie Scott	Are You Lonely For Me		
320	1	1	Mar-67	Motown	The Supremes	Love Is Here and Now You're Gone		
321	9	1	Mar-67	Atlantic	Aretha Franklin	I Never Loved a Man (The Way I Love You)		
322	2	2	Apr-67	Atlantic	Arthur Conley	Sweet Soul Music	Redding-Conley-Cooke	Alabama
323	19	3	Apr-67	Motown/Tamla	Marvin Gaye & Tammi Terrell	Ain't No Mountain High Enough	Ashford-Simpson	Detroit
324	1	1	May-67	Atlantic	Aretha Franklin	Respect	Otis Redding	New York
325	56	16	May-67	Stax	Sam & Dave	Soothe Me	Cooke	Memphis
326	23	5	May-67	Motown/Tamla	Smokey Robinson & The Miracles	More Love	William Robinson Jr.	Detroit
327	7		Jun-67	Soul City	The Fifth Dimension	Up Up And Away	Jimmy Webb	
328	15		Jun-67	ABC/TRC	Ray Charles	Here We Go Again	Don Lanier, Red Steagall	
329	6	1	Jul-67	Brunswick	Jackie Wilson	Your Love Keeps Lifting Me Higher & Higher	Jackson-Smith-Miner	Chicago
330	31	1	Jul-67	Atlantic	Joe Turner	Shake Rattle & Roll	Charles E. Calhoun	New York
331	2	1	Jul-67	Motown	Stevie Wonder	I Was Made To Love Her		
332	21	1	Jul-67	Money	Bettye Swann	Make Me Yours		
333	7	1	Aug-67	King	James Brown & the Famous Flame	Cold Sweat	James Brown-Alfred Ellis	Cincinnati
334	4	1	Aug-67	Atlantic	Aretha Franklin	Baby I Love You		
335	2	1	Sep-67	Motown	Gladys Knight & The Pips	I Heard It Through The Grapevine	Whitfield-Strong	Detroit
336	33	6	Sep-67	Atco	King Curtis	Memphis Soul Stew	Curtis Ousley	Memphis
337	4	3	Sep-67	Philly Int'l	Soul Survivors	Expressway to your Heart	Gamble-Huff	Philadelphia
338	33		Sep-67	ABC/TRC	Ray Charles	In The Heat Of The Night	Bergman, Bergman, Quincy Jones	
339	8	1	Sep-67	Atlantic	Wilson Pickett	Funky Broadway		
340	4		Oct-67	Motown/Tamla	Smokey Robinson & The Miracles	Second That Emotion	Robinson-Cleveland	Detroit
341	8	2	Oct-67	Atlantic	Aretha Franklin	A Natural Woman (You Make Me Feel)	Goffin-King-Wexler	
342	4	8	Nov-67	Scepter	Dionne Warwick	I Say A Little Prayer		New York
343	40	11	Nov-67	King	James Brown & the Famous Flame	Get it Together	Brown-Ellis-Hobgood	Cincinnati
344	10	2	Nov-67	Dial	Joe Tex	Skinny Legs And All		
345	28	4	Dec-67	King	James Brown & the Famous Flame	I Can't Stand Myself	James Brown	Cincinnati
346	4	1	Dec-67	Motown/Gordy	The Temptations	I Wish It Would Rain	Whitfield-Strong-Penzabene	Detroit
347	25		Dec-67	ABC/TRC	Ray Charles	Yesterday	John Lennon, Paul McCartney	
348	2	1	Jan-68	Atlantic	Aretha Franklin	Chain of Fools		

#	Pop	R&B	Year	Label	Artist	Song	Writer	Place
349	29	5	Feb-68	Motown/Gordy	Bobby Taylor & The Vancouvers	Does Your Mother Know About Me	Baird-Chong	Detroit
350	2	13	Feb-68	Scepter	Dionne Warwick	(Theme from) Valley of the Dolls		New York
351	36	3	Feb-68	King	James Brown & the Famous Flame	There Was A Time	James Brown-Bud Hobgood	Cincinnati
352	9	4	Feb-68	Stan	Sam & Dave	I Thank You	Hayes-Porter	Memphis
353	6	1	Mar-68	King	James Brown & the Famous Flame	I Got The Feelin	James Brown	Cincinnati
354	8	1	Mar-68	Motown/Tamla	Marvin Gaye & Tammi Terrell	Ain't Nothing Like The Real Thing	Ashford-Simpson	Detroit
355	8	1	Mar-68	Epic	Sly & The Family Stone	Dance To the Music	S. Steward	
356	6	1	Mar-68	Philly Int'l	The Intruders	Cowboys To Girls	Gamble-Huff	Philadelphia
357	14	1	Mar-68	ABC Paramount	The Impressions	We're A Winner		
358	1	1	Mar-68	Volt	Otis Redding	(Sittin' On) The Dock of The Bay		
359	1	1	Apr-68	Atlantic	Archie Bell & The Drells	Tighten Up	Buttier-Bell	Houston
360	10	23	Apr-68	Scepter	Dionne Warwick	Do You Know The Way To San Jose		New York
361	11	6	Apr-68	Atlantic	Percy Sledge	Take Time To Know Her		
362	5	1	Apr-68	Atlantic	Aretha Franklin	(Sweet Sweet baby) Since You've Been Gone		
363	48	20	May-68	Stan	Sam & Dave	You Don't Know What You Mean To Me	Floyd-Cropper	Memphis
364	14	2	Jun-68	King	James Brown & the Famous Flame	Licking Stick	Brown-Ellis-Byrd	Cincinnati
365	9	1	Jun-68	Motown	Stevie Wonder	Shoo-Be-Doo-Be-Doo-Da-Day		
366	3	2	Jun-68	Soul City	The Fifth Dimension	Stoned Soul Picnic	L. Nyro	
367	7	1	Jun-68	Atlantic	Aretha Franklin	Think		
368	54	19	Jul-68	Stax	Sam & Dave	Can't You Find Another Way	Banks-Jackson	Memphis
369	13	1	Jul-68	Motown	The Temptations	I Could Never Love Another (After Loving You)		
370	1	1	Jul-68	Uni	Hugh Masekela	Grazing in the Grass		
371	35	1	Jul-68	ABC/TRC	Ray Charles	Eleanor Rigby	John Lennon, Paul McCartney	
372	5	5	Aug-68	Philly Int'l	Archie Bell & The Drells	I Can't Stop Dancing	Gamble-Huff	Philadelphia
373	15	3	Aug-68	Brunswick	Barbara Acklin	Love Makes a Woman		New York
374	6	2	Aug-68	Atlantic	Clarence Carter	Slip Away		New York
375	10	1	Aug-68	Cadet	The Dells	Stay in My Corner	Armstrong-Terrell-Daniel	
376	7	1	Aug-68	Motown	Marvin Gaye & Tammi Terrell	You're All I Need To Get By		
377	1	2	Sep-68	Motown	Diana Ross & The Supremes	Love Child	Taylor-Wilson-Sawyer-Richards	Detroit
378	10	1	Sep-68	King	James Brown	Say it Loud, I'm Black and I'm Proud	James Brown - Alfred Ellis	Cincinnati
379	5	21	Oct-68	JAD	Johnny Nash	Hold Me Tight	J Nash	
380	2	2	Oct-68	Motown/Tamla	Marvin Gaye	I Heard It Through The Grapevine	Whitfield-Strong	Detroit
381	2	2	Oct-68	Motown/Tamla	Stevie Wonder	For Once In My Life	Miller-Murden	Detroit
382	6	2	Oct-68	Motown/Gordy	The Temptations	Cloud Nine	Whitfield-Strong	Detroit
383	41	18	Nov-68	Stax	Sam & Dave	Soul Sister, Brown Sugar	Hayes-Porter	Memphis
384	16	1	Nov-68	Vee-Jay	Jerry Butler	Hey, Western Union Man		
385	5	1	Nov-68	Stax	Johnnie Taylor	Who's Making Love		
386	31	9	Dec-68	King	James Brown	Goodbye My Love		
387	8	3	Dec-68	Motown/Tamla	Smokey Robinson & The Miracles	Baby Baby Don't Cry	Robinson-Cleveland-Johnson	Detroit
388	3	3	Dec-68	Brunswick	Young Holt Unlimited	Soulful Strut		New York
389	21	6	Jan-69	Atlantic	Archie Bell & The Drells	Ther's Gonna Be A Showdown	Tyson-Sigler-Felder	Philadelphia
390	9	2	Jan-69	Motown	David Ruffin	My Whole World Ended (The Moment You Left	Bristol-Fuqua-Sawyer-Roach	Detroit
391	6	1	Jan-69	Motown/Gordy	Edwin Starr	Twenty-Five Miles	Bristol-Fuqua-Starr	Detroit
392	1	1	Jan-69	Epic	Sly & The Family Stone	Everyday People	S. Steward	
393	5	1	Jan-69	Brunswick	Tyrone Davis	Can I Change My Mind		New York
394	7	1	Feb-69	Scepter	Dionne Warwick	This Girl's In Love With You		New York
395	15	1	Feb-69	King	James Brown	Give It Up or Turn It Loose	Charles Bobbit	Cincinnati
396	4	1	Mar-69	Philly Int'l	Jerry Butler	Only The Strong Survive	Gamble-Huff-Butler	Philadelphia
397	1	6	Mar-69	Soul City	The Fifth Dimension	Aquarius/Let The Sunshine In	Rado-Ragni-MacDermot	
398	6	1	Mar-69	Motown	The Temptations	Run Away Child Running Wild		

	Pop	R&B	Year	Label	Artist	Song	Writer	Place
399	20	3	Apr-69	King	James Brown	I Don't Want Nobody To Give me Nothing	James Brown	Cincinnati
400	4	1	Apr-69	Motown	Jr. Walker & The All Stars	What Does It Take (To Win Your Love)	Bristol-Fuqua-Bullock	Detroit
401	22	6	Apr-69	Epic	Sly & The Family Stone	Stand	S. Steward	
402	2	1	Apr-69	T-Neck	The Isley Brothers	It's Your Thing		
403	13	1	May-69	Sound Stage	Joe Simon	The Chokin' Kind		
404	11	1	Jun-69	King	James Brown	Mother Popcorn	James Brown-Alfred Ellis	Cincinnati
405	30	11	Jun-69	King	James Brown	The Popcorn	James Brown-Alfred Ellis	Cincinnati
406	4	1	Jun-69	Motown	Marvin Gaye	Too Busy Thinking About My Baby		
407	68	15	Jul-69	Philly Int'l	The O'Jays	One Night Affair	Gamble-Huff	Philadelphia
408	14	1	Jul-69	Motown	The Originals	Baby, I'm For Real	Gaye-Gaye	Detroit
409	1	1	Jul-69	Motown/Gordy	The Temptations	I Can't Get Next To You	Whitfield-Strong	Detroit
410	1	1	Aug-69	Epic	Sly & The Family Stone	Hot Fun In The Summertime	S. Steward	
411	21	1	Aug-69	Curtom Records	The Impressions	Choice of Colors		
412	13	1	Aug-69	Atlantic	Aretha Franklin	Share Your Love With ME		
413	37	8	Sep-69	King	James Brown	Man's World Part 1	James Brown-Betty Newsome	Cincinnati
414	10	1	Sep-69	Cadet	The Dells	Oh What a Night		
415	23	23	Oct-69	Soul City	The Fifth Dimension	Wedding Bell Blues	L. Nyro	
416	1	1	Oct-69	Motown	The Jackson 5	I Want You Back	Perren-Mizell-Gordy-Richards	Detroit
417	21	2	Nov-69	King	James Brown	Let a Man Come in and Do the Popcorn		Cincinnati
418	24	3	Dec-69	King	James Brown	Ain't it Funky Now	James Brown	Cincinnati
419	1	1	Dec-69	Motown	Diana Ross & The Supremes	Someday We'll Be Together		New York
420	4		Jan-70	Cotillion	Brook Benton	Rainy Night in Georgia	White	
421	6	17	Jan-70	Scepter	Dionne Warwick	I'll Never Fall In Love Again	Bacharach-David	New York
422	40	4	Jan-70	King	James Brown	Let A Man Come in and Do the Popcorn Pt 2		Cincinnati
423	39		Jan-70	JAD	Johnny Nash	Cupid	S Cooke	Kingston, JAM
424	1	1	Jan-70	Epic	Sly & The Family Stone	Thank You	S. Steward	San Francisco
425	12	4	Jan-70	Motown	The Originals	The Bells	Gaye-Gaye-Gordy-Stover	Detroit
426	76	30	Feb-70	Philly Int'l	Dusty Springfield	Silly, Silly Fool	Gamble-Huff	Philadelphia
427	32	2	Feb-70	King	James Brown	It's a New Day	James Brown	Cincinnati
428	1	1	Feb-70	Motown	The Jackson 5	ABC	Perren-Mizell-Gordy-Richards	Detroit
429	10	5	Feb-70	Motown	The Supremes	Up The Ladder To The Roof	DiMarco-Wilson	Detroit
430	51	20	Mar-70	King	James Brown	Funky Drummer	James Brown	Cincinnati
431	13	1	Mar-70	Atlantic	Aretha Franklin	Call Me		New York
432	2	20	May-70	Invictus	Freda Payne	Band of Gold	Holland-Dozier-Holland	
433	32	2	May-70	King	James Brown	Brother Rapp	James Brown	Cincinnati
434	2	1	May-70	Motown	The Jackson 5	The Love You Save	Perren-Mizell-Gordy-Richards	Detroit
435	3	2	May-70	Motown/Tamla	The Temptations	Ball Of Confusion	Whitfield-Strong	Detroit
436	3	1	May-70	Dakar	Tyrone Davis	Turn Back the Hands of Time	Daniels-Thompson	Chicago
437	3	1	May-70	Stang	The Moments	Love On a Two-Way Street	Keyes/Robinson	New York
438	1	3	Jun-70	Motown/Gordy	Edwin Starr	WAR	Whitfield-Strong	Detroit
439	38	14	Jun-70	Epic	Sly & The Family Stone	I Want To Take You Higher	S. Steward	San Francisco
440	3	1	Jun-70	Motown/Tamla	Stevie Wonder	Signed Sealed & Delivered	Wonder-Garrett-Wright-Hardaway	Detroit
441	14	4	Jun-70	Motown/VIP	The Spinners	It's A Shame	Wonder-Garrett-Wright	Detroit
442	1	1	Jul-70	Motown	Diana Ross	Ain't No Mountain High Enough	Ashford-Simpson	Detroit
443	11	4	Aug-70	Motown	Four Tops	Still Water	Robinson-Wilson	Detroit
444	15	2	Aug-70	King	James Brown	Get Up, I Feel Like Being a Sex Machine	Brown-Byrd-Lenhoff	Cincinnati
445	7	20	Aug-70	Rare Earth	Rare Earth	I Know I'm Losing You	Holland-Whitfield-Grant	Detroit
446	1	1	Sep-70	Motown/Tamla	Smokey Robinson & The Miracles	The Tears Of A Clown	Cosby-Robinson-Wonder	Detroit
447	1	1	Sep-70	Motown	The Jackson 5	I'll Be There	Gordy-West-Davis-Hutch	Detroit
448	29	3	Oct-70	Curtom	Curtis Mayfield	(Don't Worry) If There's A Hell Below	Curtis Mayfield	Chicago

	Pop	R&B	Year	Label	Artist	Song	Writer	Place
449	9	1	Oct-70	Motown	Gladys Knight & The Pips	If I Were Your Woman	Ware-Sawyer-McMurray	Detroit
450	13	1	Oct-70	King	James Brown	Super Bad	James Brown	Cincinnati
451	7	1	Oct-70	Motown	The Supremes	Stoned Love	Wilson-Samoht	Detroit
452	2	4	Nov-70	Bell	The Fifth Dimension	One Less Bell To Answer	Bacharach-David	San Francisco
453	34	4	Jan-71	King	James Brown	Get Up, Get into It, Get Involved	Brown-Byrd-Lenhoff	Cincinnati
454	2	1	Jan-71	Motown/Tamla	Marvin Gaye	What's Going On	Gaye-Ctevelans-Benson	Detroit
455	1	1	Jan-71	Motown/Tamla	The Temptations	Just My Imagination (Running Away With Me)	Whitfield-Strong	Detroit
456	17	2	Jan-71	Philly Int'l	Wilson Pickett	Don't Let The Green Grass Fool You	Aikenes-Bellman-Drayton-Turner	Philadelphia
457	6	1	Jan-71	Chimneyville	King Floyd	Groove Me	King Floyd	Los Angeles
458	4	1	Feb-71	Liberty	Ike & Tina Turner	Proud Mary	J Fogerty	St Louis
459	25	1	Feb-71	Stax	Rufus Thomas	(Do The) Push and Pull	Rufus Thomas	Memphis
460	28	1	Feb-71	Stax	Johnnie Taylor	Jody's Got Your Girl and Gone	Baker-Wilson-Davis	Memphis
461	29	3	Mar-71	King	James Brown	Soul Power	James Brown	Cincinnati
462	2	1	Mar-71	Motown	The Jackson 5	Never Can Say Goodbye	Clifton Davis	Detroit
463	16	8	Apr-71	Motown	The Supremes	Nathan Jones	Wakefield-Caston	Detroit
464	2	2	May-71	United Art	Cornelius Bros & Sister Rose	Treat Her Like a Lady	E. Cornelius	Florida
465	17	2	May-71	Motown	Gladys Knight & The Pips	I Don't Want To Do Wrong	Bristol-Knight-Guest-Knight-Schaffn	Detroit
466	51	10	May-71	Philly Int'l	The Ebonys	You're The Reason Why	Gamble-Huff	Philadelphia
467	3	2	May-71	Motown/Gordy	The Undisputed Truth	Smiling Faces Sometimes	Whitfield-Strong	Detroit
468	6	1	May-71	Atlantic	Aretha Franklin	Bridge Over Troubled Water	Paul Simon	New York
469	1	1	May-71	Hot Wax	The Honey Cone	Want Ads	Holland-Dozier-Holland	Los Angeles
470	12	3	Jun-71	Invictus	Freda Payne	Bring The Boys Home	Holland-Dozier-Holland	
471	25	6	Jun-71	People	James Brown	Escapism	James Brown	Cincinnati
472	4	1	Jun-71	Motown/Tamla	Marvin Gaye	Mercy Mercy Me	Marvin Gaye	Detroit
473	7	30	Jun-71	Motown/RareEarth	Rare Earth	I Just Want To Celebrate	Rzesses-Fekaris	Detroit
474	13	1	Jun-71	Atlantic	Wilson Pickett	Don't Knock My Love	Pickett-Shapiro	Memphis
475	15	1	Jul-71	People	James Brown	Hot Pants	James Brown-Fred Wesley	Cincinnati
476	9	3	Jul-71	Volt	The Dramatics	Whatcha See Is Whacha Get	Tony Hester	Detroit
477	1	1	Jul-71	Stax	Jean Knight	Mr. Big Stuff	Broussard/Washington/Williams	Memphis
478	2	1	Aug-71	Atlantic	Aretha Franklin	Spanish Harlem	Leiber-Spector	New York
479	22	1	Sep-71	Polydor	James Brown	Make it Funky	James Brown-Charles Bobbit	Cincinnati
480	11	1	Sep-71	Hot Wax	The Honey Cone	Stick Up	Holland-Dozier-Holland	Los Angeles
481	69	13	Oct-71	Curtom	Curtis Mayfield	Get Down	Curtis Mayfield	Chicago
482	115	32	Oct-71	Curtom	Curtis Mayfield	We Got To Have Peace	Curtis Mayfield	Chicago
483	1	1	Oct-71	Enterplse	Isaac Hayes	Theme from Shaft	Isaac Hayes	Memphis
484	15	1	Oct-71	Atco	The Persuaders	Thin Line Between Love & Hate	Members-Poindexter-Poindexter	New York
485	13	1	Oct-71	Westbound	Denise LaSalle	Trapped By a Thing Called Love	D. LaSalle	Jackson, MS
486	9	2	Nov-71	Atlantic	Aretha Franklin	Rocksteady	Aretha Franklin	New York
487	11	3	Nov-71	Philly Int'l	Joe Simon	Drowning In The Sea of Love	Gamble-Huff	Philadelphia
488	4	4	Nov-71	Motown	Michael Jackson	Got To Be There	Willensky	Detroit
489	1	1	Nov-71	Epic	Sly & The Family Stone	Family Affair	S. Steward-Stone	San Francisco
490	1	1	Nov-71	Motown	Marvin Gaye	Inner City Blues (Make Me Wanna Holler)	Marvin Gaye	Detroit
491	3	1	Nov-71	Brunswick	The Chi-Lites	Have You Seen Her	Acklin/Record	Chicago
492	35	7	Dec-71	Polydor	James Brown	I'm a Greedy Man	James Brown-Charles Bobbit	Cincinnati
493	1	1	Jan-72	Stax	Staple Singers	I'll Take You There	Green-Jackson-Mitchell	Memphis
494	1	1	Jan-72	Hi	Al Green	Let's Stay Together		Memphis
495	27	1	Feb-72	Polydor	James Brown	Talking Loud & Saying Nothing	James Brown-Bobby Byrd	Cincinnati
496	2	1	Feb-72	Dial	Joe Tex	I Gotcha	Joe Tex	Memphis
497	23	14	Feb-72	Epic	Sly & The Family Stone	Running Away	S. Steward	San Francisco
498	1	4	Mar-72	Atlantic	Roberta Flack	The First Time Ever I Saw Your Face		New York

	Pop	R&B	Year	Label	Artist	Song	Writer	Place
499	5	1	Mar-72	Volt	The Dramatics	In the Rain	Tony Hester	Detroit
500	4	2	Apr-72	Hi	Al Green	Look What You Done For Me	Green-Jackson-Mitchell	Memphis
501	40	6	Apr-72	Polydor	James Brown	King Heroin	Brown-Bobbit-Matthews-Rosen	Cincinnati
502	43	4	Apr-72	Polydor	James Brown	There It Is	James Brown	Cincinnati
503	1	1	Apr-72	MGM	Sammy Davis Jr.	The Candy Man	Bricusse-Newley	Los Angeles
504	1	1	Apr-72	Brunswick	The Chi-Lites	Oh Girl	E Record	Chicago
505	8	28	Apr-72	Bell	The Fifth Dimension	Last Night I Didn't Get Any Sleep At All	T. Macaulay	San Francisco
506	5	1	May-72	Atlantic	Aretha Franklin	Day Dreaming	Aretha Franklin	New York
507	44	7	May-72	Polydor	James Brown	Honky Tonk	James Brown	Cincinnati
508	2	1	Jun-72	United Art	Cornelius Bros & Sister Rose	It's Too Late to Turn Back Now	E. Cornelius	Florida
509	58	7	Jun-72	Philly Int'l	Harold Melvin & The Blue Notes	I Miss You	Gamble-Huff	Philadelphia
510	2		Jun-72	Motown	Michael Jackson	Rockin Robin	Thomas	Detroit
511		2	Jun-72	Philly Int'l	The O'Jays	When The World's At Peace	Gamble-Sigler-Hurtt	Philadelphia
512	60	1	Jun-72	United Art	Bobby Womack	Woman's Gotta Have It	Carter-Womack-Womack	
513	1	1	Jul-72	Sussex	Bill Withers	Lean On Me		
514	2	1	Jul-72	A&M	Billy Preston	Outa-Space	Greene-Preston	
515	4	2	Jul-72	Curtom	Curtis Mayfield	Freddie's Dead (Theme from Superfly)	Curtis Mayfield	Chicago
516	44	3	Jul-72	Polydor	James Brown	I Got A Bag of My Own	James Brown	Cincinnati
517	3	1	Jul-72	Philly Int'l	The O'Jays	Back Stabbers	McFadden-Whitehead-Hutt	Philadelphia
518	64	17	Jul-72	Buddah	The Trammps	Zing Went The Strings Of My Heart	Baker/Felder/Harris/Young	Philadelphia
519	3	1	Jul-72	Koko	Luther Ingram	(If Loving You Is Wrong) I Don't Want To Be Rig	Banks-Hampton-Jackson	Memphis
520	5	2	Aug-72	Atlantic	Roberta Flack & Donny Hathaway	Where is the Love	MacDonald-Slater	New York
521	13	1	Aug-72	Hi	Al Green	I'm Still in Love with You	Green-Jackson-Mitchell	Memphis
522	11	1	Aug-72	Spring	Joe Simon	Power of Love	Gamble-Huff-Simon	Philadelphia
523	1	1	Sep-72	Chess	Chuck Berry	My Ding-A-Ling	J Nash	
524	18	1	Sep-72	Polydor	James Brown	Get On The Good Foot	Brown-Wesley-Mims	Cincinnati
525	78	12	Sep-72	Philly Int'l	Johnny Williams	Slow Motion (Part 1)	Gamble-Huff	Philadelphia
526	3	2	Sep-72	RCA	Main Ingredient	Everybody Plays the Fool	Bailey-Clark-Williams	New York
527	1	5	Sep-72	Motown	Michael Jackson	Ben	Black/Scharf	Detroit
528	1	1	Oct-72	Philly Int'l	Billy Paul	Me & Mrs Jones	Gamble-Huff-Gilbert	Philadelphia
529	8	5	Oct-72	Curtom	Curtis Mayfield	Superfly	Curtis Mayfield	Chicago
530	3	1	Oct-72	Philly Int'l	Harold Melvin & The Blue Notes	If You Don't Know Me By Now	Gamble-Huff	Philadelphia
531	1	38	Oct-72	Epic	Johnny Nash	I Can See Clearly Now	J Nash	Kingston, JAM
532	3	1	Oct-72	Atlantic	The Spinners	I'll Be Around	Bell-Hurtt	Detroit
533	57	13	Nov-72	Philly Int'l	The O'Jays	992 Arguments	Gamble-Huff	Philadelphia
634	3	1	Dec-72	Hi	Al Green	You Ought To Be With Me	Green-Jackson-Mitchell	Memphis
535	1	1	Jan-73	Philly Int'l	The O'Jays	Love Train	Gamble-Huff	Philadelphia
536	1	1	Jan-73	Motown	Stevie Wonder	Superstition	Stevie Wonder	Detroit
537	3	1	Jan-73	Glades	Timmy Thomas	Why Can't We Live Together	Timmy Thomas	Miami
538	27	4	Feb-73	Polydor	James Brown	I Got Ants in My Pants and I want to Dance	James Brown	
539	1	2	Feb-73	Atlantic	Roberta Flack	Killing me Softly with His Song	Fox-Gimbel	New York
540	4	1	Feb-73	Atlantic	The Spinners	Could It Be I'm Falling In Love	Steals-Steals	Detroit
541	10	2	Mar-73	Decca	Al Green	Call Me (Come Back Home)	Green-Jackson-Mitchell	Memphis
542	5	42	Mar-73	Hi	Dobie Gray	Driftaway		
543	63	12	Mar-73	Philly Int'l	Harold Melvin & The Blue Notes	Yesterday I Had The Blues	Gamble-Huff	Philadelphia
544	12		Mar-73	Epic	Johnny Nash	Stir It Up	B. Marley	Kingston, JAM
545	1	3	Mar-73	Tamla	Stevie Wonder	You are the Sunshine of my Life	Stevie Wonder	Detroit
546	2	1	Mar-73	Soul	Gladys Knight & The Pips	Neither One Of Us (Wants To Be The First To Say Goodbye)		
547	79	29	Apr-73	Philly Int'l	Billy Paul	Am I Black Enough For You	Sigler-Hurtt	Philadelphia
548	7	1	Apr-73	Motown	The Temptations	Masterpiece	Norm Whitfield	Detroit

#	Pop	R&B	Year	Label	Artist	Song	Writer	Place
549	36	6	May-73	Philly Int'l	The Intruders	I'll Always Love My Mama	McFadden-Whitehead-Gamble-Huff	Philadelphia
550	15	1	May-73	Westbound	Ohio Players	Funky Worm	Fisher-Preston	
551	1	10	May-73	A&M	Billy Preston	Will It Go Round In Circles	Jackson-Yancy	
552	21	1	May-73	Wand	The Independents	Leaving Me		
553	3	1	May-73	20th Century	Barry White	I'm Gonna Love You Just A Little More Baby	Barry White	Los Angeles
554	10	4	Jun-73	London	Bloodstone	Natural High	McCormick	Kansas City
555	39	11	Jun-73	Curtom	Curtis Mayfield	Future Shock	Curtis Mayfield	Chicago
556	11	1	Jun-73	Atlantic	The Spinners	One of a Kind (Love Affair)	Jefferson	Detroit
557	10	2	Jul-73	Hi	Al Green	Here I Am (Come And Take Me)	Green-Hodges	Memphis
558	1	1	Jul-73	Motown	Diana Ross	Touch Me In the Morning	Masser-Miller	Detroit
559	28	15	Jul-73	Buddah	Gladys Knight & The Pips	Where Peaceful Waters Flow	Jim Weatherly	
560	12	1	Jul-73	Epic	Sly & The Family Stone	If You Want Me To Stay	S. Steward	San Francisco
561	22	1	Jul-73	People	Fred Wesley & The JBs	Doing it to Death		
562	11	1	Jul-73	Stax	Johnnie Taylor	I Believe in You (You Believe In Me)	Davis	Memphis
563	6	1	Aug-73	T-Neck	Isley Brothers	That Lady (Part 1)	Isley Brothers	Cincinnati
564	20	1	Aug-73	Atlantic	Aretha Franklin	Angel		New York
565	1	1	Aug-73	Motown	Marvin Gaye	Let's Get It On	Marvin Gaye	Detroit
566	1	1	Sep-73	Buddah	Gladys Knight & The Pips	Midnight Train to Georgia	Jim Weatherly	
567	7	1	Sep-73	Philly Int'l	Harold Melvin & The Blue Notes	The Love I Lost	Gamble-Huff	Philadelphia
568	50	6	Sep-73	Polydor	James Brown	Sexy, Sexy, Sexy	James Brown	Cincinnati
569		1	Sep-73	Philly Int'l	The O'Jays	Now That We Found Love	Gamble-Huff	Philadelphia
570	4	1	Sep-73	Motown	Stevie Wonder	Higher Ground	Stevie Wonder	Detroit
571		1	Oct-73	Philly Int'l	The O'Jays	Don't Call Me Brother	Gamble-Huff	Philadelphia
572	1	1	Oct-73	Motown	Eddie Kendricks	Keep On Truckin'	Caston-Wilson	Detroit
573	7	2	Nov-73	20th Century	Barry White	Never, Never Gonna Give You Up	Barry White	Los Angeles
574	88	16	Nov-73	Curtom	Curtis Mayfield	Can't Say Nothin'	Curtis Mayfield	Chicago
575	4	1	Nov-73	A&M	Billy Preston	Space Race	Billy Preston	
576	1	1	Dec-73	Buddah	Gladys Knight & The Pips	I've Got To Use My Imagination	Goffin-Goldberg	
577	1	1	Dec-73	20th Century	Love Unlimited Orchestra	Love's Theme	Barry White	Los Angeles
578		75	Dec-73	Philly Int'l	The Trammps	Love Epidemic	Harris-Green	Philadelphia
579	9	1	Dec-73	Stax	Staple Singers	If You're Ready (Come Go With Me)	Staple Singers	Memphis
580	8	1	Dec-73	Motown	Stevie Wonder	Living for the City	Stevie Wonder	Detroit
581	4	2	Jan-74	De-Lite	Kool & The Gang	Jungle Boogie	Bayyan-Kool & the Gang	Los Angeles
582	3	1	Jan-74	Atlantic	Aretha Franklin	Until You Come Back To Me (That's What I'm Gonna Do)		New York
583	19	1	Jan-74	Hi	Al Green	Livin' For You	Green-Mitchell	Memphis
584	27	1	Feb-74	Motown	The Temptations	Let Your Hair Down	Norm Whitfield	Detroit
585	2	1	Feb-74	Motown	Eddie Kendricks	Boogie Down	Caston-Poree-Wilson	Detroit
586	3	1	Mar-74	Buddah	Gladys Knight & The Pips	Best Thing That Ever Happened To Me	Jim Weatherly	
587	10	8	Mar-74	RCA	Main Ingredient	Just Don't Want To be Lonely	Barrett-Eli-Freeman	New York
588	1	1	Mar-74	Philly Int'l	MFSB (Feat. The Three Degrees)	TSOP (The Sound of Philadelphia)	Gamble-Huff	Philadelphia
589	20	1	Mar-74	Atlantic	The Spinners	Mighty Love	Hawes-Jefferson-Simmons	Detroit
590	10	1	Apr-74	United Art	Bobby Womack	Lookin' For A Love	Bacharach-David	
591	26	1	Apr-74	Polydor	James Brown	The Payback	Brown-Wesley-Starks	Cincinnati
592	5	2	Apr-74	Avco	Stylistics	You Make Me Feel Brand New	Bell/Creed	Philadelphia
593	9	3	Apr-74	Philly Int'l	The O'Jays	For The Love of Money	Gamble-Huff-Jackson	Philadelphia
594	40	3	May-74	Curtom	Curtis Mayfield	Kung Fu	Curtis Mayfield	Chicago
595	2	1	May-74	Motown	The Jackson 5	Dancing Machine	Davis-Fletcher-Parks	Detroit
596	19	1	May-74	Atlantic	Aretha Franklin	I'm In Love		New York
597		28	Jun-74	Philly Int'l	Bunny Sigler	Love Train	Gamble-Huff	Philadelphia
598	1	1	Jun-74	T.K.	George McCrae	Rock Your Baby	Casey-Finch	

	Pop	R&B	Year	Label	Artist	Song	Writer	Place
599	5	1	Jun-74	Buddah	Gladys Knight & The Pips	On & On	Curtis Mayfield	Philadelphia
600	1	1	Jun-74	RCA	Hues Corporation	Rock the Boat	W. Holmes	Washington
601	4	1	Jun-74	Roxbury	William DeVaughn	Be Thankful For What You Got	Williams DeVaughn	Los Angeles
602	6	1	Jun-74	De-Lite	Kool & The Gang	Hoolywood Swinging	Kool & the Gang-West	
603	8	1	Jun-74	Atco	Blue Magic	Sideshow	Barrett/Eli	Chicago
604	17	1	Jun-74	Curtom	The Impressions	Finally Got Myself Together (I'm a Changed Ma	Curtis Mayfield	New York
605	1	2	Jul-74	Atlantic	Dionne Warwick	Then Came You		Philadelphia
606	85	42	Jul-74	Philly Int'l	MFSB	Love is The Message	Gamble-Huff	Chicago
607	3	1	Jul-74	ABC	Rufus & Chaka Khan	Tell me Something Good	Stevie Wonder	Cincinnati
608	29	1	Aug-74	Polydor	James Brown	My Thang	James Brown	New York
609	1	1	Aug-74	Atlantic	Roberta Flack	Feel Like Making Love	McDaniels	Cincinnati
610	31	1	Sep-74	Polydor	James Brown	Papa Don't Take No Mess	James Brown	
611	13	2	Sep-74	Mercury	Ohio Players	Skin Tight	Brown-Wesley-Starks-Bobbit	Philadelphia
612	2	4	Sep-74	Philly Int'l	The Three Degrees	When Will I See You Again	Gamble-Huff	Los Angeles
613	1	1	Sep-74	20th Century	Barry White	Can't Get Enough Of Your Love, Babe	Barry White	Detroit
614	1	1	Sep-74	Motown	Stevie Wonder	You Haven't Done Nothin'	Stevie Wonder	
615	6	11	Oct-74	Back beat	Carl Carlton	Everlasting Love		Cincinnati
616	44	4	Oct-74	Polydor	James Brown	Funky President	James Brown	Brooklyn
617	2	1	Oct-74	Roadshow	B.T. Express	Do It ('Til You're Satisfied)	Nichols	Los Angeles
618	37	2	Oct-74	De-Lite	Kool & The Gang	Higher Plane	Bayyan-Kool & the Gang	Memphis
619	7	2	Nov-74	Hi	Al Green	She La La (Make Me Happy)	Al Green	Los Angeles
620	2	2	Nov-74	20th Century	Barry White	You're The First, The Last My Everything	Radcliffe-Sepe-White	
621	1	1	Nov-74	20th Century	Carl Douglas	Kung Fu Fighting		Miami
622	31	1	Nov-74	Glades	Latimore	Let's Straighten It Out	Latimore	
623	22	1	Nov-74	Truth	Shirley Brown	Woman to Woman		
624	21	1	Nov-74	Buddah	Gladys Knight & The Pips	I Feel a Song (In My Heart)	Camillo-Sawyer	
625	9	34	Dec-74	MGM	Gloria Gaynor	Never Can Say Goodbye	Davis	
626	1	1	Dec-74	Mercury	Ohio Players	Fire	Beck-Bonner-Jones-Middlebrook-Ohio Players-Satch	Philadelphia
627	48	17	Dec-74	Philly Int'l	The O'Jays	Sunshine	Sigler-Hurtt	Chicago
628	11	1	Dec-74	ABC	Rufus & Chaka Khan	You Got the Love	Khan-Parker	New Bedford
629	50	1	Dec-74	Capitol	Tavares	She's Gone	Hall-Oates	Detroit
630	3	1	Dec-74	Motown	Stevie Wonder	Boogie On Reggae Woman	Stevie Wonder	Philadelphia
631	1	1	Feb-75	Epic	Labelle	Lady Marmalade	Crewe-Nolan	Brooklyn
632	12	1	Feb-75	Vibration	Shirley & Company	Shame, Shame, Shame	Sylvia Robinson	Memphis
633	4	1	Feb-75	Roadshow	B.T. Express	Express	Lomas-Risbrook-Rowe-Thompson-N	Los Angeles
634	13	1	Mar-75	Hi	Al Green	L-O-V-E	Al Green	New York
635	8	1	Mar-75	20th Century	Barry White	What Am I Gonna Do With You	Barry White	Los Angeles
636	5	1	Mar-75	Atlantic	Ben E. King	Supernatural Thing-Part I		Philadelphia
637	1	1	Mar-75	Columbia	Earth Wind & Fire	Shining Star	White-Bailey-Dunn	London, UK
638	15	4	Mar-75	Philly Int'l	Harold Melvin & The Blue Notes	Bad Luck	McFadden-Whitehead-Carstarphen	
639	8	1	Mar-75	Big Three	Hot Chocolate	Emma	Brown-Brown	Detroit
640	8	1	Mar-75	Spring	Joe Simon	Get Down, Get Down (Get on the Floor)		Chicago
641	26	1	Mar-75	Tamla	Smokey Robinson	Baby That's Backatcha	Robinson	New York
642	10	4	Mar-75	ABC	Rufus & Chaka Khan	Once You Get Started	Wright	
643	5	1	Apr-75	Atlantic	Major Harris	Love Won't Let Me Wait	Barrett-Eli	New York
644	11	5	May-75	Buddah	Gladys Knight & The Pips	Try To Remember/The Way We Were	Schmidt-Hamlish-Bergman-Bergman-Jones	Philadelphia
645	1		May-75	Avco	Van McCoy	The Hustle	Van McCoy	Philadelphia
646		25	Jun-75	Philly Int'l	Archie Bell & The Drells	I Could Dance All Night		
647	9	1	Jun-75	Cat	Gwen McCrae	Rockin' Chair	Tyson-Sigler-Felder	
648	42	1	Jun-75	Philly Int'l	Harold Melvin & The Blue Notes	Hope That We Can Be Together Soon	Gamble-Huff	

	Pop	R&B	Year	Label	Artist	Song	Writer	Place
649	7	1	Jul-75	Philly Int'l	Archie Bell & The Drells	Let's Groove (Part 1)	Tyson-Sigler-Felder	Philadelphia
650	67	9	Jul-75	Curtom	Curtis Mayfield	So In Love	Curtis Mayfield	Chicago
651	4	1	Jul-75	T-Neck	Isley Brothers	Fight The Power (Part 1)	Isley-Isley-Isley-Isley-Jasper	Cincinnati
652	11	1	Jul-75	Philly Int'l	People's Choice	Do It Any Way You Wanna	Leon Huff	Philadelphia
653	10	1	Aug-75	Capitol	Tavares	It Only Takes A Minute	Lambert-Potter	New Bedford
654	5	1	Aug-75	Atlantic	The Spinners	They Just Can't Stop It the (Games	Hawes-Jefferson-Simmons	Detroit
655	38	1	Sep-75	Warner	Graham Central Station	Your Love		
656	6	1	Oct-75	Capitol	Natalie Cole	This Will Be	Jackson-Yancey	Los Angeles
657	1	1	Oct-75	Mid. Int'l	Silver Convention	Fly Robin Fly	Levay-Prager	Munich
658	28	1	Nov-75	Hi	Al Green	Full of Fire	Al Green	Memphis
659	1	1	Nov-75	Motown	Diana Ross	Theme from Mahogany (Do You Know	Goffin-Masser	Detroit
660	22	8	Nov-75	Buddah	Gladys Knight & The Pips	Part-Time Love	D. Gates	
661	12	1	Nov-75	Philly Int'l	Harold Melvin & The Blue Notes	Wake Up Everybody	McFadden-Whitehead-Carstarphen	Philadelphia
662		1	Nov-75	Mercury	Ohio Players	Love Roller Coaster	Beck-Bonner-Jones-Middlebrook-Satchel-Williams	
663	1	1	Nov-75	Curtom	Staple Singers	Let's Do It Again	Staple Singers	Chicago
664	5	1	Dec-75	Philly Int'l	The O'Jays	I Love Music	Gamble-Huff	Philadelphia
665	2	3	Dec-75	Casablanca	Donna Summer	Love to Love you baby	Bellotte-Moroder-Summer	Munich
666	5	1	Dec-75	Columbia	Earth Wind & Fire	Sing A Song	White- MacKay	Los Angeles
667	3	1	Dec-75	Big Three	Hot Chocolate	You Sexy Thing	Brown	London, UK
668	32	1	Dec-75	Capitol	Natalie Cole	Inseparable	Jackson-Yancey	Los Angeles
669	5	1	Feb-76	Motown	Commodores	Sweet Love	Comodores	Detroit
670	35	10	Feb-76	Buddah	The Trammps	Hold Back The Night	Baker/Felder/Harris/Young	Philadelphia
671	5	1	Feb-76	ABC	Rufus & Chaka Khan	Sweet Thing	Khan-Maiden	Chicago
672	1	1	Mar-76	Columbia	Johnnie Taylor	Disco Lady	Davis-Scales-Vance	Memphis
673	2	1	Mar-76	United Art	Maxine Nightingale	Right Back Where We Started	Edwards-Stubbs	London, UK
674	1	1	Mar-76	Capitol	Sylvers	Boogie Fever	Perren-Saint Lewis	Memphis
675	20	1	Mar-76	Philly Int'l	The O'Jays	Livin' For The Weekend	Gamble-Huff-Gilbert	Philadelphia
676	79	18	Mar-76	Philly Int'l	The O'Jays	Stairway To Heaven	Gamble-Huff	Philadelphia
677	3	2	Apr-76	Malaco	Dorothy Moore	Misty Blue	Montgomery	Jackson, MS
678	1	1	Apr-76	Mid. Int'l	Silver Convention	Get Up And Boogie	Levay-Prager	Munich
679	14	1	May-76	United Art	Brass Construction	Movin'	Muller-Williamston-Wong	
680	3	1	May-76	A&M	Brothers Johnson	I'll Be Good To You	Johnson	Los Angeles
681	6	1	May-76	ARC	Earth Wind & Fire	Boogie Wonderland	Lind-Willis	Los Angeles
682	1	1	May-76	Columbia	Manhattans	Kiss & Say Goodbye	Lovett	New York
683	25	1	May-76	Capitol	Natalie Cole	Sophisticated Lady	Jackson-Yancey	Los Angeles
684	15	5	Jun-76	Casablanca	Parliament	Tear The Roof Off The Sucker		
685		8	Jul-76	Curtom	Curtis Mayfield	Only You Babe	Curtis Mayfield	Chicago
686	45	4	Jul-76	Polydor	James Brown	Get Up Off A That Thing	Brown-Brown-Jenkins	Cincinnati
687	2	1	Jul-76	Philly Int'l	Lou Rawls	You'll Never Find Another Love Like Mine	Gamble-Huff	Philadelphia
688	15	3	Jul-76	Capitol	Tavares	Heaven Must Be Missing An Angel	Perren-Saint Lewis	New Bedford
689	1	10	Jul-76	Private Stock	Walter Muphy & Big Apple Band	A Fifth of Beethoven	Walter Murphy	New York
690	1	1	Aug-76	Motown	Diana Ross	Love Hangover	McLeod-Sawyer	Detroit
691	12	1	Aug-76	Columbia	Earth Wind & Fire	Getaway	Taylor-Cor	Los Angeles
692	7	1	Oct-76	Motown	Commodores	Just to be Close to You	Lionel Ritchie	Detroit
693	1	1	Oct-76	ABC	Marilyn McCoo & Billy Davis Jr	You Don't Have to be A Star	Dean-Glover	Los Angeles
694	6	2	Oct-76	Philly Int'l	The Jacksons	Enjoy Yourself	Gamble-Huff	Philadelphia
695	2	1	Oct-76	Atlantic	The Spinners	The Rubberband Man	Bell-Creed	Detroit
696	3	1	Nov-76	Bang	Brick	Dazz	Hargis-Irons-Ransom	
697	1	1	Dec-76	MCA	Rose Royce	Car Wash	Norm Whitfield	Los Angeles
698	1	1	Dec-76	Tamla	Stevie Wonder	I Wish	Stevie Wonder	Detroit

	Pop	R&B	Year	Label	Artist	Song	Writer	Place
699	1	1	Jan-77	Tamla	Thelma Houston	Don't Leave Me This Way	Gamble-Gilbert-Huff	Detroit
700	5	1	Feb-77	Capitol	Natalie Cole	I've Got Love On my Mind	Jackson-Yancey	Los Angeles
701	30	1	Feb-77	ABC	Rufus & Chaka Khan	At Midnight (My Love Will Lift You Up)		Chicago
702	10	3	Mar-77	MCA	Rose Royce	I Wanna Get Next To You	Norm Whitfield	Los Angeles
703	22	1	Mar-77	Capitol	Tavares	Whodunit		New Bedford
704	12	7	Apr-77	Dial	Joe Tex	Ain't Gonna Bump No More (With no Big Fat Woman)		Memphis
705	1	1	Apr-77	Tamla	Stevie Wonder	Sir Duke	Stevie Wonder	Detroit
706	28	6	Apr-77	Philly Int'l	The Jackson	Show You The Way To Go	Gamble-Huff	Philadelphia
707	5	3	May-77	Capitol	Sylvers	Hot Line	Perren-Saint Lewis	Memphis
708	4	1	Jun-77	Motown	Commodores	Easy	Lionel Ritchie	Detroit
709	5	1	Jul-77	A&M	Brothers Johnson	Strawberry Letter 23	Otis	Los Angeles
710	2	5	Aug-77	Epic	Heatwave	Boogie Nights	Rod Temperton	Germany
711	5	1	Sep-77	Motown	Commodores	Brick House	Comodores	Detroit
712	29	1	Sep-77	Curtom	Curtis Mayfield	Do Do Wap Is Strong In Here	Curtis Mayfield	Chicago
713	6	9	Sep-77	Casablanca	Donna Summer	I Feel Love	Bellotte-Moroder-Summer	
714	4	1	Oct-77	20th Century	Barry White	It's Estacy When You Lay Down Next To Me	Paris-Pigtord	Los Angeles
715	18	3	Oct-77	Drive	Peter Brown	Do Ya Wanna Get Funky With Me	Brown-Rans	
716	4	1	Nov-77	A&M	L.T.D.	Everytime I Turn Around	Grey-Hanks	Los Angeles
717	6	6	Dec-77	Atlantic	CHIC	Dance Dance Dance	Rodgers-Edwards	New York
718	18	2	Dec-77	Epic	Heatwave	Always And Forever	Rod Temperton	Germany
719	24	21	Feb-78	Philly Int'l	Lou Rawls	Lady Love	Gray-Marshall	Philadelphia
720	10	1	Feb-78	Capitol	Natalie Cole	Our Love	Jackson-Yancey	Los Angeles
721	16	1	Feb-78	Casablanca	Parliament	Flash Light		
722	8	1	Feb-78	Arista	Ray Parker Jr & Raydio	Jack & Jill	Ray Parker	Detroit
723	1	1	Feb-78	RSO	Yvonne Elliman	If I Can't Have You	Gibb/Gibb/Gibb	New York
724	11	9	Mar-78	Atlantic	The Trammps	Disco Inferno	Green/Kersey	Philadelphia
725	32	36	Apr-78	Capitol	Tavares	More than a Woman	Gibb	New Bedford
726	8	5	May-78	Drive	Peter Brown	Dance With me	Brown-Rans	
727	38	12	Jun-78	Atlantic	CHIC	Everybody Dance	Rodgers-Edwards	New York
728	3	5	Jun-78	Casablanca	Donna Summer	Last Dance	Jabara	
729	2	1	Jun-78	Epic	Heatwave	The Groove Line	Rod Temperton	Germany
730	4	1	Jun-78	Philly Int'l	The O'Jays	Use Ta Be My Girl	Gamble-Huff	Philadelphia
731	1	1	Jul-78	Motown	Commodores	Three Times a Lady	Lionel Ritchie	Detroit
732	9	1	Jul-78	RCA	Evelyn "Champagne" King	Shame	Cross/Fitch	
733	1	1	Jul-78	Capitol	Taste of Honey	Boogie Oogie Oogie	Johnson-Kibble	Los Angeles
734	25	1	Jul-78	Philly Int'l	Teddy Pendergrass	Close the Door	Gamble-Huff	Philadelphia
735	25	1	Jul-78	Casablanca	Village People	Macho Man	Belolo-Morali-Whitehead-Willis	New York
736	9	1	Aug-78	Columbia	Earth Wind & Fire	Got To Get You Into My Life	Lennon-McCartney	Los Angeles
737	1	20	Aug-78	Philly Int'l	Teddy Pendergrass	Come Go with Me	Gamble-Huff	Philadelphia
738	1	8	Sep-78	Casablanca	Donna Summer	MacArthur Park	Jimmy Webb	
739	19	4	Sep-78	Fantasy	Sylvester	Dance (Disco Heat)	Perren-Saint Lewis	
740	1	1	Nov-78	Atlantic	CHIC	Le Freak	Rodgers-Edwards	New York
741	28	1	Nov-78	Warner	Funkadelic	One Nation Under A Groove	Clinton-Morrison-Shider	Memphis
742	2	32	Nov-78	Casablanca	Village People	Y.M.C.A.	Belolo-Morali-Willis	New York
743	8	1	Dec-78	ARC	Earth Wind & Fire	September	McKay/White/Willis	Los Angeles
744	6	1	Dec-78	Infinity	Hot Chocolate	Every 1's a Winner	Brown	London, UK
745	1	1	Dec-78	Casablanca	Parliament	Aqua Boogie		
746	2	1	Dec-78	Planet	Pointer Sisters	Fire	Springsteen	
747	12	3	Jan-79	Columbia	Cheryl Lynn	Got To Be Real	Foster-Lynn-Paich	
748	4	10	Jan-79	Casablanca	Donna Summer	Heaven Knows	Bellotte-Moroder-Summer	

	Pop	R&B	Year	Label	Artist	Song	Writer	Place
749	1	1	Jan-79	Polydor	Gloria Gaynor	I Will Survive	Fekaris-Perren	
750	5	4	Jan-79	Polydor	Peaches & Herb	Shake Your Groove Thing	Fekaris-Perren	
751	32	5	Jan-79	Whitfield	Rose Royce	Love Don't Live Here Anymore	Gregory	Los Angeles
752		3	Jan-79	T.K.	T-Connection	At Midnight		Miami
753	26	32	Feb-79	Capitol	Gonzales	I Haven't Stopped Dancing Yet	Coakley-MacKey	
754	36	46	Feb-79	Fantasy	Sylvester	You Make Me Feel (Mighty Real)	Orsborn-Wirrick	San Francisco
755	7	20	Feb-79	Atlantic	CHIC	I Want Your Love	Rodgers-Edwards	New York
756	7	5	Mar-79	Epic	Jackson 5	Shake Your Body Down To The Ground	Jackson-Jackson	Philadelphia
757	1	1	Mar-79	Polydor	Peaches & Herb	Reunited	Fekaris-Perren	
758	9	1	Mar-79	Cotillon	Sister Sledge	He's The Greatest Dancer	Rodgers-Edwards	New York
759		28	Mar-79	T.K.	T-Connection	Saturday Night	Coakley	Miami
760	7	3	Mar-79	Epic	The Jacksons	Shake Your Body Down To the Ground	Jackson-Jackson	Los Angeles
761		1	Mar-79	GRP	Tom Browne	Funkin' For Jamaica	Tom Browne	New York
762	3	30	Mar-79	Casablanca	Village People	In the Navy	Belolo-Morali-Willis	New York
763	1	3	Apr-79	Juana	Anita Ward	Ring My Bell	Bellotte-Faltermeyer-Forsey	Memphis
764	2	1	May-79	Cotillon	Sister Sledge	We Are Family	Casey-Finch	
765	1	1	May-79	Casablanca	Donna Summer	Bad Girls	Rodgers-Edwards	New York
766	1	1	Jun-79	Brunswick	McFadden & Whitehead	Ain't No Stopping Us Now	Esposito-Hokenson-Sudano-Summer	
767	13	14	Jun-79	Arista	Curtis Mayfield w. Linda Clifford	You Can't Change That	Cohen-McFadden-Whitehead	Philadelphia
768	9	18	Jun-79	Arista	Dionne Warwick	America The Beautiful	Ray Parker	Detroit
769		5	Jul-79	MCA	Ray Charles	Good Times	Katherine Lee Bates, Samuel Ward	
770	1	1	Jul-79	Atlantic	CHIC	Between You Baby & Me	Rodgers-Edwards	New York
771		14	Jul-79	Curtom	Curtis Mayfield w. Linda Clifford	I'll Never Love This Way Again	Curtis Mayfield	Chicago
772	5	18	Jul-79	Arista	Dionne Warwick	After The Love Is Gone	Jennings-Kerr	New York
773	2	1	Jul-79	Columbia	Earth Wind & Fire	Lead Me On	Champlin-Foster-Graydon	Los Angeles
774	5	37	Jul-79	Windsong	Maxine Nightingale	Turn Off the Lights	Lasley/Willis	London, UK
775	50	2	Jul-79	Philly Int'l	Teddy Pendergrass	Sail On	Gamble-Huff	Philadelphia
776	4	1	Aug-79	Motown	Commodores	(no just) Knee Deep	Lionel Ritchie	Detroit
777		77	Aug-79	Warner	Funkadelic	Dim All The Lights	Clinton-Morrison-Shider	
778	2	13	Sep-79	Casablanca	Donna Summer	Don't Stop 'til You Get Enough	Donna Summer	
779	1	1	Sep-79	Epic	Michael Jackson	Still	Jackson/Jackson	Los Angeles
780	1	1	Oct-79	Motown	Commodores	Street Life	Lionel Ritchie	Detroit
781	36	17	Oct-79	MCA	Crusaders	Do You Love What You Feel	Joe Sample	Los Angeles
782	30	1	Oct-79	ABC	Rufus & Chaka Khan	Ladies Night		Chicago
783	8	1	Nov-79	De-Lite	Kool & The Gang	Rock With You	Bayyan-Kool & the Gang	Los Angeles
784	1	1	Nov-79	Epic	Michael Jackson	Cruisin'	Rod Temperton	Los Angeles
785	4	4	Nov-79	Tamla	Smokey Robinson	Send One Your Love	Robinson-Tarplin	Detroit
786	4	5	Nov-79	Tamla	Stevie Wonder	I Wanna Be Your Lover	Stevie Wonder	Detroit
787	11	1	Dec-79	Warner	Prince	On The Radio	Prince	Minneapolis
788	5	9	Jan-80	Casablanca	Donna Summer	Rapper's Delight	Moroder-Summer	New York
789	36	4	Jan-80	Sugar Hill	The Sugar Hill Gang	Stomp	Rodgers-Edwards	Los Angeles
790	7	1	Feb-80	A&M	Brothers Johnson	Shining Star	Johnson-Johnson-Johnson-Temperti	New York
791	5	4	May-80	Columbia	Manhattans	Can't We Try	Graham-Richmond	Philadelphia
792	52	5	May-80	Philly Int'l	Teddy Pendergrass	Love TKO	Hirsch-Miller	Philadelphia
793	50	2	Jun-80	Philly Int'l	Teddy Pendergrass	One in a Million You	D. Wansel	Los Angeles
794	9	4	Aug-80	Warner	Larry Graham	Master Blaster	Dees	Detroit
795	52	1	Sep-80	Tamla	Stevie Wonder	Lady (You Bring Me Up)	Stevie Wonder	Detroit
796	8	1	Jul-81	Motown	Commodores	Oh No	Lionel Ritchie	Detroit
797	4	1	Oct-81	Motown	Commodores	Let's Groove	Lionel Ritchie	Los Angeles
798	3	1	Oct-81	Columbia	Earth Wind & Fire	Unforgettable	Earth-White	
799	14		May-91	Capitol	Nat King Cole duet w. Nathalie Cole		Irving Gordon	

Top 480 Artists — R&B Charts — Dec 31, 2000

#	ARTIST	PTS	#	ARTIST	PTS	#	ARTIST	PTS
1	James Brown	8,566	81	Maze Featuring Frankie Beverly	1,913	161	Teena Marie	1,302
2	Aretha Franklin	7,485	82	Rufus Featuring Chaka Khan	1,896	162	Jay-Z	1,299
3	The Temptations	6,450	83	Atlantic Starr	1,866	163	Little Walter	1,297
4	Stevie Wonder	6,419	84	Millie Jackson	1,861	164	Skyy	1,294
5	Louis Jordan	6,269	85	Chuck Berry	1,852	165	Run-D.M.C	1,289
6	Ray Charles	5,821	86	Tavares	1,842	166	2 Pac	1,281
7	Marvin Gaye	5,345	87	Pointer Sisters	1,840	167	Roy Brown	1,279
8	Gladys Knight & The Pips	5,203	88	Curtis Mayfield	1,824	168	Jimmy Reed	1,278
9	The Isley Brothers	5,153	89	Levert	1,814	169	Gerald Levert	1,275
10	Fats Domino	4,936	90	Ohio Players	1,811	170	Charles Brown	1,271
11	B.B. King	4,483	91	George Benson	1,807	171	Salt-N-Pepa	1,270
12	The O'Jays	4,222	92	Lionel Richie	1,802	172	Blackstreet	1,264
13	Michael Jackson	4,106	93	Ivory Joe Hunter	1,797	173	Midnight Star	1,262
14	Prince	4,103	94	Lloyd Price	1,792	174	Duke Ellington	1,258
15	Bobby Bland	3,960	95	The Stylistics	1,786	175	Toni Braxton	1,239
16	Nat "King" Cole	3,709	96	Little Richard	1,775	176	Erskine Hawkins	1,235
17	Dinah Washington	3,590	97	Jr. Walker & The All Stars	1,769	177	Dazz Band	1,234
18	Kool & The Gang	3,579	98	Deniece Williams	1,767	178	Brandy	1,234
19	Four Tops	3,520	99	Hank Ballard & The Midnighters	1,763	179	Xscape	1,230
20	Earth, Wind & Fire	3,519	100	Etta James	1,762	180	Dru Hill	1,226
21	The Miracles	3,474	101	Joe Turner	1,746	181	M.C. Hammer	1,224
22	Diana Ross	3,459	102	Amos Milburn	1,737	182	Carla Thomas	1,220
23	Luther Vandross	3,442	103	Ray Parker Jr./Raydio	1,734	183	Glenn Jones	1,217
24	Janet Jackson	3,425	104	Eddie Kendricks	1,732	184	The Dominoes	1,216
25	Whitney Houston	3,399	105	Solomon Burke	1,723	185	Vanessa Williams	1,214
26	Jerry Butler	3,380	106	The Platters	1,720	186	Little Willie John	1,213
27	Barry White	3,241	107	Martha & The Vandellas	1,712	187	The Notorious B.I.G	1,210
28	The Impressions	3,200	108	The Staple Singers	1,703	188	Surface	1,210
29	Wilson Pickett	3,191	109	Babyface	1,691	189	The Coasters	1,210
30	The Supremes	3,157	110	Jeffrey Osborne	1,679	190	Heavy D & The Boyz	1,208
31	Jackson 5/Jacksons	3,156	111	Johnny Gill	1,670	191	Clyde McPhatter	1,207
32	Joe Simon	3,069	112	Jermaine Jackson	1,642	192	Full Force	1,205
33	Dionne Warwick	3,061	113	Isaac Hayes	1,620	193	Monica	1,205
34	Brook Benton	3,030	114	Ink Spots	1,620	194	Wynonie Harris	1,203
35	Jackie Wilson	3,019	115	Evelyn "Champagne" King	1,612	195	The Detfonics	1,196
36	The Whispers	3,001	116	The Emotions	1,600	196	Starpoint	1,191
37	Spinners	2,902	117	Anita Baker	1,590	197	James Ingram	1,191
38	Patti LaBelle	2,879	118	Johnny Otis	1,580	198	Billy Eckstine	1,191
39	The Drifters	2,865	119	War	1,569	199	Karyn White	1,189
40	Elvis Presley	2,808	120	Little Milton	1,555	200	Chubby Checker	1,188
41	Smokey Robinson	2,789	121	Lou Rawls	1,555	201	The Brothers Johnson	1,176
42	Johnnie Taylor	2,783	122	Roy Milton	1,539	202	Alexander O'Neal	1,173
43	Tyrone Davis	2,751	123	Con Funk Shun	1,536	203	Luther Ingram	1,161
44	Sam Cooke	2,737	124	Sly & The Family Stone	1,518	204	El DeBarge	1,152
45	The Dells	2,725	125	Harold Melvin/The Blue Notes	1,500	205	Sister Sledge	1,151
46	Parliament/Funkadelic	2,618	126	Tevin Campbell	1,500	206	After 7	1,143
47	The Manhattans	2,616	127	Tony! Toni! Tone!	1,489	207	Al B. Sure!	1,137
48	Peabo Bryson	2,606	128	KC & The Sunshine Band	1,483	208	The Shirelles	1,136
49	Cameo	2,603	129	Quincy Jones	1,482	209	Lisa Lisa & Cult Jam	1,135
50	Freddie Jackson	2,592	130	The Marvelettes	1,475	210	Regina Belle	1,132
51	Bobby Womack	2,553	131	Candi Staton	1,473	211	Bull Moose Jackson	1,126
52	Al Green	2,480	132	LaVern Baker	1,456	212	Archie Bell & The Drells	1,121
53	Teddy Pendergrass	2,441	133	Mary Wells	1,455	213	The Main Ingredient	1,120
54	The Moments	2,424	134	One Way	1,453	214	Shanice	1,116
55	R. Kelly	2,418	135	Bobby Brown	1,438	215	Chuck Jackson	1,113
56	The Chi-Lites	2,401	136	En Vogue	1,437	216	Al Jarreau	1,113
57	The Gap Band	2,384	137	Joe Liggins	1,436	217	Chuck Willis	1,107
58	Commodores	2,366	138	The Intruders	1,433	218	Leon Haywood	1,095
59	Natalie Cole	2,328	139	Bill Withers	1,419	219	The Five Stairsteps	1,089
60	Mariah Carey	2,259	140	Ben E. King	1,414	220	Cheryl Lynn	1,088
61	Keith Sweat	2,251	141	Faith Evans	1,413	221	Lowell Fulson	1,085
62	Stephanie Mills	2,199	142	Puff Daddy	1,408	222	Kashif	1,084
63	Ruth Brown	2,196	143	Esther Phillips	1,392	223	Muddy Waters	1,081
64	Joe Tex	2,135	144	Jody Watley	1,392	224	L.T.D.	1,081
65	New Edition	2,098	145	Ike & Tina Turner	1,391	225	Lakeside	1,069
66	Rick James	2,095	146	Clarence Carter	1,384	226	Sam & Dave	1,057
67	Mary J. Blige	2,082	147	Ella Fitzgerald	1,380	227	BeBe & CeCe Winans	1,056
68	The Dramatics	2,075	148	The S.O.S. Band	1,377	228	Mase	1,055
69	Ashford & Simpson	2,064	149	Jodeci	1,371	229	Rose Royce	1,051
70	Donna Summer	2,041	150	Fatback	1,366	230	Buddy Johnson	1,050

ARTIST	PTS		ARTIST	PTS		ARTIST	PTS
71 Gene Chandler	2,032	151	Larry Graham/Graham Central S	1,356	231	Edwin Starr	1,046
72 Bar-Kays	2,027	152	SWV (Sisters With Voices)	1,355	232	Lucky Millinder	1,045
73 LL Cool J	1,969	153	Shalamar	1,348	233	Tammi Terrell	1,044
74 Chaka Khan	1,963	154	Johnny Moore's Three Blazers	1,347	234	Howard Hewett	1,029
75 Boyz 11 Men	1,959	155	Stacy Lattisaw	1,344	235	Roger	1,028
76 Otis Redding	1,949	156	TLC	1,325	236	Billy Preston	1,028
77 Roberta Flack	1,946	157	Phyllis Hyman	1,324	237	Major Lance	1,018
78 Melba Moore	1,941	158	Peaches & Herb	1,311	238	The New Birth	1,018
79 The Clovers	1,918	159	Lionel Hampton	1,309	239	Chic	1,017
80 Betty Wright	1,915	160	Billy Ocean	1,307	240	Troop	1,004
241 Barbara Mason	1,002	321	Bill Doggett	787	401	Sonny Thompson	643
242 Eddie Floyd	993	322	O.V. Wright	786	402	The System	638
243 Force M.D.'s	991	323	Whodini	786	403	Enchantment	637
244 David Ruffin	990	324	Busta Rhymes	781	404	Christopher Williams	636
245 Zapp	990	325	Vesta	777	405	Eric B. & Rakim	635
246 Patti Austin	985	326	The Soul Children	776	406	The "5" Royales	635
247 Julia Lee	984	327	AWB (Average White Band)	776	407	Jade	634
248 Miki Howard	983	328	Mint Condition	774	408	Fat Boys	631
249 Guy	973	329	Brick	772	409	Fantastic Four	626
250 George Michael/Wham E	964	330	Lenny Williams	769	410	Five Star	626
251 Johnny "Guitar" Watson	958	331	Laura Lee	768	411	Big Daddy Kane	624
252 Donny Hathaway	958	332	The Time	764	412	Change	624
253 Sade	956	333	Albert King	763	413	The Controllers	623
254 William Bell	952	334	Percy Sledge	760	414	Shirley Murdock	619
255 Mills Brothers	952	335	Naughty By Nature	756	415	Aaron Hall	619
256 DeBarge	952	336	Latimore	752	416	Detroit Emeralds	618
257 Johnny Ace	952	337	Betty Everett	750	417	Nas	617
258 Carl Carlton	949	338	The Boys	748	418	Lee Dorsey	616
259 Slave	946	339	Immature	746	419	The Charms	614
260 Snoop Doggy Dogg	943	340	Yarbrough & Peoples	745	420	Doug E. Fresh & The Get Fresh Crew	612
261 Ready For The World	940	341	EPMD	741	421	Dee Dee Sharp	612
262 Ice Cube	936	342	Herbie Hancock	741	422	Alyson Williams	611
263 Rufus Thomas	935	343	Joe	739	423	Kool Moe Dee	608
264 Booker T. & The MG's	934	344	Walter Jackson	737	424	Billy Paul	606
265 Tina Turner	934	345	Mtume	737	425	Norman Connors	603
266 Daryl Hall & John Oates	929	346	Soul 11 Soul	733	426	Kurtis Blow	601
267 William "Bootsy" Collins	926	347	The Undisputed Truth	730	427	Roy Ayers	601
268 K-Ci & JoJo	925	348	Klymaxx	728	428	Billy Stewart	601
269 Luke/2 Live Crew	919	349	The Ravens	722	429	Jon B	601
270 Randy Crawford	918	350	The Trammps	714	430	Barbara Acklin	599
271 Grandmaster Flash/Melle Mel/Fur	916	351	Denise LaSalle	714	431	Jean Carn	599
272 Syl Johnson	914	352	Angela Bofill	714	432	Kris Kross	599
273 The Orioles	914	353	Z.Z. Hill	711	433	Michael Cooper	594
274 Total	913	354	Tony Terry	708	434	Club Nouveau	594
275 Roy Hamilton	911	355	Madonna	707	435	Richard "Dimples" Fields	592
276 Usher	907	356	Little Anthony & The Imperials	707	436	Bobby Darin	591
277 Brian McKnight	906	357	B.T. Express	706	437	The Persuaders	589
278 George Duke	902	358	Jackie Moore	705	438	Steve Arrington	584
279 Blue Magic	901	359	MC Lyte	702	439	Maxine Brown	584
280 112	899	360	D Train	702	440	Sounds Of Blackness	581
281 Method Man	898	361	The Meters	701	441	The Independents	580
282 Rene & Angela	894	362	Tracie Spencer	699	442	The Moonglows	580
283 Silk	891	363	Thelma Houston	698	443	O'Bryan	579
284 Master P	881	364	Ricky Nelson	698	444	Changing Faces	579
285 Little Junior Parker	870	365	Jonathan Butler	695	445	Count Basie	579
286 Brenda & The Tabulations	869	366	Missy "Misdemeanor" Elliott	692	446	T-Bone Walker	577
287 R.J.'s Latest Arrival	863	367	Bo Diddley	690	447	Sylvia	576
288 Nellie Lutcher	862	368	The Blackbyrds	690	448	King Floyd	576
289 Michael Henderson	857	369	Ronnie Dyson	688	449	Johnny Bristol	573
290 Cherrelle	857	370	D.J. Jazzy Jeff & The Fresh Prin	686	450	Shai	573
291 Pebbles	857	371	Silkk The Shocker	686	451	Timmy Thomas	568
292 The 5th Dimension	855	372	Jennifer Holliday	686	452	Sybil	567
293 Bloodstone	855	373	Ralph Tresvant	684	453	Memphis Slim	567
294 Nancy Wilson	853	374	The Jets	683	454	Shabba Ranks	564
295 Hi-Five	853	375	Fred Wesley & The J.B.'s	681	455	The Crusaders	562
296 The Sylvers	852	376	OutKast	680	456	Shirley Brown	561
297 Dr. Dre	850	377	Percy Mayfield	680	457	Marv Johnson	559
298 Ann Peebles	847	378	Slick Rick	679	458	Tamia	557
299 Redman	845	379	John Lee Hooker	677	459	Chocolate Milk	557
300 Montell Jordan	842	380	Dorothy Moore	676	460	Switch	557

	ARTIST	PTS		ARTIST	PTS		ARTIST	PTS
301	Patrice Rushen	840	381	Lisa Stansfield	676	461	Gwen McCrae	554
302	Loose Ends	833	382	Kenny G	675	462	GQ	554
303	Herb Alpert	832	383	Public Enemy	675	463	Junior	552
304	Bell Biv DeVoe	831	384	Paul Williams	674	464	Charles Wright	551
305	Brass Construction	828	385	Ce Ce Peniston	672	465	George McCrae	550
306	The Everly Brothers	824	386	Narada Michael Walden	670	466	King Curtis	550
307	Ramsey Lewis	821	387	Margie Joseph	670	467	First Choice	547
308	Da Brat	820	388	The Honey Cone	669	468	Heatwave	545
309	Queen Latifah	818	389	Baby Washington	666	469	De La Soul	544
310	Aaliyah	817	390	H-Town	666	470	Connie Francis	543
311	Meli'sa Morgan	813	391	Jimmy Castor Bunch	663	471	A Taste Of Honey	543
312	O.C. Smith	812	392	Chairmen Of The Board	661	472	Gerald Alston	542
313	Bone Thugs-N-Harmony	809	393	Lillo Thomas	657	473	Eric Gable	542
314	The Three Degrees	808	394	Willie Hutch	654	474	Faye Adams	541
315	Angela Winbush	807	395	Jesse Johnson	652	475	Crown Heights Affair	540
316	DMX	805	396	Eugene Wilde	650	476	The Five Keys	540
317	George Clinton	804	397	Linda Clifford	649	477	Rude Boys	540
318	Grover Washington, Jr	802	398	Johnny Mathis	649	478	Lloyd Glenn	540
319	Zhane	802	399	Hamilton Bohannon	647	479	Lil' Kim	539
320	Deborah Cox	801	400	Too Short	644	480	Will Downing	537